1994

The Untold Story of a Tragic and Controversial F1 Season

Photo: Motorsport Images/LAT

Dedicated to the memory of
Roland Ratzenberger
(1960 to 1994)

First Published January 2019
Copyright Text copyright Ibrar Malik
Page layout and graphics copyright Performance Publishing Ltd

ISBN 978-0-9576450-3-5

Author Ibrar Malik
Designer Sarah Scrimshaw

Printed by The Manson Group Ltd, Hertfordshire AL3 6PZ

 Publisher Performance Publishing Ltd
Unit 3 Site 4 Alma Park Road,
Alma Park Industrial Estate,
Grantham, Lincolnshire NG31 9SE, Great Britain

ACKNOWLEDGEMENTS

Thanks to...

There are so many people who deserve recognition for their help with this book, like Paul West. Discussing 1994 with him was one of the highlights of this project. In this day and age, true gentlemen are a rare breed but Paul is certainly one of them. As is Willem Toet, perhaps the main inspiration behind this book. Simply put, if Willem had not posted his amazing 1994 articles on LinkedIn, you would not be reading this book right now. I've also asked Willem some very challenging questions about Benetton's possibly illegalities, but no matter how difficult my questions Willem always replied with helpful responses.

Frank Dernie received an approach out of the blue from an unknown budding author and, unlike so many people, he responded, for which I am eternally grateful. Another highlight of this project was whenever his emails popped up. As you would expect from such a legendary F1 engineer, his insight was exceptional. Mark Blundell was another kind soul who went out of his way to help me. There is only so much one can learn from books and magazines, so Mark's contribution helped fill in the gaps. I also know both Frank Dernie and Mark Blundell are helping other unknown authors, doing so not for the publicity but purely for the love of their sport.

I am forever indebted to Simon Morley for using this book to share his account of that dreadful Hockenheim fire and its aftermath. Not only for the exclusive material he has kindly provided, but Simon's contributions also gave me additional motivation because once he put his trust in me to deliver his amazing story, I didn't want to let him down.

Antony John Dennis provided many of the book's rare photos and unique insights. He also read through the manuscript and suggested important changes, all of which were acted upon. Furthermore, Antony was fondly remembered by everyone who worked with him, and upon meeting him it became immediately apparent why. Another key contributor was Joan Villadelprat because he made me realise how much had yet to be published about 1994. Quite often, his insider knowledge completely blew me away. Indeed, he was so helpful, it was a challenge ensuring all of his material made it into the final cut of the book.

Christian Silk and Richard Wise were others who provided some great insider anecdotes. It's simple acts like this that keep you motivated whenever the going gets tough. This book would not be half as good without the ridiculous generosity that David Baker has shown in lending his magazines to assist the research. Likewise, Kevin Turner of *Autosport* also helped by allowing the use of various quotes and extracts from the magazine. These are the sort of acts which restore your faith in humanity.

Darren Banks (author of *Stephen South – The Way it Was*) and Mike Fairholme were other vital contributors and I really enjoyed our various conversations. Their help and advice was truly touching and will never be forgotten. Neil White, Rupert Potter, CN Condron and Rob Negri have all been true stars in proof-reading chapters and providing great ideas – the ideal beta readers.

Alastair Ladd's photos improved the book no end and to overcome various computer issues he went above what most people would do to ensure I had his photos before the print deadline. Károly Méhes (author of *Gilles Villeneuve, His Untold Life*), Pete Hennessy, Dave Sheddon and Rob Seymour all provided great material and it was a pleasure dealing with them. As were Mark Hughes, Robin Horton, Tim Holmes from Ford Motor Company and Simon Arron of *Motor Sport* magazine. Martin Zusak (Author of Tamburello) and Christiaan W Lustig (co-author of *Senna v Schumacher*) were major inspirations and sources of help when I was starting out.

Sarah Antar deserves massive praise for not only listening to me banging on about 1994 and pretending to be interested, but also helping me through some personal issues. Only she and another former work colleague, Dave Cooney, truly know how stressfully this book has been. Dave also provided some great feedback after reading an early version of the manuscript.

Trying to find a publisher is nigh on impossible when you are an unknown author with no writing experience. So huge credit must go to Adam Wilkins of Performance Publishing for taking a chance with me, when so many others weren't willing to do so. Adam's professionalism, input and advice all elevated the book to a much higher level than I could ever do by myself. Likewise, Performance Publishing's designer, Sarah Scrimshaw, was amazing at spotting photos issues, laying out the book and generally turning it into a product one can be proud of.

Thanks to all the photo contributors, their amazing pictures really do bring this book to life and I am also grateful to the book's 'informed sources' who wish to remain anonymous. A special thanks to those who have been following the book's progress on social media, and hopefully it inspires others to write about their passion. Apologies if I have forgotten anyone, there were simply too many people who assisted with the production of this book to remember, but you have my eternal gratitude.

Writing a book is tough, no doubt about it, and this project would never have seen the light of day without everyone's help. So from the bottom of my heart, my sincerest thanks and I hope you are proud of the end result.

CONTENTS

1994

"There is no point having a mind unless you are willing to change it"
James O'Brien

Frank Dernie (left, and pictured in 1993) was Benetton's Chief Engineer in 1994. His expertise provides great insight for readers.
Photo: Motorsport Images/LAT

Mark Blundell shares his opinion on the 1994 accusations within the book. ***Photo: Alastair Ladd***

INTRODUCTION

A tragic and controversial F1 season

Schumacher was banned or disqualified from a quarter of 1994 grands prix due to various rule infringements. Despite this, he clinched the F1 title under the most acrimonious circumstances. It meant he and his team, Benetton, narrowly escaped exclusion from the championship on three separate occasions that year. Yet today, ex-Benetton staff feel liked scapegoats for what happened 1994. Why? F1's darkest season has confused fans for the last 25 years. This book provides some much needed answers by asking those involved.

The 1994 season was complicated and, today, it's often viewed with the benefit of hindsight which inevitably adds to the confusion. Rumours, accusations and people misremembering events all mean we are increasingly becoming in danger of the facts being replaced by fiction. If you repeat a lie often enough, it becomes the truth. Therefore, the best way to resolve the many mysteries of 1994 is by understanding the backdrop of F1 at the time and detailing how events unfolded, race by race. This is what the book does while also helping you understand important correlations between certain controversies and politics.

Readers will come to appreciate why Benetton was not punished over some things, but treated harshly in other cases. It is understandable conspiracy theories have arisen since, because the official version of events make little sense, but are they true?

For example, how did Benetton escape exclusion from the F1 championship after the Hockenheim fire despite pleading guilty to altering its refuelling equipment without written authorisation? It is rumoured that this was because the sport needed a German world champion in 1994 for commercial reasons. The conspiracy theorists would also have you believe Benetton was treated harshly during their other cases to even things out.

Anthony John Dennis, a Benetton Ford electronics expert, gives his view on the 1994 controversies.

Simon Morley, Benetton's Hockenheim refueller, opens up about that incident.

Whereas others have indicated Benetton and Schumacher's troubles were largely related to a clash between their boss and the FIA president. A by-product of this, they argue, was the exciting championship conclusion which assisted TV ratings. All of these theories are discussed. However, the book goes further in understanding the circumstances behind those individual cases and how Benetton's penalties compared to similar infringements by others.

Moreover, readers will learn the background under which the various 1994 allegations were made (this is important to help you assess their validity). Also telling was which rules were quietly changed afterwards. Where debatable points exist, readers are given both sides to any arguments

Willem Toet, Benetton's Head of Aerodynamics in 1994, has helped uncover some of the book's exclusive findings. **Photo: Willem Toet**

Paul West (left) was Hill's mechanic in 1994. He's with Schumacher mechanics, Kenny Handkammer and Max Fluckiger. **Photo: Paul West**

Schumacher and Benetton committed an infringement at Silverstone and then ignored a black flag . Their original fine was increased twentyfold, which many felt was politically motivated. The book fully explains. **Photo: Motorsport Images/LAT**

along with all corresponding evidence, thereby allowing you to decide what happened. The 1994 controversies are a bit like a jigsaw puzzle. If you only see part of the picture then it's easy to conclude one thing. However, once consideration is given to other factors, such as the politics, then a much more interesting picture emerges. In summary, this book merely presents you with all the jigsaw pieces you need. What picture you see at the end is left up to you.

As a devoted F1 fan, I thought I knew everything about the 1994 season before starting this project. But since interviewing those involved, it soon became apparent how much had yet to be made public. Willem Toet, Benetton's Head of Aerodynamics in 1994, summed it up: "Perhaps time has allowed people to say what they think." Therefore, the book's emphasis is on uncovering those hitherto unpublished details about 1994.

For instance, the book contains a previously undiscussed theory over what Senna heard on Schumacher's car at Aida. This is supported by Willem Toet, telemetry traces and in the words of former F1 driver, Mark Blundell, "that all makes a lot of sense". Since Blundell was also taken out of that first corner in Aida, his words carry weight because, like Senna, he would have also heard Schumacher's Benetton trackside. The book's theory also explains why Schumacher would have been much faster than his various teammates and why they all found the

car especially twitchy. It is also consistent with race footage that readers can check for themselves online.

Another exclusive is that Simon Morley, Benetton's refueller during 1994 and the so-called 'junior employee' blamed for the Hockenheim fire, gives his account of it and the subsequent investigation within the book. Simon literally had his life put at risk by that fire and, apart from a few select quotes in 2004, he has not publicly spoken about it until now. So it is important his story is told – and I'm not afraid to admit that Simon's account brought a tear to my eye. I couldn't even begin to imagine how scary that incident was for him. Indeed, reading his story makes you more appreciative why things panned out the way they did and he has kindly provided some rare images and documents.

Furthermore, you'll also learn just how many times Schumacher's Benetton was spot-checked after races, and for what in particular and the results. All of this is just a taste of what is unearthed.

This was a watershed year for F1, not only because of the tragic accidents which forced the sport's safety to improve drastically and immediately. However, it was the changing of the guard within the sport. Senna (part of the old generation) and Schumacher (part of the new generation) were about to fight it out for the 1994 title until fate sadly intervened. This book helps readers decide whether Schumacher was beating Senna fairly in those opening rounds or not.

BACKDROP

June 1993 to December 1993

"We must finish the season with active [suspension]. It makes no sense to change the car in the middle of the season."
Flavio Briatore, Benetton Commercial Director,
Autosport, 22 July 1993

"The Concorde Agreement hasn't been broken at all. It's just that the changes were made a bit late, that's all."
Bernie Ecclestone, F1 commercial supremo,
Autosport, 22 July 1993

Many teams struggled financially during the early 1990s following a global financial crisis. This forced F1 bosses to reduce costs, but their methods would be questioned. *Photo: Martin Lee*

Standings before the 1993 Canadian Grand Prix

DRIVERS' CHAMPIONSHIP		
Pos	Driver	Points
1	Ayrton Senna	42
2	Alain Prost	37
3	Damon Hill	18

CONSTRUCTORS' CHAMPIONSHIP		
Pos	Constructor	Points
1	Williams-Renault	55
2	McLaren-Ford	44
3	Benetton-Ford	19

Active suspension shown on the 1993 Williams. Unlike conventional springs, it was able to keep the ride height consistent by… *Photo: Neil Thompson via www.williamsdb.com*

…using computers and actuators to predict and counteract body roll and pitch variation under cornering, accelerating and braking. *Photo: Morio*

Can you name a major international sporting event that threatened to ban every team from competing, apart from one? Answer: the 1993 Canadian Grand Prix where officials declared 24 out of the 26 cars illegal. Only the Lola team, consistently the slowest cars in the field, complied with the rules in a race jokingly dubbed 'The Illicit Grand Prix'. Much to the relief of paying speculators, common sense prevailed and officials allowed the 24 questionable cars to race. However, those teams were warned in a few weeks' time (15 July) the powers-that-be were likely to throw them out of the championship. Should that happen, then F1's top teams might miss the proceeding races as they altered their cars drastically and at great expense in order to comply. In other words, F1 was about to shoot itself in the foot with a very large gun, but why?

Two electronic driver aids were behind all this, and those cars deemed illegal were running at least one of them. Active suspension was a device which maintained a constant height of the car while on track to maximise grip and therefore performance. FISA (F1's governing body) declared this outside the regulations because they deemed it to be a movable aerodynamic device. While traction control allowed a driver to merely floor the throttle and rely on

computers to eliminate wheelspin, this was considered illegal because propulsion systems were not under the control of the driver at all times. Both points were certainly open to interpretation, however many were confused as to why FISA chose this particular moment to clamp down given neither device was new or secretive. F1 technology had long since moved on, hence the reason 24 out of 26 cars would have been affected by the ban.

In fact, active suspension first took to the F1 track as early as 1983, in the Lotus Type 92, driven by Nigel Mansell. Whereas traction control made its debut at the start of 1992 in the Williams FW14B, again driven by the same driver. Indeed, 'Our Nige', as he became affectionately known won the 1992 world championship using both devices. His boss at the time, Frank Williams, took a verbal pot-shot at FISA: "We sincerely hope the validity of Nigel Mansell's World Drivers' Championship and the Williams Renault World Constructors' Championship is not called into question. The team's suspension system has been identical for the past 22 grands prix – that is since the beginning of 1992 World Championship and its conformity with the regulations has never been called into question until today."[1] So why the bombshell ruling now?

The answer was that it was part of a much bigger political battle. In February 1993, FISA proposed banning these devices for 1994. However, some teams blocked this because the notice period was insufficient. It broke the timescales required under the Concorde Agreement – a legal document stipulating how changes are to be made within the sport. Therefore certain teams argued that the ban on active suspension and traction control couldn't be implemented until 1995 at the earliest. Despite meetings between the two sides agreement couldn't be reached so FISA seemingly used another tactic – namely declaring the majority of cars competing at the Canadian Grand Prix illegal.

Lola was declared the only legal car at the 1993 Canadian Grand Prix. Was this politics at play? *Photo: Martin Lee*

1. *Autosport*, 17 June 1993

Chapter 1

This was allegedly an attempt to railroad teams into accepting the proposed changes for 1994. Williams Technical Director Patrick Head explained why: "Charlie Whiting [FISA's technical delegate] came up with something incredibly spurious. Basically, he's been told by his master to find a way of making active ride cars illegal, but I don't think it will stand up. The regulation was worded identically in 1987, and Nelson Piquet won the 1987 World Championship with three victories in an active ride car... It seems odd to suddenly want to re-interpret what they choose to mean by that rule now."[2] The Canada ruling bypassed the Concorde Agreement and its timescales because the cars were said to have contravened existing F1 regulations, not future ones. FISA appeared to be telling constructors: use your clever legal argument to block our 1994 proposals, we'll just rule your cars illegal until you agree to them. Who says rules and regulations are no fun?

The Concorde Agreement was drawn up after a civil war within the sport[3] and its purpose was to prevent rules being forced upon participants at short notice. The issue some teams had wasn't so much the banning of the aforementioned driver aids, but the way the Concorde Agreement timescales were being sidestepped by FISA. Constructors like Williams claimed they needed as much time as possible to remove their car's active suspension system because it was an enormous job. There would also be unforeseen knock-on effects on their cars' aerodynamics, with potentially tragic consequences (as we shall find out later). Teams argued that, if these timescales were not observed, then anarchy would follow. Ironically, one of the key architects of the Concorde Agreement in the early 1980s was Max Mosley – the very person who appeared to be bypassing its timescales, a ploy Mosley tacitly admitted a year later.

Interestingly, two days before the Canada ruling, Mosley had been elected president of the FIA, following an acrimonious battle with a rival candidate. At that time, the FIA was in the process of replacing FISA as F1's governing body, and the takeover would be completed

McLaren (pictured) and Williams won every race bar one in 1993. Their main advantage came from expensive electronics. *Photo: Alastair Ladd*

by October 1993. Mosley was the son of Sir Oswald, the controversial former leader of the British Union of Fascists. He secured his position as president after replacing Jean Marie Balestre – a former French SS member during World War Two. Mosley had previously worked as a lawyer, and then within UK politics before becoming part of the FISA establishment. Therefore if teams thought the new president would be a pushover, they were in for a big shock. Mosley astonished respected F1 journalist Nigel Roebuck when asked about the Canada ruling at the following race. "In the end, these controversies only have an effect if the press writes about them," Mosley said. "If you all ignore them, and treated them as a bit of gossip, while the real business is on the track, this would minimise the damage."[4]

Many felt if consensus was reached on the 1994 rules then FISA, under Mosley's command, would drop the Canada ruling. That would mean teams could return to the more important matter of going around in circles quicker than their neighbours, spending millions of dollars in pursuit of this most worthy endeavour. However, a storm of the brown variety had been kicked up by the

Wheelspin was undesirable during an F1 race start and traction control prevented it. In Canada in 1993, all but one team (Lola) either had traction control or active suspension on their cars. *Photo: Alastair Ladd*

Patrick Head of Williams believed active suspension wasn't a "driver aid" because it didn't drive the car for the driver, instead it merely raised its performance potential.
Photo: Alastair Ladd

Teams like March (pictured), Brabham, Fondmetal, AGS, Modena Lamborghini and Andrea Moda had all folded in recent years. ***Photo: Alastair Ladd***

two top teams of the day, Williams and McLaren, who refused to be bullied like this. They had the most to lose from banning active suspension because both pioneered the system since 1992. Moreover, Williams and McLaren tailored their car's aerodynamics to maximise its effect, something others could only dream of. This was a key reason they dominated F1 at the time.

Williams and McLaren agreed to outlaw traction control and anti-lock brakes (ABS) for 1994, but they stood firm on retaining active suspension until 1995 despite the Canada ruling. Effectively, they were calling FISA's bluff and threatening to go legal on the matter via the International Court of Appeal. This action would delayed a resolution by months and be damaging for the sport, because it caused uncertainty for the poorer teams who needed to work on their 1994 cars immediately.

The richer teams (like Williams and McLaren) had contingency plans in place, so could accept the uncertainty if there was a chance of keeping their active suspension advantage for 1994. Under the backdrop of a financial crisis, it was feared this posturing might cause the smaller teams to go out of business. However, FISA had good reasons why they couldn't back down on this issue either.

There had been growing concerns from TV audiences that the sport was becoming too predictable as the richer teams kept winning due to their electronic gizmos, like active suspension. American Indycar racing was growing in popularity at the time and

Poorer teams, like Minardi, couldn't afford expensive gizmos like active suspension so the 1994 ban helped them. ***Photo: Martin Lee***

becoming a serious rival for F1. Nigel Mansell, Mario Andretti and Emerson Fittipaldi all raced in the US series and even Ayrton Senna had investigated a move stateside during the winter of 1992/93. A declining public interest would seriously hurt F1's income, something the powers-that-be were keen to avoid.

Therefore, FISA felt it had to force a ban on active suspension for 1994 in order to protect the future of F1 as Mosley later alluded to. "A lot of that I didn't discuss with Ecclestone beforehand because it was very last minute, particularly the decision to say that was what we were going to do, Concorde Agreement or no Concorde Agreement. It was a very risky thing to do, but I decided that, in the final analysis, I had to stake my FISA presidency on getting the changes through. The teams wouldn't agree, so it couldn't be done by negotiation. Therefore it had to be done by force. When Patrick Head and others, say they didn't like the methods I used, I agree – but it was a choice between doing that and not doing it at all. And I felt absolutely that the changes had to be made. F1 was in a nosedive of escalating costs and declining spectacle."[5] Trouble at mill was brewing.

The deadlock remained when the World Motor Sports Council (the decision-makers) met on 15 July. Unsurprisingly to some, the Canada ruling was ratified, meaning active suspension and traction control needed to be removed from cars by the 1993 Hungarian Grand Prix – the next race but one. Essentially, FISA had just upped the stakes and thrown the bluff back into Williams' and McLaren's faces. Unsurprisingly, they were outraged because rules had been changed halfway through a season. If they wanted to continue to fight their corner and still compete in the Hungarian Grand Prix, their only realistic option was to undertake significant and expensive modifications to their cars. Because their legal challenge via the International Court of Appeal couldn't be concluded before Hungary. Williams found the decision "disgusting" and threatened not to race because of the amount of work demanded of them. FISA might have won this particular battle, but at what cost?

2. *F1 News*, 22 June 1993
3. FISA v FOCA war of 1980 to 1982
4. *Autosport*, 22 July 1993
5. *Autosport*, 7 April 1994

Bernie Ecclestone was called upon to resolve all the politics. ***Photo: Ryan Bayona***

Ferrari had been in the doldrums ever since active suspension became a necessity in Formula One, so its ban for 1994 helped them. ***Photo: Martin Lee***

Journalists naturally questioned the decision, citing the example: halfway through Wimbledon, you don't have the authorities deciding that the larger racquets that have been used for several years are suddenly illegal and that everyone using them are disqualified. "We've probably been a bit slow in catching up on this, I'm ready to admit that" Mosley responded. "So we are going to change our procedures slightly so we are more up to date on what the teams are doing... At Wimbledon, you have two bats, a ball and a net and it really isn't that difficult. With us, the ball is something of enormous technical complexity. Just to describe the ball as a F1 car you have a thick book of regulations which even the teams don't fully understand. It's a very difficult sport from that point of view. We do our best and most of the problems disappear by mutual agreement but they arise all the time, as you would expect with something so complicated."[6]

As an aside the "change of procedure" referred to above-involved teams consulting FISA about the legality of new devices prior to their use. During an interview in January 1994, Mosley admitted this was a shrewd political move because it gave them more control over teams. For example, dominant or trouble-making teams might find it difficult getting their new technology declared legal. The sport's

Ironically, the active suspension ban delayed the new Simtek car, which had to be completely reworked afterwards. ***Photo: Giovanni Talli***

governing body could also determine the future direction of F1 with their judgements. Previously teams had controlled this latter point under the Concorde Agreement because they wrote the technical regulations and the sport's governing body only policed them. But Mosley's move seemed to be a power grab from under the teams' noses because it gave the FISA the final say on vague matters. At the time, teams were busy fighting against the active suspension ban and amongst themselves, perhaps too busy to notice the full implications of Mosley's "change of procedure".

Some failed to understand why, if active suspension and traction control were deemed illegal since Canada, could the cars affected retain points won since then? F1 was quickly becoming increasingly hard-to-understand soap opera. Williams and McLaren appealed the ban – but that wasn't expected to be successful and their other legal challenge wouldn't be resolved before the Hungarian Grand Prix. Therefore, F1 was facing subsequent races without any top drivers or teams – a suicidal move for the sport. In order to resolve the crisis and prevent anarchy at upcoming races, Bernie Ecclestone stepped in to broker a deal.

Ecclestone is one of F1's most colourful characters, the sort of person who would go into a revolving door behind you yet come out in front of you. He was a master negotiator with an innate ability to exploit his leverage at the most opportune time. From a humble background, Ecclestone became one of the richest men in the UK by promoting F1 to the world. His roles in 1993 included representing the teams' interest as FOCA boss, yet he also held power at FISA, as FIA vice president. Therefore questions were raised as to whose side Ecclestone was on over this issue, which in many ways is typical of him – never showing his hand until absolutely necessary.

Mosley and Ecclestone worked well together as F1's two power brokers and formed their successful alliance throughout the early 1970s. Together they fought and won many battles for control of the sport most notably the FISA v FOCA (or FIASCO) war of 1980 to 1982. Mosley was the legal eagle, well versed in politics who appeared to be pressuring teams in 1993 to achieve the FIA's goals.

Williams claimed removing active suspension during the middle of 1993 was an enormous job. **Photo: Martin Lee**

Whereas Ecclestone, intentionally or otherwise, appeared to fuel the controversy fear and paranoia by not publicly stating which side he was on. By now, teams were sick of this saga so were prepared to concede ground to achieve a resolution. "They specialise in creating chaos and then coming in with an edict to resolve it," fumed Patrick Head of Williams. "We've never been asked to get together in a room and say what we think is good or bad."[7]

Coincidentally, Ecclestone suggested meeting the teams before the German Grand Prix – the final race before the ban took effect – which on the face of things seemed to be F1's Commercial Supremo coming to everyone's rescue at the eleventh hour to negotiate a settlement. Dubbed the 'Hockenheim crisis meeting', it took five hours to thrash out this issue. Ecclestone even admitted to bullying some teams into line, because the richer and poorer teams were not united. Eventually, a proposal was reached which overturned the looming ban on active suspension and traction control. It had to be accepted by FISA, but that was a mere formality since Ecclestone could use his considerable influence. Initially, the richer teams were delighted and considered the meeting a victory for them because the potential crisis of having to rebuild their cars had been averted. Little did they know what trouble lay ahead of them.

For instance, teams were forced to agree some very unpalatable longer term proposals like accepting the active suspension ban for 1994. Despite their earlier resistance, Williams and McLaren now obliged. If Mosley and Ecclestone had applied pressure as a tactic, it seemed to work because the concessions teams were forced to agree didn't finish there. Ecclestone, acutely aware of team's

desperation by this stage, forced through another proposal: mid-race refuelling for 1994. It was something he had been trying to introduce for years but most teams objected due to the serious risk of fire it presented to their mechanics. Would you want to refuel a car at 12 litres per second under extreme time pressure when the merest drop could ignite from the car's hot brakes? Moreover, refuelling added additional expense for teams since they would have to maintain and transport all the equipment to the various races across the world.

Ecclestone, however, loved refuelling because it spiced up the show thereby making F1 an easier sell for TV companies. Furthermore, sponsors' logos on cars would have increased exposure during the longer refuelling stops. Ecclestone sold the idea to teams by promising a cool down meeting later if they gave their provisional agreement at the Hockenheim crisis meeting. If every team was still against refuelling at that cool down meeting Ecclestone promised to drop the idea, so what did teams have to lose? Some failed to appreciate Ferrari were not going to vote against refuelling at this cool down meeting because it helped their thirsty V12 engine. Rather than having to carry additional fuel (in comparison to their rivals) during races, something which adversely affects lap times. If that fuel could instead be kept at the pits until it was needed, that would be an easy way to instantly increase Ferrari's competitiveness.

6. *A Season With McLaren*, episode six (1993)
7. *Autosport*, 15 July 1993

Refuelling helped Ferrari and its thirsty V12 engine. Incidentally, the Italian team proved more competitive in 1994 than previous years.
Photo: Storem

Williams also alleged the powerbrokers in F1 wanted to help Ferrari return to a competitive position, which was another reason behind mid-race refuelling and the banning of active suspension. The Italian team had been in the doldrums ever since active suspension became a necessity in F1. According to Ecclestone's biography, it was he who Ferrari should recruit Jean Todt. On 1 July 1993, Todt became the first non-Italian to become General Manager of the racing division at the Scuderia and, under his leadership, Ferrari enjoyed their most successful period in its illustrious history. At the time of writing, Todt is the current FIA president.

Once ratification was granted by FISA to the Hockenheim proposals, Williams' and McLaren's previous appeals against the ban on active suspension were redundant and FISA annulled reprimands it had previously issued to both teams. It seemed peace had finally broken out. Paul West, a former Williams mechanic, recalled how the 1993 Constructors' Champions had not lost their humour throughout events. "I do remember someone at Williams putting a sticker which said 'Jurassic Park' on the door to the room where all that stuff was assembled and then a few weeks later a 'Back to the Future' sticker took its place." One wonders how

Mid-race refuelling (shown here in 2004) was controversially introduced for 1994 despite most teams expressing concern it was too expensive and dangerous. A notable exception was Ferrari. **Photo: Fabio Alessandro Locati**

many sleepless nights certain team bosses had following the crisis. However, below the surface tensions were still bubbling away.

Following the Hockenheim crisis meeting, the teams (apart from Ferrari) united to try to remove refuelling and its associated dangers from the 1994 regulations. Williams and McLaren team leaders even met with Mosley and Ecclestone during the Italian Grand Prix weekend where it is believed they discussed the issue. According to *Autosport* magazine, the meeting was described as "stormy" and "even to the casual observer it was clear they were not in agreement". Afterwards, none of the four present was willing to discuss what had been said. A couple of weeks later at the cool down meeting, held in Estoril, predictably Ferrari stood in the way of other teams' efforts to outlaw refuelling for 1994.

Because the teams couldn't unanimously agree between them this meant FISA – now in the process of being restructured to become the FIA – could act without consensus. Which is precisely what it did when voting through refuelling for 1994 two weeks later at the newly formed FIA World Motor Sports Council meeting on 15 October.

Frank Williams summed up the situation: "Bernie brought it [refuelling] up at the end of the crisis meeting at Hockenheim. Because everyone there was desperate for an agreement – so as to keep active suspension for the balance of the season – refuelling went through. We made a number of decisions too quickly, and without enough thought. Then at a meeting in Estoril, we told Bernie we really didn't want refuelling: it would be dangerous, and expensive – at a time we're supposed to be saving money. Let's undo it, we said and Bernie didn't object because it was going to cost him a lot too. But one other team refused to vote to undo it, so we're stuck with it."[8]

Once refuelling was confirmed for 1994, many F1 folk feared it wasn't a case of *if* an accident would happen but when – and whether it could be contained? Refuelling was previously banned on safety grounds after the 1983 season. In their defence, there was pressure being placed on Ecclestone and Mosley to introduce it because Indycar racing was becoming a serious threat to F1. Refuelling, safety cars and stop-go penalties were all Indycar features Ecclestone and Mosley adopted into F1 around the time to improve the spectacle. Whether improving the show became a more important aspect than safety in 1993 is debatable. The

Indycars, which included stars like Mansell, was rivalling F1 in 1993. Refuelling was therefore introduced to spice up grand prix racing.
Photo: Rick Dikeman

A non-refuelling practice pit stop from 1993. Mechanics did not need fireproof overalls and less personnel were involved.
Photo: Antony John Dennis

question on everyone's lips as 1994 approached was whether refuelling would give the spectacle that was intended, or a much more frightening one?

My personal view is the political manoeuvring which resulted in refuelling appears largely engineered rather than by accident. In 1992, a similar situation occurred when F1's fuel regulations suddenly changed mid-season causing Elf to accuse Mosley of "imposing rules by force" and a "totally unfounded interpretation of the rules." Whatever your opinion, teams found themselves at the Hockenheim crisis meeting effectively forced to agree to refuelling for 1994. It was either that or accept the ban on active suspension from the next race onwards, which would have caused those teams huge problems. In other words, pain today or pain tomorrow.

On the flip side, things didn't need to get to that point because it was well known Mosley and other prominent figures had been trying to rid F1 of expensive technology as early as 1992. Senna (a McLaren driver at the time) famously sent Mosley a Christmas card in 1992 lamenting electronic aids, and demanding they be banned immediately. Mosley took this as a call to arms, and by February 1993 all the teams knew of FISA's intention to rid F1 from driver aids by 1994. It was felt F1's emphasis had moved away from driver skill and the spectacle. Understandably, FISA wanted to redress this balance in order to protect F1's future during the global recession of the 1990s.

It could be argued because the richer teams continually blocked the ban on their technological advantage, they were effectively putting themselves ahead of the sport. Their stubbornness ultimately led to that Hockenheim crisis meeting. However in their defence around March 1993 it was unclear that "driver aids" also incorporated active suspension. F1 insiders believed Ferarri struggling with their active ride thus becoming uncompetitive as a result was a key reason behind it being outlawed.

All this was just a foretaste of the politics and infighting that occurred in one of F1's most controversial and tragic seasons: 1994.

8. *Autosport*, 10 February 1994

Chapter 2

PRE-SEASON
January 1994 to March 1994

"The consequences for any team or driver found to be cheating will be mind-blowing."

**Max Mosley, FIA President,
Autosport, 6 January 1994**

"I'm fairly confident we are kosher."

**Ross Brawn, Benetton's Technical Director,
The Independent, 4 September 1994**

Schumacher and Benetton won a single race in 1993. Therefore nobody
considered them serious 1994 title challengers. ***Photo: Martin Lee***

Standings after the 1993 Season

DRIVERS' CHAMPIONSHIP		
Pos	Driver	Points
1	Alain Prost	99
2	Ayrton Senna	73
3	Damon Hill	69

CONSTRUCTORS' CHAMPIONSHIP		
Pos	Constructor	Points
1	Williams-Renault	168
2	McLaren-Ford	84
3	Benetton-Ford	72

The above warning from FIA president Max Mosley towards teams was in response to a fresh war brewing within F1. Teams believed the 1994 ban on driver aids couldn't be policed because the new regulations didn't define what those aids were. "The driver must drive the car alone and unaided" was all the rules said on the matter, and teams felt this was too vague to be enforced. Mosley's comment above appeared to show he felt otherwise. In my opinion, keeping the rules vague was a deliberate strategy by the FIA because it gave them the final say over what constituted a driver aid whenever questionable devices appeared. It also allowed the FIA to determine what penalties were applicable in such cases. This would prove one of the most contentious issues throughout the year, with many believing the FIA used these powers to manipulate the 1994 F1 championship. Had the term 'driver aids' been clearly defined in the rules along with the associated penalties, how could the FIA influence decisions?

Some readers may wonder why it wasn't obvious what a driver aid was? For instance, the following were *not* considered driver aids: power steering, semi-automatic gearboxes, speed limiter buttons (for pitlane use), pre-programmed buttons to select specific gears and a brake balance adjuster. Nor was a hydraulic differential banned under the 1994 rules, which some considered a rudimentary form of traction control. Conversely, an anti-roll bar adjuster, a device that had been in use in F1 since 1974, was now deemed to be a driver aid. Confusingly, there seemed little logic behind these decisions and it would catch out at least two of the top teams in F1 during 1994 (fully explained later). *Autosport* magazine felt it ultimately boiled down to one man – FIA technical delegate Charlie Whiting – and his opinion on the day. Granted he did consult outside experts, but Whiting's opinions were those of one man – with all the quirks and foibles that implied.

Not a satisfactory situation from a team's point of view due to the uncertainty. They constantly invent new technologies which stray into grey areas otherwise they wouldn't be competitive. So without a clear definition of the rules, certain devices may be legal to one person but not to another. F1 history is littered with such examples some of which occurred in 1994 and will be explained later. According to Willem Toet, Benetton's Head of Aerodynamics at the time: "There are split approaches to how a team should check the legality of their various systems. One is to lay it out and explain every detail. The other is to prepare your explanation of why it is legal and just run it." In early 1994 the FIA didn't have the resources to keep up with the former approach, particularly in light of all the queries being thrown up by the various bans. So the latter approach was adopted by participants which partly explains the various controversies later on.

The banning of various electronic gizmos created another issue which also wasn't clarified. Because the rules didn't stipulate that outlawed driver aid programmes, such as launch control, must be removed from the car's on-board engine control units (ECUs),[9] teams only disarmed these systems, because they felt purging them might create unforeseen errors elsewhere. Both actions had the same outcome, but removing illegal functions was time-consuming and, rightly or wrongly, teams wanted to focus their resources elsewhere. They believed that, provided this software was made

Some teams only disarmed launch and traction control from their ECUs, rather than removing it, believing that complied with the ban. This proved highly controversial. **Photo: Ford**

redundant, leaving traces of them within their black boxes would be deemed acceptable. This point would come back to haunt one top team in particular.

Likewise, the now illegal anti-roll bar adjuster wasn't removed from the Williams cockpit, again because the rules didn't say they had to. Williams, therefore, kept it in place, because they used this adjuster during private testing in 1994. These loopholes were open to exploitation as was the defence "what we've done must be legal because it's not specifically outlawed in the rules." The FIA felt these points were covered by placing the onus on teams to prove their cars were legal at all times. We shall see later how this pans out, but at the time the FIA would only give advice on vague areas of the rules before races, rather than a definitive ruling. Partly due to the lack of FIA resources mentioned earlier.

Thus teams were placed in the incredible situation of turning up to races not knowing if their cars would be declared 100 percent legal by those making the decisions. Some magazines joked that the 1994 championship might be decided before an F1 car ever turned a wheel in anger, such was the uncertainty. "I agree in principle with the step the FIA has taken to improve the racing," said Patrick Head of Williams, "but I don't necessarily agree with the methods used. When it comes to implementing the new regulations, the FIA will be very tough and I only hope that its toughness is fairly and evenly directed. There'll be lots of screaming and shouting at first, but in the end, the FIA will win. It'll say: 'it's our championship and if you don't like it you can go somewhere else.'"[10]

9. AKA black boxes, they contain software which related to engine controls, driver displays and telemetry. The ECU discussed was the sole responsibility of Benetton (not Cosworth or Ford).
10. *Autosport*, 24 March 1994

Chapter 2

The problem appeared to stem from the legal and political battles throughout the second half of 1993 as detailed in chapter one. Because there was such wrangling over active suspension and then mid-race refuelling, it seems this left less time to finalise the rest of the 1994 regulations. In the end, they largely consisted of what was agreed during the Hockenheim crisis meeting. Since the new rules were rushed through it appears there was no time to consider the implications. As the reality sunk in, it became apparent just how vague they were.

Autosport magazine felt some wanted to deliberately keep the rules vague because F1 was benefitting from the additional publicity caused from the squabbling during the offseason. Furthermore, it would ensure a shake-up in the pecking order and therefore an exciting season ahead. If the new rules were clear, then Williams would have had a better chance of dominating for the third season running. As a result, Williams had no option but to go conservative with its interpretation of the rules. Perhaps they felt a team or driver dominating in 1994 might not be given the leeway of a smaller team on a contentious point. In his autobiography, Mosley said judges have more power when the law is less clear. The race stewards were the judges in F1 and their decision would be based on advice from the FIA. If the matter was appealed then the FIA's World Council became the final judge.

The constructors allowed this power grab because they couldn't agree on clearly defined rules amongst themselves within the timeframe available. Changes to the regulations needed the signed off by every team. As we saw in the case of refuelling, unanimous

Was Jean Todt's letter the reason behind the fly-by-wire throttle ban?
Photo: Tony Harrison

agreement was nigh on impossible. Mosley also admitted in his autobiography "sometimes the rather narrow outlook of some team principles could be helpful." Vagueness could be found in other 1994 rules as well.

Take the regulation "traction control is forbidden" for example. Did this mean electronic fly-by-wire throttles were legal or illegal? By 1993, the top teams had developed them so whenever the throttle was pressed an electronic command was sent to the engine instead of moving a traditional cable. During the 1993 Japanese Grand Prix weekend, Whiting told Williams a fly-by-wire system would be legal next year. Since there was nothing in the regulations to the contrary

Traction control was banned for 1994 because it prevented wheelspin (shown above), but the vague ruling threw up many questions.
Photo: Eric McCombs FormulaCarChallenge.com

Questions were raised over Ferrari's front suspension and fuel.
Photo: Martin Lee

Was Williams' streamlined shroud (circled in red) a moveable aerodynamic device? **Photo: Morio**

the recently crowned constructors' champions went ahead and spent £250,000 on developing a 1994 fly-by-wire device only to be told it was now deemed illegal because it *might* conceal an illegal traction control device. This U-turn would have hurt Williams more than others because they had an extremely powerful engine, so a fly-by-wire throttle would have helped make it more driveable.

Autosport reported this change of stance by the FIA was initiated by a letter from Jean Todt, the Ferrari sporting director. Apparently using fly-by-wire throttles rendered teams unable to prove their cars were legal at all times, as required. It's a bit like seizing £250,000 off someone on the basis that they may commit fraud – not because they actually did. Under this logic why were semi-automatic gearboxes, where drivers shifting paddles to change gears, also banned? Like fly-by-wire they relied on electronics, which might conceal an illegal device. Later, we will learn of one of the frontrunners being found guilty of a driver aid concealed within their gearbox. Not only did said team go unpunished, during the investigation a fault within the engine management software was discovered by the FIA and highlighted to them, giving the guilty offender a potential performance bonus.

McLaren boss, Ron Dennis, was furious over the change in stance by the FIA, stating he fully intended to go to the first race with fly-by-wire throttles. Effectively calling the bluff of race stewards to throw his team out. Jean Todt said he expected the fly-by-wire to be declared illegal. Eventually, McLaren conceded and brought the older cable throttle to Brazil, which ironically caused the team persistent problems all weekend – partly due to a lack of testing with it. A side effect of the unclear rules was paranoia was growing among everyone that cheating was rife, and so began the season-long slinging of mud.

Patrick Head of Williams said Ferrari's front suspension contravened the regulations "in black and white". Rivals considered a streamlined shroud containing the Williams rear suspension to be a "moveable aerodynamic device" which was against the rules. The FIA raised questions over Ferrari's new performance fuel (codenamed F10) after a batch failed to come up to the required standard. However, it was later approved following a retest. Adding to this volatile mix was the alleged favouritism towards Ferrari that many believed existed and the bad feeling towards the Italian outfit

from others following the reintroduction of refuelling. It was little wonder accusations were thrown around F1 at the time and would continue throughout the season.

As if there wasn't enough controversy, the new-for-1994 refuelling equipment arrived for testing. The rig itself was a ghastly steel box, about the size of a bottle bank and had pipes and pumps sticking out of it. Various mechanics approached it like a caveman might approach a mirror. Jordan was the first team to overcome their bewilderment and try out the equipment, only to immediately suffer a fuel leak. John Walton, Jordan's Team Manager, explained: "The nozzle proved a bit tricky to get on and off. When it did come off, fuel leaked out, which is a bit worrying. The guys from Intertechnique – who build the system – said the nozzle is just tight because it's new. A lot of people are still wary and are not 100 percent keen on having to use it... The equipment is very cumbersome. It takes two guys to pick up the hose. I guess this is for safety reasons – it certainly doesn't make the process any easier. But you've got to have the safest equipment available because, however good it is, there's always a chance of an accident. And when you've got 20 of your guys standing around the car you have to be careful... Most important from the safety point of view, the nozzle drips when it is pulled off the car."[11]

Older males might appreciate what a problem that the last point might be. Whiting admitted there was "a small problem with the fuel valve" and during a later meeting with Ecclestone, teams highlighted this incident as a last ditch attempt to block refuelling for 1994. However, Ferrari upset others by not adding their voice to this latest lobby, an action which confirmed refuelling would remain despite the fierce objection against it. The upset teams also tried revising the Concorde Agreement during that meeting, specifically the clause which was allowing refuelling. So instead of requiring unanimous agreement, they were seeking a consensus of 70 percent to enable future changes to be passed. Presumably, they had learnt from their mistake although it seemed the damage was done.

11. *Autosport*, 24 February 1994

Chapter 2

By now even Ecclestone was reportedly having second thoughts on refuelling. He agreed to supply one set of apparatus to each team but it became apparent that would be an expensive promise. So he invoiced teams for the equipment. When challenged Ecclestone said, "I said I was going to supply them, I didn't say I was going to pay for them."[12] As usual in F1, the situation was more complicated than it first appeared. By this stage, teams had unveiled their new cars which were built with refuelling in mind, which didn't have large enough tanks to race without refuelling. Having to shorten races wasn't what the money men of F1 wanted to see happen. Even if their tanks were large enough teams had to refuel, because Ferrari was intending to. Otherwise, they simply wouldn't be competitive.

This didn't stop safety concerns continuing to build up during pre-season testing. Bob Dance of Lotus was showered with fuel during testing at Silverstone. The shut-off value proved troublesome for McLaren at Estoril as did the nozzle itself for Ferrari during testing at Imola. Ligier was so concerned about a pitlane fire that it decided to simulate a mistake in the pits based on the hose spraying for about four seconds. "It was terrifying, like a bomb going off" concluded their team manager Dany Hindenoch. Max Mosley stepped into the fiery debate (excuse the pun) with the following:

"I think that the team owners are being a little disingenuous. Whatever their excuses, they all requested refuelling in the first place and when they say it's crazy, it does invite the question: why did they sign for it? Would they have signed, for example, if, at the end of the meeting Ecclestone had said he wasn't going to give them any more prize money? I admit that, had the matter of refuelling been left entirely to me, I'd have thought very long and hard about it. People say now the FIA could simply take away the equipment, and that would settle the matter, but I know that there would be cries of 'there he goes again' and having forced through the technical changes we wanted, I don't want to do it again unless I really have to."[13]

Did the banning of fly-by-wire throttles contribute towards Williams' traction problems in 1994? *Photo: Alastair Ladd*

Mosley also pointed out after the Hockenheim crisis meeting, teams came to him with the settlement package which included refuelling, not the other way around, implying you therefore cannot blame the FIA for introducing it. Granted, but was that the whole picture? By late September 1993, no team wished to proceed with it, except Ferrari. Moreover, it was widely believed the idea originated from Ecclestone, but who was he representing when proposing refuelling? Was it the teams under his role as chairman of the F1 Constructors' Association (FOCA) or was it the FIA under his role as vice-president of the body? "I would say Ecclestone remains very much the teams' man, not only as FOCA chairman but also within the FIA," said Mosley. In light of the way refuelling was seemingly thrust upon them perhaps some participants might have disagreed with that particular assessment.

On top of the aforementioned problems, some teams also found metallic swarf (tiny debris produced during the manufacturing

Benetton was a smaller team than its rivals, but somehow its 1994 car proved quick in the hands of Schumacher. *Photo: Ford*

Few betted against Senna becoming 1994 champion during pre-season.
Photo: Alastair Ladd

Most teams brought two refuelling tanks to 1994 races, whereas the above suggests Ferarri had four tanks. **Photo: Ersek Zsolt**

stage) within the refuelling apparatus. According to *Motor Sport* magazine, this contributed towards the fuel rig problems Lotus and Jordan had experienced during pre-season in 1994. To overcome this issue, a filter was retrofitted to the equipment around March 1994. This would become highly significant later on. Simon Morley, Benetton's refueller at the time, adds: "Before the 1994 season and even before fuel rig delivery, Intertechnique hosted a training session for all the teams. Each team sent representatives that would be responsible for the maintenance of their rigs, as the refueller I made it my responsibility to maintain my own rigs after all it was in my own interest as well as my teammates'."

"The training session consisted of two or three days of lectures and hands-on component strip down and rebuild. With this being a French company and the French tradition of long lunches the training days were quite short. By the time most teams received their rigs it was only a week before freight had to leave for Brazil and the training sessions were well in the past, yes you had plenty of notes, but the hands-on experience was faded. The rigs and valves were serviced after every event and sometimes during the events with new seals and slide rings each time – no compromise. The nozzle [part that connects to car] was quite often extremely sensitive to slight variations in seals or slide rings."

Despite being a book about the 1994 F1 season, the various races will not be covered in detail since that information can be found

from numerous other sources. However, on-track performances will be referenced when it is relevant or adds context for those readers who are not familiar with the drama that awaits you, and now is such a time. Coming into the year Williams was the team to beat. They had been so dominant in 1992 that triple World Champion Ayrton Senna was offering his services to them for free! Williams was unable to sign him for 1993 due to a complicated contractual situation, however the Brazilian persisted and eventually got his dream drive for 1994. As they say, be careful what you wish for.

Senna's chief rival in 1993 had been Alain Prost who, at the age of 38, old by F1 standards, cruised to his fourth championship within a Williams before retiring. With Prost out of the way, conventional wisdom said Senna was going to dominate 1994. However, the challenge facing the Brazilian was far greater than anyone anticipated. Williams' dominance had partly been based on its ability to master the electronic gizmos necessary for F1 success. So it had most to lose once they were outlawed for 1994, which ironically was something Senna had been lobbying for. One of the reasons driver aids had been banned was to give Williams' rivals a chance at winning, ie to 'spice up' the show.

12. *No Angel: The Secret Life of Bernie Ecclestone* by Tom Bower (2011)
13. *Autosport*, 7 April 1994

Chapter 2

Indeed Williams had manipulated active suspension, the system which maintained a constant ride height of the car, in a specific way which exploited its aerodynamics. This was due to having greater recent experience with active suspension, while also employing the acknowledged guru on F1 aerodynamics, Adrian Newey. However, the 1993 constructors' champions would become complacent. In his recent autobiography, Newey admitted not enough prior thought and work went into adapting things for the new for 1994 passive suspension (which is one that merely reacts to the road's surface, similar to your road car). As a consequence, Williams found the aerodynamics on its 1994 car, the FW16, too peaky and sensitive to changes in ride height. Meaning the FW16 was unpredictable to drive in practice, certainly in those early 1994 grands prix.

By Newey's own admission, it took Williams a few races into the season to remarry the aerodynamics to passive suspension. Until then, the FW16 also proved difficult to set up during race weekends and the drivers reported it was inconsistent over bumps. During a *Motor Sport* magazine podcast in February 2018 Dickie Stanford, Williams' chief mechanic at the time, explained because there was such a big change from the previous year's car, Williams didn't spend enough time testing the car pre-season. The FW16 was one of the last 1994 F1 cars to hit the track. Anti-lock brakes were also banned for 1994, which hurt Williams more than most because it had been using a highly developed version whereas Benetton had not used any system in 1993.

Perhaps Williams was also hurt by the 1994 regulations being finalised so late, which was partly due to Williams' and McLaren's efforts to keep active suspension and the subsequent wrangling explained earlier. *Autosport* magazine felt this battle wasn't solely about active suspension, but was also about who ran the sport – the teams or the FIA? If true, this may explain why the dispute lasted so long. Whatever the case, the upshot was Williams was now paying the price. Interestingly, McLaren also suffered a dip in form from

Benetton, a fashion company, was not a traditional F1 team like Williams, McLaren and Ferrari. *Photo: Pete Hennessy*

1993 to 1994. However, in that case things were complicated by the loss of Senna and their new Peugeot engine proving uncompetitive. Ferrari, unsurprisingly, was a major winner of the 1994 rules shake-up and an added bonus was that its new 412T1 car looked and sounded stunning. The sound of a mid-1990s Ferrari V12 truly makes the hairs on the back of your neck stand up.

While Ferrari, Williams and McLaren had been throwing allegations of cheating at one another or threatening to go legal over rule changes, the fourth biggest team in F1 had quietly been getting on with the job. Benetton made a conscious effort in early 1993 to limit the development of that season's car, the B193, and instead focus up to 90 percent of its resources on its successor. Martin Walters, Cosworth's Chief Engineer, confirmed that the team also took the same approach with the new-for-1994 Ford Zetec R engine: paying particular attention to improving things like driveability and fuel consumption.[14] Things that would play a crucial role given traction control and fly-by-wire throttle ban.

Ross Brawn, Benetton's Technical Director, detailed the reasoning: "Active suspension was going, which meant the

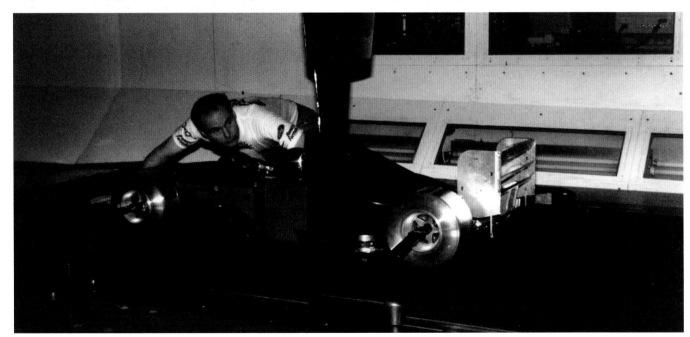

Willem Toet believes Benetton's advantage came from developing usable aerodynamics. *Photo: Willem Toet*

The B194 was one of the first cars to hit the track in 1994, allowing the team to adapt its aerodynamics to passive suspension. **Photo: Ford**

Richard Wise (circled in red) in early 1994. **Photo: Richard Wise**

aerodynamic regulations were changing. There was a whole raft of new rules. At the beginning of 1993, I said to Rory Byrne [designer] that this was our big opportunity... We had a brilliant driver in Michael, enough money to do the job and a works Ford engine. We should be up there."[15] Unlike Williams and McLaren, Benetton didn't fight the active ban – instead, it choose to plan for it. FISA's intentions that F1 would go back to basics for 1994 became known in February 1993, meaning the Enstone team was likely to have gained a massive head start as a result. It was a gamble because Benetton would have been on the back foot had Williams and McLaren successfully kept active for 1994, but they didn't so it paid off.

Consequently, Benetton was testing its 1994 challenger several weeks before Williams, which proved invaluable in rectifying any problems before the first race. "At Benetton, we worked hard on making the downforce usable," explains Head of Aerodynamics, Willem Toet. "In 1993, we were using active suspension and that allowed us to have aerodynamic parts that were a bit more on a knife edge. It was clear at Barcelona (pre-season testing) – Benetton found ways to minimise the aero damage done by the regulation changes." By the time the Williams FW16 first took to the track in late February, the new Benetton B194 had racked up the miles and blitzed the 1993 pole time at Barcelona. Aerodynamics were more of a factor than any illegal concealed devices at Barcelona because the majority of corners were high speed, where traction control make little difference.

One of Benetton's biggest assets was a young Schumacher, who was seen as the hottest property in F1 since Senna. Some even believed the German would have the Brazilian's measure had they been teammates. However, questions were raised whether Schumacher and Benetton could sustain a season-long threat to Senna and Williams. In Benetton's favour was its engineering team, led by Ross Brawn and Rory Byrne, who would both go on to win multiple world championships subsequently. However, at the start of 1994 it wasn't generally appreciated just how strong Benetton's technical team was. Likewise, Schumacher would eventually become F1's most successful driver ever. It is worth remembering the achievements of Schumacher, Brawn and Byrne outside of 1994 when forming an opinion over the controversies that are to come.

Williams, Ferrari and Benetton all participated in a FOCA[16] arranged pre-season test held two weeks before the opening race.

It was a four-day test, held between 8 and 11 March, and the first chance to see how the new cars compared against one another. The circuit hosting the test, Imola, was considered a power track and primarily consisted of slow/medium speed corners. The new passive suspensions would also be put through their paces on Imola's high kerbs and bumpy road surface. In hindsight, it now clear this track didn't entirely suit Williams because the bumps exposed the FW16's aerodynamic problems. However, at the time not many knew of Williams' issues – therefore it was assumed the Didcot team would easily top the times, given Imola's power demands. This explains why observers were shocked by Williams' lack of performance during this test relative to Schumacher's Benetton Ford.

Often, lap times set during testing can be deceiving because the cars are not always running the same amount of fuel or type of tyre etc. What's more, they're not on track at the same time, so conditions and track temperatures are different. However, this Imola test was significant because *Autosport* magazine reported the final hour on the final day became a "mini-qualifying session" meaning every car ran together, with lowest fuel, softest available tyres and drivers trying to set their best laptime. It therefore provided the best opportunity yet to compare the 1994 pecking order of the teams and drivers. Below are the results from that day:

Schumacher topped the timesheets, which registered with onlookers because his Ford V8 engine wasn't best suited to the power demands of Imola. Instead, its strengths were in driveability, size, weight, fuel consumption and packaging (ie smaller cooling radiators which upset the aerodynamics less). Nevertheless, Schumacher had been consistently quick throughout the four days, suggesting he might be a threat to title favourites Senna and Williams in the early races at least. Richard Wise was Williams' timekeeper in 1994: "I remember at the end of the Imola test, while I was collating all my times from the day, Ayrton came in to the truck to go through the times with me. Again it was just him and me and I will always remember and look back at this moment." The German's surprising pace then gave rise to other, darker, predictions as Brawn later recalled:

14. Eurosport's coverage of the 1994 Canadian Grand Prix weekend
15. Monaco: Inside F1's Greatest Race by Malcolm Folley (2017)
16. F1 Constructors' Association

1994 PRE-SEASON IMOLA TEST RESULTS

	Driver	Team	Lap Time	Gap	Date Set
1	Schumacher	Benetton-Ford	1m21.078	—	11/3/1994
2	Senna	Williams-Renault	1m21.244	+0.166	11/3/1994
3	Hill	Williams-Renault	1m21.825	+0.747	11/3/1994
4	Berger	Ferrari	1m21.865	+0.787	11/3/1994
5	Alesi	Ferrari	1m23.324	+2.246	11/3/1994
6	Verstappen	Benetton-Ford	1m23.648	+2.570	9/3/1994
7	Lehto	Benetton-Ford	1m32.590	+11.512	8/3/1994

1994 SAN MARINO GP QUALIFYING RESULTS

	Driver	Team	Friday Qualifying	Saturday Qualifying	Gap
1	Senna	Williams-Renault	1:21.548	no time	—
2	Schumacher	Benetton-Ford	1:22.015	1:21.885	+0.337
3	Berger	Ferrari	1:22.113	1:22.226	+0.565
4	Hill	Williams-Renault	1:23.199	1:22.168	+0.620
5	Lehto	Benetton-Ford	1:22.717	1:24.029	+1.169
6	Larini	Ferrari	1:22.841	1:23.006	+1.293

"At the Imola test before the season started, we did a mock race run – not many people were doing that at the time. So we did this mock race run and you cannot sandbag [ie hide performance] in that because the fuel runs down, the tyres change. Others were coming on to the pit wall and watching the lap times. They were stunning. Then the accusations started: 'You are running underweight, you have done this, that and the other.' It's an easy excuse to make."[17] Despite this, rival teams seemingly didn't have enough conviction within their belief that Benetton was doing something questionable, to report it to the FIA or media. Meaning, Benetton was the only top team not to be accused of breaking the rules in some way before the Imola pre-season test in either *Motor Sport*, *F1 News* or *Autosport* magazines. In fact, the latter described Benetton as "squeaky clean" at the time, but how long would that last for?

"Well, so much depends on what results people are getting" Brawn replied at the time. "Ferrari, for instance, has a new front suspension system. Some people think it's legal, others don't. If they started to run away with the races, I'm sure the other teams would become more vociferous in their objections. But if they aren't competitive, people will tend to overlook it."[18] Given all the mudslinging between Ferrari, Williams and McLaren – the expected front-runners for 1994 prior to the Imola test –how surprising was it accusations of cheating were thrown Benetton's way once Schumacher started beating others? It was around this time suspicions started to emerge that Schumacher was using an illegal traction control.

Whether there is any truth behind these allegations is something explored in detail later. However, video footage of this Imola test can be found online. Within this footage, those cars present can be heard with perfect clarity since there is no disruptive crowd noise or trackside PA systems usually found during race weekends. During testing sessions like this one, the silence is only shattered by the glorious wail of proper F1 engines and traction control has a very distinctive sound – a rough, gargling or popping engine note – which is noticeable whenever cars equipped with it launch out of slow corners. Readers might be interested to seek out this footage, and decide for themselves whether Schumacher's Benetton makes any such sounds under heavy acceleration when exiting corners like Tosa.

After the Imola pre-season test, both Schumacher and Berger admitted they were 100 percent on the limit to achieve their best lap times. Whereas Senna said he could go faster but didn't want to show his hand. For comparison purposes, below are the qualifying times, held weeks after the Imola test:

The gap between Schumacher and Berger at the March test was 0.8sec. However, the gap between the two drivers after the qualifying session reduced to 0.2sec. This is understandable considering Ferrari made significant improvements to its handling imbalance during the intervening period. The two Williams also proved faster during the race weekend relative to Schumacher's Benetton, because they had a better understanding of their aerodynamic flaws so were now starting to unleash the FW16's hidden potential. The point being those who believed

At the final pre-season test Senna was 0.16sec slower than Schumacher at Imola... **Photo: Giovanni Talli**

...This was surprising given Benetton's Ford engine was less powerful than the Renault in Senna's Williams. **Photo: Ford**

Verstappen debuted in F1 amid huge hype but little car racing experience. **Photo: Ford**

Lehto joined Benetton for 1994 but suffered a neck-breaking accident only weeks before the Imola test. **Photo: Alastair Ladd**

Schumacher ran illegal traction control during the race weekend must by implication believe he used it during the Imola test because Schumacher was slower at the race weekend relative to Senna and Berger compared to the pre-season test. The aforementioned video footage of the Imola pre-season tests, may prove interesting to some.

During that test Lehto, in the second Benetton, was slow because he broke his neck during a testing accident only 48 days prior and this was his first time back in the car since. "My neck was hurting over the bumps and in the corners," explained Lehto, who only completed 11 laps. "The muscles have been dead for a month and the first time that I braked I heard a cracking noise in my neck. I can drive but not quickly enough... I was due to drive again but I didn't want my recovery to go backwards."[19]

Lehto had rushed his return to F1 because he was terrified of losing his Benetton seat – 1994 was the Finn's first top F1 drive after five years within the sport, and adding to his pressure was he only had a one-year contract. Having seen how quick the B194 was in Schumacher's hands from earlier tests, Lehto would have known this was a make or break year for him in F1 – but his injury had forced him to sit on the sidelines until the San Marino Grand Prix. Replacing Lehto in the meantime was an extremely young and raw Jos Verstappen – the father of current F1 star Max Verstappen.

After karting, Verstappen only had two seasons of car racing experience behind him prior to 1994. At the time this was an unprecedented rise through the ranks to race the fastest and

most dangerous cars on earth. It was almost half the car racing experience Senna and Schumacher each had before getting to F1. While Verstappen had shown considerable promise testing for Footwork in September 1993, it was a car fitted with the fully suite of permitted driver aids. Even so, Jos crashed the Footwork heavily forcing the test to be ended prematurely. Nevertheless he impressed Benetton enough to be appointed as their test driver when the B194 was launched in early January, and then came to call to replace Lehto in the opening two races. A

Given the circumstances behind his unusually rapid ascent from karting to a Benetton race seat, the B194 wouldn't have been designed with Verstappen or his driving style in mind. Indeed, the new 1994 breed of F1 cars were much harder to drive than their 1993 counterparts, adding to the Dutchman's steep learning curve. Verstappen would also be in the same team as the highly rated Schumacher, in a car increasingly built around the German – a situation which destroyed the careers of numerous F1 drivers before and since. Verstappen was well and truly being thrown in at the deep end, and perhaps his 1994 crash record would prove this. They say start as you mean to go on, and Verstappen certainly did this in Brazil, by arguably causing one of the most horrific looking multi-car pile-ups ever seen in F1.

17. *Monaco: Inside F1's Greatest Race* by Malcolm Folley (2017)
18. *The Independent*, 4 September 1994
19. *Autosport*, 17 March 1994

BRAZIL AND PACIFIC

March and April 1994

"It's going to be a season with lots of accidents, and I'll risk saying that we'll be lucky if something really serious doesn't happen."

Ayrton Senna, Williams driver

"Touch wood we haven't killed anybody at a Grand Prix for 11 years now."

Max Mosley, FIA President
(speaking in 1993)

Senna was concerned how unstable the 1994 cars were.

Photo:Károly Méhes

Pre-season predictions for the 1994 season

DRIVERS' CHAMPIONSHIP	
Pos	Driver
1	Ayrton Senna
2	Michael Schumacher
3	Damon Hill

CONSTRUCTORS' CHAMPIONSHIP	
Pos	Constructor
1	Williams-Renault
2	Benetton-Ford
3	Ferrari

Alesi was forced to miss two races following his Mugello accident. **Photo: Tony Harrison**

The Benetton mechanics were closely watched by Senna in Brazil. **Photo: Martin Lee**

Although the new cars were less stable due to the ban on driver aids and active suspension, they proved quicker than their 1993 predecessors. However, safety wasn't a major talking point at the start of 1994 because there had not been any fatal accidents during a race weekend in the previous 12 years. With multiple drivers emerging unscathed from major accidents in previous years, it seemed figures in the sport had become complacent about safety by 1994. This was about to be shattered in a manner that the sport would never forget.

While the popular driver, Elio de Angelis, had been killed during a test session at Paul Ricard in 1986, that tragedy was put down to a lack of medical facilities onsite. Multiple major accidents had taken place since 1982, including Nelson Piquet and Gerhard Berger who both had high-speed accidents at the Tamburello corner in 1987 and 1989. Alex Zanardi crashed heavily during the practice sessions for the 1993 Belgian Grand Prix, yet recovered fully from his injuries. On 21 January 1994, JJ Lehto broke his neck and was lucky not to have been killed following a testing accident in his Benetton at the Silverstone circuit. The immediate reaction wasn't one on what safety lessons could be learnt: instead, the press was more eager to know when the Finn would be back in the car and whether Jos Verstappen, despite his inexperience, would be thrust into a race seat.

Similarly, a few days after the Brazilian Grand Prix, Jean Alesi injured his neck after a high-speed crash during a test at Mugello which forced him to miss the next two races. Despite the Ferrari driver claiming "I'm lucky to be alive," no action to improve safety standards was taken in the immediate aftermath. While this attitude may sound startling given current attitudes towards safety, it was considered normal at the time. The F1 paddock had become accustomed to drivers escaping unscathed from horrific looking accidents. Derek Warwick crashed heavily in both the 1990 Italian Grand Prix and 1993 German Grand Prix, yet neither accident prevented him from racing the same day. It would be wrong to say that there had been no improvements in safety standards in this period though.

Towards the end of the 1980s and early 1990s, the FIA had introduced stricter front impact and roll hoop tests, along with stricter fuel cell standards in 1991. In 1992, the first front crash test that imposed restrictions on the maximum deceleration that drivers should experience was introduced, while in 1993 the headrests were increased in size from 80 to 400sq cm to increase head protection. However, it could also be argued that side impact regulations had not kept pace with the improvements in the front impact test requirements.

Mosley later claimed the culture within F1 was hostile to any substantial safety improvements before 1994. "You were always up against the argument that for all practical purposes accidents with injuries had been limited. There had not been a death [at a grand prix] for 12 years."[20] While crash testing standards had gradually improved over the years, luck also played a major role why the last fatality was 184 grands prix ago.

The first race of the season was held in Senna's home city of Sao Paulo, Brazil, this was where the talking would stop and teams would finally show one another their hand. Could anyone live with Senna in the Williams? Would any cars be declared illegal? Would the refuelling equipment prove unsafe? The teams practised the refuelling procedure as much as possible to minimise the risk and, by the end of the weekend, fortunately no incidents had occurred. "I do know that after the first race of 94, there was a huge collective sigh of relief from the whole paddock knowing that refuelling had been completed incident free," said Benetton's refueller Simon Morley. "As subsequent races went on it just became the norm that nothing would go wrong, not saying that we all became complacent but the fear of something happening reduced as time progressed."

Once again Mosley warned if someone "deliberately cheated – not that they interpreted the rule differently to you or there was some debatable point which they may be wrong about – then I think draconian penalties are completely correct". With all the bickering between teams, havoc was expected in the scrutineering bays at Brazil, but come the moment of reckoning all was surprisingly quiet. It seemed teams were waiting until after the race to protest about one another in order to inflict the maximum damage on their rivals.

20. *Motorsport*, February 1995

Chapter 3

Senna watched Schumacher's car closely during practice in Brazil. Its competitiveness and stability out of slow corners increasingly convinced the Brazilian his rival was using illegal traction control. In Senna's mind, there was no other explanation why the German should be so close to his Williams. According to former Benetton mechanic, Steve Matchett, in his book entitled *Life in the Fast Lane*, each time Senna drove past their pits he would slow down lift his visor and study the B194 or the mechanics should Schumacher be out on the track himself.

Nevertheless, it was local boy Senna who beat Schumacher to pole position by 0.3sec, although this was nothing like the margin Williams enjoyed in previous years. Senna's car looked unpredictable on the limit and he had used all of his considerable talent to achieve that lap time. By comparison, the well-honed Benetton looked comfortable over the bumpy track and Schumacher, despite suffering from flu, felt he could have gone quicker had the rain not affected the final qualifying session. Underlining what a difficult car the Williams was at this stage of the season Hill, who also had flu, was fourth and 1.6sec slower than his teammate. Further back, Verstappen had shown his lack of experience by spinning several times during practice and qualifying only ninth.

Before the race, the cars undertook a formation lap[20] where Schumacher transgressed a rule stipulating drivers must maintain grid order, as he overtook pole man, Senna, along the back straight approaching turn three. Neither Schumacher nor Benetton were penalised for this misdemeanour, nor were they given any warning not to do it again. Interestingly, no TV commentators or press reporters picked up on this infringement afterwards. Why?

Because this rule wasn't well known. Indeed, until 1994 no F1 driver had been penalised for a breach. It was therefore common to see drivers briefly overtaking one another during the formation lap. This rule would be brought sharply into focus during a subsequent race, and on that occasion many would be angered over it being infringed (detailed later on). Meanwhile, few cared it had been broken in Brazil and cynics might argue killing off a potentially exciting race and championship battle by penalising Senna's only challenger, Schumacher, at the first race wouldn't help TV ratings. Remember 'spicing up the show' had been the buzz phrase of F1 coming into 1994.

Senna led from pole, while Schumacher made a poor getaway and dropped behind Alesi's Ferrari – everything seemed to be working out for the local favourite after all. However, Schumacher immediately passed Alesi and chased after the Brazilian, drawing a little closer with each passing lap: nobody expected this! The exciting battle between the superstar of F1 and the young pretender was interrupted on lap 21 with the first round of refuelling pit stops. Senna and Schumacher came into the pits together but Benetton was quicker in getting their man out first, which handed Schumacher the lead.

Afterwards, the German initially pulled away but Senna, spurred on by his home crowd, chipped away at Schumacher's lead. However, it was evident the triple world champion was right on his and the car's limit in doing so. When being lapped by the two leaders, Irvine remarked just how stable the Benetton looked in comparison to Senna's Williams. On lap 55 it finally got too much for the Brazilian and he spun out. "I was pushing too hard – it was my mistake," Senna later conceded. This gifted the win to Schumacher who considered this as one of his greatest wins because he and Senna had been racing at qualifying pace throughout their battle.

Mario-Alberto Bauér, an F1 journalist at the time, revealed: "I spoke to Ayrton about his spin on Monday evening after Brazil and

In Brazil, the bargeboard stays (circled in red) proved a bone of contention for Schumacher's winning Benetton. *Photo: Martin Lee*

For 1995, many teams including Williams (pictured) and McLaren adopted a high nose concept, similar to that on the 1994 Benetton. **Photo: Morio**

Benetton (pictured in 1996) had a quicker pitstops than Williams. Greater practice, or them removing a fuel filter? **Photo: Andrew-44-19**

he basically summed it up as the FW16 being especially tricky in the circumstances. On why his sudden, uncontrollable mid-corner snap-oversteer occurred, it was definitely an aero problem and probably related to the radical front end of the car... He also made a side-remark about how easily the Benetton was handling with a high-nose front end layout. He didn't go much into details, but he clearly knew something the rest of us would find out later."

In view of later events, the pit stops at this race would come under close scrutiny. Benetton achieved faster refuelling stops than Williams for a number of reasons. Firstly, they were using a lighter and more fuel efficient Ford V8 engine compared to the powerful Renault V10 used by Williams. This consumption advantage meant a lower fuel load was required during pit stops. Benetton's Technical Director, Ross Brawn, also noted Schumacher had a tendency to use less fuel than teammates during his time in sports car racing,[21] suggesting the German may have conserved fuel at some point during the race while behind Senna.

Key figures at Benetton like Schumacher, Walkinshaw and Brawn all had prior refuelling experience from sports car racing during the early 1990s. Brawn explains the benefits: "Strategy was a key part of things [there] but in F1 it was only getting started then. When I returned to F1 I was amazed at how poorly some teams used the pit stops to work for them strategically. In 1994, we were often able to beat Williams through simple strategic moves. The fuel rigs were much slower then. We could stay with them carrying 10 more kilos of fuel so we could put less in. So our pit stops would be a couple of seconds quicker than theirs and we would come out in front. All sorts of accusations went flying around, and our fuel cells were stripped three or four times that season. But the calculations were simple. It was just something we were more familiar with because of sports car racing."

Hill also confirmed Williams had not grasped the subtleties of refuelling pit stops,[22] while his mechanic Paul West explained: "Another reason for Benetton being so quick at their pit stops was they had a quick release and reset for the wheel locking mechanism to stop the wheel nuts from coming undone. We used a metal clip which had to be pulled out and refitted by hand, very time consuming, theirs was released by the socket going onto the

nut and all the gunman had to do was pull it out to reset it. It was that attention to detail, plus Ross's experience in sports cars, that gave them an edge." West also confirms Williams didn't use a quick release jack in 1994, whereas Benetton had. This was yet another example of Benetton's time-saving initiatives during pit stops.

Williams had usually been poor at pit stops before 1994, the most famous example being the 1991 Portuguese Grand Prix where a botched pit stop contributed to Mansell losing that year's championship. It wasn't until 1996 when Williams could finally compete with Benetton in terms of quick pit stops and strategic planning. Benetton, on the other hand, practised pit stops more than any other team, helping to shave those vital tenths of a second. During 1993, Benetton was consistently the fastest team in the pitlane. In that year's Belgian Grand Prix, Benetton claimed to have turned Patrese's car around in 3.2sec, a record which due to refuelling being introduced in 1994, would last until 2012.

"I think that Williams just didn't give pit stops and refuelling enough practice," said Paul West. "Looking back Benetton could see that time could be made up by getting the driver 'in the zone' by constant practice either testing or at a race. Whereas I think Williams and some of the other teams didn't see the advantage that could be gained or were slow to pick up on what Benetton was doing. On our part, it may have been a misplaced confidence that we had been, mostly, so dominant in previous years that a slow stop could be made up for in the performance of the car on track and then 1994 comes along and that window has slammed shut."

Simon Morley, Benetton's refueller in 1994, highlights another benefit pit stop practice gave: "We had the refueller and a hose holder behind him. The hose holder was a very important and integral part of the refuelling procedure. Not only did he support most of the weight he also tried to give the correct angle for the nozzle to connect to the car. This set-up between the refueller and the hose holder was practiced without compromise, during pit stop practice, in the evenings or on our own with which ever car was available to plug in to, most often the spare car."

20. Cars drive a slow lap in grid order which acts as a final system check
21. *Motorsport*, April 2007
22. *Watching the Wheels: My Autobiography*, Damon Hill (2016)

Chapter 3

"Once everyone was happy the pitlane was marked with our starting positions, these positions were not far from the final plugging in position because if we had moved much, then valuable time was lost during the pit stop. The refueller would stand as close as possible to where the car would stop without hopefully having his foot run over! I did get hit a few times across the toes of my shoes by the bargeboards[23] as the car came to a stop. "If I remember correctly, we came up with the procedure of the fuel hose being plugged into the car before the car was jacked up for the tire change, by doing this it meant less of a moving target for the feeler to hit. Generally the fuel was always slower than the tires so it also made sense to get the fuel flowing as soon as possible."

Another Benetton insider added: "For me, the reason we [Benetton] had fast stops with Schumacher was that I trusted him. He could come into the pitlane crossed up and I wouldn't move because he'd always had it under control." Pat Symonds of Benetton adds: "The final part of the equation was that we had a driver [Schumacher] who was capable of driving three sprint races during a grand prix, and he was bloody good at that."[24] The above factors may not sound significant individually, but collectively they all contributed and the 1994 Brazilian Grand Prix was effectively won by the time saved in the pits. Despite the above, many claimed Benetton's quicker pitstops in Brazil was due to them tampering with their refuelling equipment, which is discussed in detail later.

There was only one protest between teams after the race, which was surprising given the arguments over interpretation over the rules pre-season. Schumacher's winning Benetton was challenged by Jordan over their bargeboards, which are used to deflect the airflow wake around the sidepods. The rules stated all bodywork viewed from beneath the car must form a solid and impervious surface, but Benetton attached their barge boards to their chassis using two stays, one at the front and one at the rear. Jordan therefore claimed that, because there was a gap in between these two stays, the bodywork didn't form an "impervious" surface.

Jordan admitted Benetton wouldn't have gained any performance advantage from this design, claiming its protest was merely to clarify ways of mounting the bargeboard. Benetton was the only team to run bargeboards in Brazil, so it is possible this point had been overlooked when the 1994 regulations were originally drawn up. The race stewards threw out Jordan's protest, presumably

After Brazil, Williams ran the number 0 for the rest of the season.
Photo: Martin Lee

because their argument might open a Pandora's box. For instance, if it had been successful then could one argue the gaps in between the suspension wishbones were "not impervious" under this rule? The regulation was later amended for 1995 specifically to allow for this gap, given more teams started to run bargeboards by then.

The timing of Jordan's protest surprised many because earlier in the weekend Charlie Whiting had invited all of the teams to raise concerns during scrutineering. Given the barge boards and their mounting points were not particularly hidden, Jordan therefore had ample opportunity to raise their concerns to the FIA prior to the race. In fact, bargeboards had been introduced the previous season by McLaren which also included gaps in between their mounting points, yet no teams protested the matter in 1993. Nobody knew why only Jordan complained about it in Brazil, however by excluding Schumacher's winning Benetton it would have elevated their star driver Barrichello, another local hero, to his and the team's first ever podium.

Conversely, Schumacher being allowed to keep his win was good for TV because it set the scene for an exciting championship battle against overwhelming favourite Senna, of course little did people know how events would unfold. Williams designer, Adrian Newey, recently implied Jordan's appeal had some substance[25] although neither he nor Williams protested at the time.

Ferrari's Aida infringement added to the paranoia that cheating was rife because electronics were difficult to police. **Photo: Károly Méhes**

Ferrari only disarmed its outlawed software in Aida, rather than removing it from the black box (circled in red). **Photo: Norbert Neutron**

The large Renault badge instead of the number 0 on the nose of Hill's car. This broke the rules. ***Photo: Motorsport Images/LAT***

Another bone of contention largely forgotten since 1994 was Williams running a large Renault badge instead of the number 0 on the nose of Hill's car. It was a clever marketing ploy since it vaguely looked like a 0, Hill's race number, from a distance. It did, however, break article 48 of the sporting regulations which stated "[A car's] race number must be clearly visible from the front and from either side of the car." Once again, no TV commentators or journalists appeared to notice this at the time. Although Williams was not penalised, it does seem they were quietly told to change this immediately because they ran a 0 for the rest of the season on Hill's car.

The most controversial incident after Brazil was Irvine being blamed for an enormous accident involving three other cars. The Jordan driver was initially given a one race ban and fined $10,000, when the team appealed this its fine was lifted but his race ban was tripled. Jordan also lost its appeal fee of c$16,500 – a bad deal all round which left the team "shattered". Many thought this ruling was incredibly harsh because Verstappen was arguably at fault yet escaped any punishment. Irvine himself felt that was the case, and believes he was blamed because the authorities wanted to teach him a lesson for an earlier misdemeanour.

During his F1 debut only a couple of races before, Irvine had unlapped himself against Senna who subsequently punched him. The Brazilian received a six month suspended penalty his action. However during the hearing it was reported Irvine had put some influential noises out of joint. Was Irvine now experiencing payback? Before 1994, the last driver to have suffered a race ban was Nigel Mansell in 1989 after he ignored a black flag. Before that Riccardo Patrese, had to miss the 1978 US Grand Prix because

the drivers (incorrectly) blamed him for causing a startline crash at the previous race which led to Ronnie Peterson's tragic death.

The next race was entitled the Pacific Grand Prix, and held on the TI Circuit (Tanaka International) in Japan. In order to hide disappointing attendance figures, organisers took inspiration from the old restaurant trick of serving tiny portions on smaller plates by dismantling several grandstands prior to the race. Before the event Ferrari upset its rivals by testing at Imola, which they were not supposed to do apparently, because it was the venue for the next Grand Prix. Ferrari's boss, Jean Todt, claimed the test was cleared by the FIA which angered McLaren's principle, Ron Dennis, who retorted: "The rule is there in black and white and Ferrari can read". Hopes that this might be the only controversy that weekend were dashed by Saturday morning.

Following the continued suspicion that some, like Schumacher's Benetton, were somehow circumventing the rules on traction control and other driver aids, the FIA's Charlie Whiting stood trackside during practice in Aida, with sound measuring equipment which carefully listened to the cars. He noticed the Ferrari had a distinctive misfiring sound from its exhaust note, a characteristic of traction control, which suggested some kind of device was in operation. He intended to see them about it but before he could Ferrari found him to explain themselves. The device in question was later ruled illegal and Ferrari disarmed it with immediate effect. To the astonishment of many the Italian team wasn't punished in any way.

23. Curved vertical piece of bodywork situated between the front wheels and the sidepods
24. *Autosport,* 7 August 2014
25. *How to Build a Race Car* by Adrian Newey (2017)

Chapter 3

In light of Mosley's pre-season promise of "draconian penalties" for any breach of the driver aids ban, many felt this decision was excessively lenient. They were let off the hook because Ferrari saw the FIA before the stewards came knocking on their door. *Autosport* reported that Berger had spotted Whiting trackside with his measuring equipment, the Ferrari driver then pitted to warn Todt of this. If true could this have prompted Ferrari to visit the FIA about their device, or maybe it was just coincidence and Ferrari was intending to see Whiting anyway. Mosley and Todt later admitted Ferrari had made a mistake in not consulting with the FIA before running its device during a race weekend.

Another reason for leniency was because the FIA didn't consider Ferrari's device to be traction control "because it wasn't influenced in any way by the behaviour of the driven wheels", in effect saying it wasn't a deliberate attempt to cheat, merely the Italian team brought something where the legality was debatable. However, the FIA admitted the device did come between a driver's right foot and the power output of the engine: precisely the reason fly-by-wire throttles were banned only weeks earlier. Benetton's Ross Brawn accused Ferrari of hypocrisy because they were against fly-by-wire throttles, yet were exploiting a similar grey area in the regulations which he believed to be analogous.

The device in question was described by Ferrari as a "just like a rev limiter... Why not have something which comes in at say 11,000rpm in first and second gears and then cuts out in higher gears? We could take all our wheel sensors off and still run the system. It's not traction control."[26] However questions were asked, why else would you have this system if it's not to aid traction? The name of the device even caught out Ferrari's substitute driver Nicola Larini (replacing the injured Alesi) who spoke of turning off his traction control to the Italian media. After the Ferrari PR

team corrected him Nicola then referred to the device as 'it' when speaking with *Autosport*. Whatever 'it' was called the net result limited wheelspin.

The FIA cited a third reason why they didn't come down like a ton of bricks over this. It was claimed the device made no difference to the performance of the car and the outcome of the race since it was only used in practice. Nevertheless, the rules clearly stated under Article 2.6 that a car must be legal in its entirety at all times during an event. Many felt this was yet another example of favouritism towards Ferrari. With the next race held in Italy, it would have been brave to ban the scarlet cars that made such a wonderful noise from their home event. Or maybe this is unfair and the FIA would have reacted in the same way had it been a dominating Williams caught. One to ponder perhaps. In view of later controversies, it is important to remember that Ferrari was allowed compete in this race with a potentially illegal device merely disarmed, and not completely removed from their engine electronic control unit.

Senna, mindful of the uphill task he had given himself after his non-finish in Brazil, took his 64th pole position ahead of Schumacher. However, once again it had not been easy for the former world champion as renowned journalist, Dennis Jenkinson, noted in his languorous style that the car "had no qualms about demonstrating its continuing distaste for slow-speed corners". Having initially traded times with Schumacher, the session finally turned in Senna's favour when Schumacher misjudged a set-up change and ultimately couldn't improve on his times.

Pole position was on the racing line usually ideal for a clean getaway. However Senna tried unsuccessfully to move it because a dragster had been in action on the other side of the grid prior to the race. Therefore a lot of rubber was laid on the tarmac, which significantly improved the traction for any cars

Schumacher won in Aida, while Verstappen qualified a lowly 10th before spinning out in supposedly the same car. *Photo: Alastair Ladd*

At the time, Autosport reported one-third of all spectators at races were there to see Ferrari. **Photo: atom69**

Nicola Larini (pictured in 2007) spoke of turning off his traction control in Aida, which caused a stir. **Photo: Morio**

After retiring from the race, Senna stood trackside. He later told close associates Schumacher's car sounded "different". **Photo: Károly Méhes**

starting from second, fourth, and sixth on the grid. After his terrible start in Brazil, Schumacher had practised them and left the line perfectly, some might say too perfectly! Hakkinen and Brundle also made great starts from fourth and sixth respectively, thereby proving the former world champion was correct to attempt to move pole position.

Senna bogged down in wheelspin which gifted the lead to Schumacher. As they approached the first corner the Brazilian, on the inside line, was unable to out brake his rival and therefore needed to lift off more than normal to make the apex. Hakkinen, who had made such a good start, didn't anticipate this and thus tapped the Williams into spin. Moments later, Larini collided with Senna's car, which ensured the furious Brazilian was out of the race there and then. To add insult to injury, Schumacher won the race commandingly.

Instead of returning to the pits, Senna chose to stand at the first corner and watch Schumacher's car lap the circuit. Williams team manager, Ian Harrison, collected Senna and later recalled: "I remember one of the things the paddock was getting obsessed with at the time was Schumacher's Benetton and its electronics. There were all sorts of paddock gossip about traction control, which seemed to be the norm at the time. Senna himself was convinced that there was something different about Schumacher's car. I know that because I'd gone to meet him after his first-corner accident at Aida in Japan and we walked back to the pits together. Senna was still on a suspended ban after decking Eddie Irvine after the race at Suzuka the year before, so I thought I'd better go and find him after the Aida crash to make sure nothing else kicked off. When I got to him, he was walking back and he was very calm. We stopped for two minutes to watch in the infield section. Senna said to me that he thought there was something different about Schumacher's car. Whether there was or not I don't know, but Senna was utterly sure that there was."[27]

The legendary driver never raised his suspicions publicly, choosing only to confide with close associates. It is debatable whether that was the right thing to do but it appears Senna wasn't alone in this view. According to the book *Fatal Weekend* by Tom Rubython the former team manager of Benetton, Peter Collins,

also had his doubts. While other F1 insiders raised similar concerns but none made any "on the record" comments at the time. While Senna's and Collins' F1 experience undoubtedly added weight to their suspicions, both had a vested interested against Benetton. Whether legally or not, Senna was losing to a Benetton driver who had already outscored him only two years earlier and was attracting a lot of attention as a potential rising star of the sport. While Benetton had won multiple races in previous years, its drivers had never been in a position to challenge for the Drivers' Championship before: Senna's pride was at stake to these upstarts.

The triple world champion also had a history of accusing opponents of cheating or accusing the governing body of favouring his rivals whenever he was being beaten. When David Leslie pipped him to an F3 pole in 1983, Senna claimed Leslie's car was illegal. When Martin Brundle started winning races that same year, the Brazilian then claimed the British authorities were against him. In 1984, Senna, competing in one of his early F1 races, looked on course to win the Monaco Grand Prix in the unfancied Toleman before the race was stopped due to adverse weather conditions. Afterwards, he accused the French authorities of fixing the race to ensure Alain Prost (a Frenchman) won. Later in his career, he frequently clashed with Jean-Marie Balestre, the former FISA president, who Senna claimed rigged title battles in favour of his main rival, Prost. These instances are well documented and part of the folklore of the sport.

Similarly, did Collins harbour a grudge against Briatore and Benetton? Collins joined Benetton in 1986, but by 1989 he had come to blows with the flamboyant Italian over Herbert's performances in the car. Collins, having spent three years supporting Herbert through junior series was adamant the Englishman should remain at Benetton in 1989, but Briatore insisted on replacing him. After failing to qualify for the Canadian Grand Prix, Herbert was promptly replaced by Emanuele Pirro and Collins left the team a few weeks later under acrimonious circumstances.

26. *Autosport*, 21 April 1994   27. *Autosport*, 29 April 2014

Chapter 3

It's well known that Senna was observing Schumacher's car from the first corner at Aida, but often overlooked is that fact that Larini, having crashed out at the first corner himself, stood alongside him to also study the Benetton. By contrast, Larini has never claimed Schumacher's Benetton sounded different because of an illegal device. Having used a "driver aid" only the day before, it could be argued that Larini would be ideally placed to hear anything amiss. On the flipside, because Larini had previously caused a minor scandal when referring to the Ferrari device as "traction control", perhaps he didn't want the aggravation of accusing Benetton. Such a tactic could risk backfiring and result in the FIA reopening their investigation into Ferrari's 412 T1.

What Senna might have heard as he studied Schumacher's car is not clear and remains a topic of debate to this day. Many believe it was the sound of an illegal traction control device at work. An alternative theory is connected with the semi-automatic gearbox which was still new technology in 1994. Ferrari introduced it in 1989, and by 1992 both Williams and McLaren were using a semi-automatic gearbox[28] whereas Benetton's system was operational a year later. Because semi-automatic gearboxes didn't require a clutch pedal/lever after the start, drivers could now modify their technique in ways that were previously not possible. At the time Schumacher was at the forefront of a driving style known as left-foot braking which he and others developed during their karting days.[29]

This involves using the throttle and brake pedals simultaneously to control the car into and through a corner to prevent lift-off oversteer. Schumacher was known to keep around 15 percent throttle throughout the majority of a braking zone, allowing him to reduce the pitch movement[30] of the car. In 2004 telemetry traces were published which compared Schumacher's left-foot braking style against his then teammate, Barrichello's, who didn't use this technique. The subject corner is the 'Old Pits hairpin' in Montreal. The traces looked similar to those in Fig 1.

Fig 2. Exhaust gases generated rear end grip via the diffuser, but required driver confidence to maintain a consistent throttle during braking and cornering. ***Photo: Rick den Ridder***

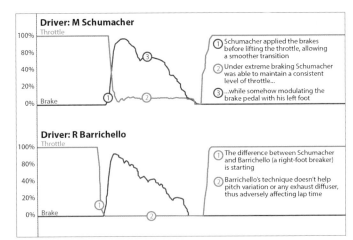

Driver: M Schumacher

① Schumacher applied the brakes before lifting the throttle, allowing a smoother transition

② Under extreme braking Schumacher was able to maintain a consistent level of throttle...

③ ...while somehow modulating the brake pedal with his left foot

Driver: R Barrichello

① The difference between Schumacher and Barrichello (a right-foot breaker) is starting

② Barrichello's technique doesn't help pitch variation or any exhaust diffuser, thus adversely affecting lap time

Fig1. These throttle and brake traces illustrate Schumacher's use of left-foot braking. ***Image: www.neilwhitedesign.co.uk***

The loss of active suspension for 1994 resulted in increased pitch movement of the cars which conversely upset its aerodynamics and grip, meaning left-foot braking became an important but difficult technique to gain performance. Leaving the throttle partially open during braking zones also kept exhaust gases flowing through the exhaust-blown diffusers (Fig 2). Not only did this provide increased rear grip, it also had the side-effect of reducing the sudden shift in handling balance that occurred when the throttle was suddenly closed. Around the time Benetton utilised a more extreme exhaust-blown diffuser than rivals (discussed in detail later) which conversely required huge driver skill and confidence to unlock its benefits. But if they could via left-foot braking, it helped the driver maintain a higher speed throughout the corner and, because the engine was closer to its optimum power band, it could accelerate on exit quicker too. Later, there is a more detailed description of this along with more telemetry traces illustrating the benefits.

Traction control and active suspension would have made left-foot braking unnecessary in 1993, because the latter maintained a consistent ride height of the car at all timesn while the former would have cut power to the driven wheels under these circumstances. Teams that didn't have those devices in 1992/93 also didn't to have semi-automatic gearboxes either, meaning those drivers had to operate a third pedal, the clutch, when downshifting through gears which rendered left-foot braking impossible. Unlike previous years, by 1994 all but one team (Simtek) had semi-automatic gearboxes, and that together with the active suspension and traction control ban gave drivers the ideal conditions for left-foot braking.

Aida was the first time in 1994 Senna stood alongside the braking zone of a slow corner to hear Schumacher's car, but why was the Brazilian so startled by what he had heard? Possibly because he mistook left-foot braking for some kind of illegal device. The triple world champion wouldn't have been aware of how Benetton's exhaust-blown diffuser worked and how the German maximised it to generate additional grip. It is also reasonable to assume that Senna would have had less recent experience than Schumacher with left-foot braking bearing in mind the latter was nine years younger, so much fresher out of karting where the two-pedal layout allowed its use. Older drivers tend also to find it harder to adapt to

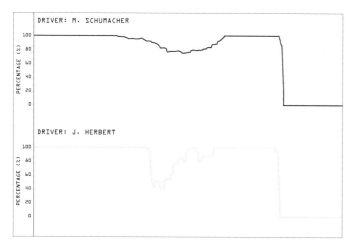

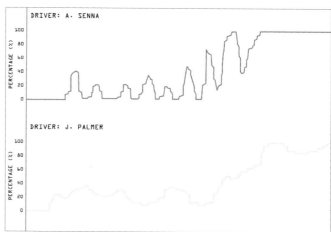

Fig 3. Schumacher's throttle application was very smooth, minimising the car's pitch movement into corners. *Image: www.neilwhitedesign.co.uk*

Fig 4. Senna's technique was to stab the throttle repeatedly mid-corner, in contrast to Jonathan Palmer. *Image: www.neilwhitedesign.co.uk*

different driving techniques because you have more to unlearn.

Schumacher also had a very progressive style on the throttle which would have continued to minimise the car's pitch movement on corner exits, while maximising its grip via the exhaust-blown diffusers. In 1995, telemetry traces were shown on a BBC documentary illustrating Schumacher's throttle technique in comparison to his then Benetton teammate, Herbert. They looked similar to Fig 3. This telemetry trace is discussed in more detail later on, however Senna famously had a completely different technique where he stabbed at the throttle rapidly and repeatedly mid-corner. In 1992 telemetry traces showing Senna's use of the accelerator in comparison to McLaren's test driver in 1991, Jonathan Palmer, was shown on BBC. It looked similar to Fig 4.

While this trace was based on data from 1991, Senna's distinctive throttle technique can be heard in 1994 at corners like Hairpin in Aida or Tosa at Imola. The upshot being Schumacher's left-foot braking along with his progressive throttle may have sounded unfamiliar to the Williams driver as he stood trackside at Aida 1994.

The 1994 passive suspensions caused fluctuations in ride heights. Techniques like left-foot braking minimised this. *Photo: Ford*

Willem Toet, Benetton's Head of Aerodynamics in 1994, believes Senna mistook this for illegal traction control. "I think it was the use of left-foot braking combined with the throttle which would have made the strange noise. There won't have been any engine cutting at all in those circumstances because the engine will not have been accelerating fast (with brakes applied as well) but it would have been strange to hear the engine working in those places on the track. That's what I believe is the most likely scenario."

Mark Blundell was a Tyrrell F1 driver that season and like Senna was also taken out at that first corner in Aida. While Blundell didn't recall any strange sounds on Schumacher's Benetton himself when walking back to the pits that day, he believes it was common knowledge their engine note was different. When asked whether the sound could have been left-foot braking, Blundell responded "in terms of your description on what the input, outputs and benefits that would all make a lot of sense. Left-foot braking was something that became a trend at that stage again. I was probably in the minority because I didn't left-foot brake, I was a conventional right-foot braker and I think Rubens [Barrichello] was like me for quite a long time... It [left-foot braking] would have made a different sound in that it would have had rpm carried into a corner, but I don't think that would have made a sound like traction control."

Driving with an exhaust-blown diffuser did allow a driver to pick up the throttle earlier but it required a bit of adaption according to Blundell. "When I was at Williams [as a test driver in 1991] I can remember driving around Imola where I had raced for Brabham the previous weekend. The Brabham didn't have a blown diffuser, whereas the Williams did and it was just an unbelievable difference! When you got on the throttle [in the Williams] the thing would just suck down at the rear and just drive you off the corner. As such you would be able to crank a lot more front wing in and get a lot more aero on the car and the grip level was sensational... Left-foot braking became an art and a trend was something you could only do if you had confidence."

28. A steering wheel mounted paddle which shifted gears without the need of a clutch pedal, thereby leaving only two pedals (brake and accelerator) inside the car.
29. Karts only have two pedals
30. The car's front and rear motion in response to acceleration and deceleration

Chapter 3

Schumacher was also known to like his mid-1990s Benetton's set-up as Blundell described above, ie very 'pointy' on the nose. So perhaps him maximising Benetton's exhaust-blown diffuser via left-foot braking was how he extracted performance from that set-up? The downside to Benetton's positioning of exhausts exits was the variation in handling balance whenever drivers were off throttle. The less the driver pressed the gas, the less the blown diffuser gave them grip at the rear. Consequently Schumacher's various teammates during 1994/95 frequently complained about the Benetton being too nervous. Was that a result of not maximising the exhaust-blown diffuser via left-foot braking?

Around the time, Williams and Ferrari worked on exhaust-blown diffusers, which made their car easier to drive off throttle but conversely offered less peak rear grip than Benetton's version (discussed in more detail later). Frank Dernie, Benetton's Chief Engineer in 1994, gives his view on Aida. "I am not sure what he [Senna] might have heard. Certainly, Schumacher left-foot braked and certainly Cosworth never permitted an engine map with any sort of torque manipulation in it, even when it was legal. My view is that Senna was searching for a reason why the Benetton had so much better traction than Williams, which I am sure was aero, and wrongly plumped for traction control. Once the great Senna had given his opinion it was taken as gospel by many, even though it was just speculation."

Christian Silk, who was race engineer to the second Benetton drivers throughout 1994, adds: "Schumacher made up a lot of his time on exit of slow corners. Possibly Jos was too new and just learning the ropes of the B194, to be worrying about the intricacies of the exhaust-blown diffuser [at Aida 1994]. Also at the start of 1994 no-one knew how good Schumacher was, hence the reason Benetton kept changing their second driver that season." Silk also believes Schumacher's driving style helped with pitch sensitivity, stability of the car, and tyre pressures, whereas his various teammates' lack of confidence with the car induced more nervousness.

Alternatively, did Senna hear Benetton's legal traction control system at work? In 2015, Willem Toet posted an article on LinkedIn explaining how Benetton created a traction control that didn't break the rules. They used an algorithm that calculated wheelspin via a number of variables (intake air pressure, engine rpm, rotational

Mike Gascoyne, Jordan's technical director in 1999, carefully phrased questions to the FIA's Charlie Whiting to ensure Jordan's traction control was legal "to the letter of the law" if not the intention. **Photo: Witherspoony**

inertia in the engine and gearbox). When this algorithm kicked in, it would cut the spark to the engine thus eliminating wheelspin if the track conditions were suitable. Toet explained: "During a race, the conditions would change rendering the system more or less useful. If the tyres went off badly or it became wet, the system wouldn't control traction. If the track got better and better, the system would cut too much power – the grip available would allow more 'engine' acceleration...

"...A good driver would use the system to learn how to apply the throttle. *Driving flat out everywhere would be fine except that it wasted fuel and made a more detectable sound*. While the team were satisfied the system was legal, it wanted to minimise visibility because they knew that would lead to 'clarifications' or regulation changes. They also didn't want other teams working out what they were doing! Of course, other teams did eventually work it out (staff transfer being one way)."[31]

It is thought less likely Senna heard this based on the italicised text because Verstappen's car should have been making the funny noises at Aida, given the Dutchman was a lesser driver than Schumacher. Nevertheless, it could have been this combined with the previous theory which Senna mistook for an illegal device.

Toet details a "legal" traction control Benetton used in 1994 which exploited a loophole. Did Senna hear this instead? **Photo: Willem Toet**

Based on all the known facts, it seems Senna may have heard Schumacher left-foot braking in Aida. **Photo: Martin Lee**

Rotational Inertia, Traction Control (when it's not permitted)

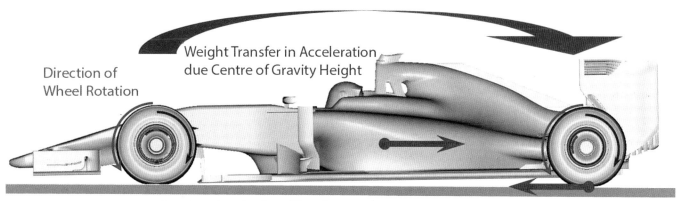

Direction of Wheel Rotation

Weight Transfer in Acceleration due Centre of Gravity Height

Acceleration "resisted" by the need to rotate significant masses such as the wheels

According to Toet: "In 1994, Benetton may have been the first to discover these loopholes but they were not the only ones." ***Photo: Willem Toet***

Readers may ask why was this system legal when the rules stated traction control was forbidden?

Toet explained: "The rule makers will often make bold and short press announcements such as – 'traction control is banned'. The reality is teams have to comply with a complex and lengthy set of technical regulations. If you can improve your car within the letter of those regulations, then you're legal even if you have 'traction control'. F1 has always worked that way and still does today... Eventually, all teams learned what to do to achieve legal (letter of law not the intent of the law) traction control."

F1 history is littered with examples of teams achieving a legal form of traction control after 1994. Most famously, during the late 1990s where anti-stall software was exploited so they effectively acted as launch control. Others were rumoured to use their pitlane speed limiters as traction control because their mandatory pitlane speed sensors where placed by the rear wheels, enabling it to inadvertently detect wheel slip. Teams were forced to move those sensors to their front wheels by the 2000 British Grand Prix, eliminating the problem because F1 cars are rear-wheel-drive. None of the teams referred to above were penalised because they could argue their devices complied with the letter of the regulations.

The FIA found policing the traction control ban became impossible as new technology appeared their regulations couldn't keep pace. The ban on traction control was eventually lifted at the 2001 Spanish Grand Prix and, by 2008, the FIA banned traction control but imposing a standard ECU thus preventing teams from encoding traction control themselves. Even so, controversies have occasionally arisen. For instance in 2008, teams introduced additional paddles on their steering wheel which allowed drivers to select different engine maps for each corner, retarding the ignition in a slower corner to reduce wheel spin. By 2011 and 2012, the FIA had to therefore tighten up the regulations on throttle maps after accusing teams of having non-linear torque curves to assist with traction in slow corners.

The reader might ask why was Benetton's legal traction control from 1994 allowed, whereas the Ferrari Aida device declared illegal?

It seems the Ferrari's system, by automatically reducing the rev limiter, didn't require any driver skill so always worked irrespective of track conditions. According to Toet, this wasn't the case with Benetton's device. "Of course the legal traction control code was carefully inspected by the FIA during 1994: "Toet added. "They came back several times with questions – but what questions and what the answers were I'm not aware of. What the team did, though, was legal to the letter of the law – that I am still convinced of today. In all teams in all years, there are long discussions about the legality or not (or the shade of grey) of potential interpretations of the regulations – 1994 was no different to any other year." Toet also insisted this system helped more with tyre life than lap time. Frank Dernie, Benetton's Chief Engineer, added: "There is nothing new about including rotational inertia in acceleration, I was doing it in 1975 for Harvey Postlethwaite at Hesketh."

Two other teams also had mutterings of traction control directed towards them after performing unexpectedly well during the opening two races. Arrows driver Morbidelli qualified in 6th at Brazil, whilst his teammate, Fittipaldi, had finished 4th in Aida.

Their designer, Alan Jenkins, guaranteed there wasn't anything untoward on the car by claiming "I'm too busy sorting the gearbox to worry about anything else." Arrows' team boss, Jackie Oliver, felt others were throwing up a smokescreen to distract from their own poor performances, maintaining "we're the quickest soft target – Ferrari is the slowest hard one." Elsewhere, a pre-season Sauber testing schedule was found by a rival that weekend, and suspiciously one item read "test 1994 specification traction control". Peter Sauber admitted his engineers had worked on such things, but he didn't allow any further testing or racing of traction control. Nevertheless, the above highlights the feeling of mistrust between constructors at the time, particularly those doing well. It was under this toxic atmosphere that events were about to take a dramatic and tragic turn.

31. William Toet LinkedIn blog, 13 November 2015

SAN MARINO

May 1994

"The team is conscious about the challenge we have to make to recover the ground over Benetton."

**Ayrton Senna, Williams driver,
BBC's coverage of the 1994 San Marino Grand Prix**

"...I met him [Senna] on Sunday twice – the main constant was safety and the fact that we he wasn't happy with the situation, thinking that the Benetton wasn't legal."

**Alain Prost, former F1 World Champion,
Autosport 1 May 2014**

The two championship contenders on the morning of the fateful San Marino Grand Prix. **Photo: Motorsport Images/LAT**

Standings before the 1994 San Marino Grand Prix

DRIVERS' CHAMPIONSHIP		
Pos	Driver	Points
1	Michael Schumacher	20
2	Rubens Barrichello	7
3	Damon Hill	6
N/A	Ayrton Senna	0

CONSTRUCTORS' CHAMPIONSHIP		
Pos	Constructor	Points
1	Benetton-Ford	20
2	Ferrari	10
3	Jordan-Hart	7

F1's blackest weekend started with Barrichello's ferocious accident.
Photo: Alan Dahl

The Jordan came to a rest upside down. Note the car's flat floor. This would be changed afterwards. *Photo: Alan Dahl*

The 1994 San Marino Grand Prix will forever be remembered as the most infamous F1 weekend in history, forcibly shaking the motor racing world to its core. Coming into the event the pressure on Senna was intense. The press were asking whether questions like "Senna: Can he take the heat?" While pointing out alarming statistics like only once before (1970) did a driver go on to become world champion having failed to finish in the opening two races. Bookmakers no longer had Senna as the favourite to take the title, Schumacher was. A massive turnaround in little over a month. Simply put, Senna had to win here, anything less would have been seen as a failure. The next race at Monaco was predicted to suit the nimble Benetton and its V8 Ford engine. Yet another reason why Senna needed to stop the rot.

Before the weekend, Italian journalists asked questions about Benetton's supposed illegal traction control. "I really cannot say much about it," Senna responded. "It's difficult to talk about things one cannot prove." The three times world champion did, however, want Williams to protest Benetton. According to Ian Harrison, the Williams team manager, they sent Richard West, their commercial manager, up onto the roof of the garages on race day to record Schumacher's starts with a video camera. If the Benetton produced no wheelspin whatsoever, then that would add weight to Senna's claims and may tempt Williams into submitting a formal protest. Meanwhile, that weekend Max Mosley found himself denying suggestions the FIA showed favouritism towards Ferrari by not punishing them for the illegal "power reduction" device.

Friday was the first sign this event would be like no other. Barrichello lost control of his Jordan and was launched over a kerb, which acted like a ramp, and the 21-year-old was thrown into a tyre barrier at 140mph (225km/h). He was extremely lucky the car didn't somersault upside down into the grandstand and instead landed nose first onto the verge beside the track. After rolling a couple of times, it eventually it came to rest upside down. The violence of the initial impact registered at 95g – enough to damage the metal and concrete wall. Rubens was knocked out by the crash but regained consciousness in the medial centre only to find Senna crying over him. In recent times, Senna had shown great compassion towards his colleagues whenever they suffered horrific accidents and this was yet another example. It might also be the first glimpse of Senna's emotional state that weekend.

Everyone was amazed to see Barrichello back at the track the next day with 'only' a bruised arm, a badly swollen nose and a few cuts. Although he took no further part in the event, he was in good spirits posing inside his car and joking that his bandaged arm didn't prevent him from driving the car. Gary Anderson, Jordan's Technical Director, highlighted the reason behind Barrichello's crash: "On the previous lap, he went through at 129mph (208km/h): at the point, he lost it he was doing 138mph (223km/h). We suggested he might like to try 133mph (215km/h) first."[32] Jordan mechanics also teased Barrichello they would let him off this time for wrecking their car but not to let it happen again.

Williams brought modified FW16s to Imola in an attempt to eradicate the car's handling problems, particularly over bumps. In the 2011 *Senna* movie there is footage of Senna complaining about the revised FW16's 'changing balance' to Adrian Newey, Williams' aerodynamics genius and David Brown, Senna's race engineer, on the Friday at Imola. At one point Newey asks him "Do you want to raise the front?" And David Brown said to Senna "You would have to brake more [into the corners]". Senna responds "No... the car is worse". In F1 jargon, this means Senna wanted the car as fast as possible even though it increased the potential for 'bottoming', which is the car's floor hitting the ground while at speed thus risking a momentary loss of grip. Senna was compromising his consistency of grip in the quest for higher cornering speed.

Both Schumacher and Senna spun at Tosa corner in almost identical fashion during Friday qualifying at Imola. During a *Motor Sport* magazine podcast from June 2011, the *Senna* movie's producer, Manish Pandey, cites the way Schumacher recovered from his spin as proof the Benetton was using traction control because he claims there was no wheelspin. This seems incorrect because Schumacher recovers with a half spin, leaving two visible black tyre marks in his wake on the outside of the corner which is evidence of wheelspin. Once the German has the car pointing in broadly the right direction, he slowly gets going. The footage is available on the internet for anyone wishing to verify this. When Senna recovers from his later spin at that same corner, he passes Schumacher's tyre marks. Real footage of Senna's spin and recovery are shown in the *Senna* film.

32. *Autosport*, 5 May 1994

Roland Ratzenberger (1960 to 1994) shortly before his fatal accident. **Photo: Sgozzi**

Fortunately Barrichello escaped relatively uninjured, and was competing at the following race. **Photo: Károly Méhes**

Sadly, the weekend took a tragic turn during Saturday qualifying. Roland Ratzenberger, just weeks into his dream job, was attempting to qualify for his second grand prix. During a fast lap he had a minor off-track excursion and, instead of coming into the pits to check for damage, he weaved the car, perhaps trying to judge for himself. Believing the front wing was OK, the popular Austrian proceeded to do another quick lap. That would prove to be a fatal error.

As he approached the fastest part of the track his front wing failed under the heavy loading, and the Simtek ploughed straight into a concrete wall at 195mph (313km/h). Ratzenberger was killed instantly and it was horrible seeing his limp head rolling from side to side, as the car bounced over a kerb and came to a stop. Ratzenberger had spent the last eleven years plugging away in the lower categories of motor racing just to get into F1. In that time

he had built himself a reputation as a likeable and hardworking driver, so it was especially sad that he couldn't reap the rewards of his efforts.

Out of respect, Ratzenberger's spot on the starting grid was left empty and his team dedicated the rest of 1994 to their fallen driver by painting his helmet colours on their air box. The sport, however, was in shock, this was the first race meeting fatality in twelve years so was a crushing blow to a generation who had never experienced such a loss. Senna was deeply affected and commandeered an official FIA car to visit the accident site as he wanted to understand what lessons could be learnt for the safety of others. It was something Senna would be chastised for before the race.

Senna then went to the medical centre where he was met by his friend Professor Sid Watkins, F1's senior doctor, who answered his questions with complete honesty. Upon hearing that Ratzenberger

Simtek paid tribute to Ratzenberger with air boxes painted in his helmet livery. **Photo: Alastair Ladd**

Simtek and Brabham bravely elected to start the race. It is what Ratzenberger would have wanted. **Photo: Alastair Ladd**

Niki Lauda spoke with Senna on race morning about improving F1 safety.

Photo: Smokeonthewater

Senna was reportedly pushing to get the FW15D (above) race ready and debut the FW16 only after a fix for its aerodynamic problems and seating position had been found. **Photo: Károly Méhes**

was beyond medical help Senna could no longer hold back the tears. "You've got nothing left to prove. Give it up and let's go fishing together," Watkins said. Senna took a long time to think about his reply "Sid, I have to go on". Those words must have haunted Watkins 24 hours later.

Perhaps the most comparable experience Senna had to draw upon was Jerez 1990 when he visited the scene of Martin Donnelly's near-fatal accident. The Ulsterman explains: "The amazing thing for me is that Senna watched all of that, saw it all first-hand, holding my crash helmet and possibly watching me die from a crash. He watched all the needles and syringes and the tracheotomy. Then he went back to his garage, put his helmet back on, visor down, and with just ten minutes left, did the fastest lap of Jerez ever of that track."[33]

Senna later reflected on Jerez 1990: "I had to put myself together, walk out, go to the racing car and do it again, and do it even better than before. Because that was the way to cover the impact it had on me." The next time Senna stepped into an F1 car after Ratzenberger's tragic accident was Sunday morning warm-up. The Brazilian topped the timesheets with a massive margin over the next car, just as he had done in Jerez 1990.

This is not to suggest the Brazilian was reckless, he was simply overcoming his fear by facing it head-on. At Imola there was an added incentive – Senna was determined to blow Schumacher

away and he wanted the German to know it. However, Benetton appeared to be playing its own mind games on Senna: in the warm-up Schumacher was a massive 2.4sec slower, suggesting he might opt for an unfancied one-stop strategy for the race. Senna's lap time suggested the more conventional two-stop strategy, but Schumacher's lack of warm-up pace must have made him wonder what his rival was up to.

According to Williams team manager, Ian Harrison: "One thing that struck me about Senna's reaction [to Ratzenberger's death] though, was that we didn't really know him – we didn't know him at all. The relationship was just beginning to get there."[34] The former world champion also had other issues on his mind that weekend – for instance, his brother was at Imola attempting to get Ayrton to split up with his 21-year-old girlfriend. It is reported that the Senna family felt she was only with him for fame and money and it has been alleged the two brothers argued over this. Also, Senna wasn't yet settled at Williams and his teammate, Damon Hill, claimed he seemed perpetually pensive. According to Adrian Newey, the FW16's aerodynamic issues were "bugging" Senna who had only learnt at the Imola race weekend what the problem behind it was.

33. *Belfast Telegraph*, 25 October 2015
34. *Autosport*, 29 April 2014

Spot the wheelspin. Whether Schumacher used launch control following the "option 13" discovery is fiercely debated today.
Photo: Motorsport Images/LAT

Newey told Senna a solution was being worked upon and it would be ready in a few races time. Perhaps at that moment, Senna felt his 1994 championship slipping away because he realised the FW16's handling issues weren't going to improve as soon as he had hoped. Some have suggested Senna wanted Williams to have raced the FW15D in those opening races instead of the FW16. The FW15D was the 1993 Williams converted to allow for the 1994 regulations and car had used it during testing before the FW16 was launched, and subsequently to undertake back-to-back comparison tests.

Jonathan Williams, the son of team owner Frank Williams, said: "I think both he [Ayrton] and Damon in those very early days of FW16 thought it [FW15D] was actually quicker. Damon didn't tell me, but he told a colleague at the time... I would have won that [the Brazilian Grand Prix] in an FW15D. But you simply have to pursue with a car which had a longer-term [potential]."[35] Senna was also unhappy with his seating position in the cockpit of the FW16 where he felt cramped and his knuckles where bashing against the top of the cockpit whenever he steered. All of which undoubtedly caused Senna to lose some enjoyment of racing in 1994.

Senna's girlfriend, Adriane Galisteu, reportedly said "In public, he [Senna] praised the team's efforts, but he privately admitted 'I feel I have arrived here two years too late. The car drives funny.' He continued: 'I went through a lot to finally be able to sit in that car. But I feel it's going to be hard. Either I haven't adapted myself to the car yet or it's the car that doesn't suit me.'"[36] In 2014, it emerged Senna was looking to terminate his Williams contract to move to Ferrari. Alain Prost claims Senna lacked the motivation to beat the younger generation of F1 drivers. Perhaps Ayrton realised he could only lose against Schumacher and Benetton because when he won a race it was expected. The press constantly reminded him of his lack of points in 1994 and, adding to Senna's burden, were additional business ventures he'd recently acquired, which some felt was planning for his life after F1.

Senna had also become increasingly concerned with F1 safety in recent times. He said in a pre-race interview how the reintroduction of refuelling in 1994 turned races into a series of sprints with low fuel levels. Senna considered this to be an unreasonable strain on both drivers and cars. He also felt this factor had not been considered when refuelling was pushed through. Niki Lauda urged Senna as F1's most famous driver to reform the Grand Prix Drivers' Association and lobby the FIA for better safety for its participants.

On the way to the pre-race drivers' briefing, Senna asked Berger and Hill to raise a complaint for him. Senna didn't want to be the instigator because he was in trouble with the FIA over his actions the previous day – namely commandeering one of the official cars to visit the scene of Ratzenberger's accident and not attending the obligatory post-qualifying press conference. So at the behest of Senna, a complaint was made about the FIA using a standard road car to lead the field around the formation lap at Aida. The road car was too slow and prevented F1 drivers from getting their tyres up to the correct temperature/pressure. This adversely affected the handling and ride height of the F1 machines during the opening laps of a race.

It presented another danger as well. During the Aida formation lap, Schumacher deliberately induced wheelspin and left two black tyre lines from his grid slot to give himself better traction from the race start. However, within a couple of seconds of doing so, he had to brake heavily otherwise he would have overtaken the FIA road car. The driver directly behind Schumacher (Hakkinen) had to, therefore, take avoiding action not to crash into the back of the Benetton before the race even started. The FIA decided not to use their road car prior to the start at Imola.

Perhaps the last person to talk with Senna before he got into the car before the race was Adrian Newey. "On the day of the race, I was in the back of the truck, close to the time when the cars leave the pitlane for grid, collecting together my notes and bit and

The Lehto/Lamy incident. Neither driver was hurt although debris did injure spectators. It also led to the safety car – an Opel Vectra – being deployed.
Photo: Motorsport Images/LAT

pieces, when in rushed Ayrton, quickly peeling off his race suit and changing his Nomex underwear. He's cutting it fine, I thought. What we now know is that on that morning he'd been talking to Alain Prost about reopening the Grand Prix Drivers' Association with the aim of improving safety. As he pulled his overalls back up, he reiterated what he'd already said in the wake of the Pacific Grand Prix – that he thought Benetton were using (illegal) traction control.

"After that Pacific race, Ferrari also had to ride out a stink regarding their own possible use of traction control, with subsequent grumbles about favouritism reaching such a peak that, by Imola, Max was forced to issue a statement categorically stating that the FIA didn't love Ferrari any more or less than it loved other teams. It wasn't Ferrari traction control rumours that concerned Ayrton, though. It was his concern over Benetton: the feeling that he was battling an illegal car-driver combination. He went into that race with all that buzzing in his head. But he went in, above all, with a desire to win. Ayrton was one of the fiercest, most passionate competitors the sport has known."[37]

On the formation lap at Imola Schumacher deliberately left an enormous amount of rubber on his grid slot in an effort to aid his

race start. For future reference, Schumacher would undertake this same trick prior to every start in dry conditions, throughout the season. At Imola Senna did the same thing – although less profound. It worked and Senna made a good start, but behind the leaders there was chaos. Lehto in the other Benetton had stalled his car and everyone avoided hitting him – expect Pedro Lamy. Although neither driver was hurt, debris hurtled into the grandstand, injuring several spectators. Everyone expected the race to be stopped due to the amount of wreckage scattered across the track surface and the high risk of punctures. It wasn't and controversially the safety car, an Opel Vectra, was brought out instead.

This was the first ever time the safety car was used at the start of a F1 race following a startline crash. It was a new idea, borrowed from Indycar, and many felt part of its purpose was to artificially boost excitement in races. As Senna had feared in the pre-race briefing, trundling along at such a slow pace behind a regular road car caused the tyres to cool down and therefore lose grip. After the slowness of the pace car at Aida, Senna told Watkins the Williams had no grip in these situations and a drop in tyre pressures lowered the ride height of the car. Senna explained the FW16 rode very low and a reduction of one or two millimetres made a difference to its handling.[38] To add to Senna's woes, his car would have still been heavy with fuel. Remember due to the set-up path he had chosen, Senna's car was already at a high risk of 'bottoming' even before the safety car. At one point an enraged Senna drove alongside the Opel Vectra gesticulating for it to go faster. The problem was it was already at its limit.

Seconds before the accident. Did Senna realise that Schumacher's Benetton was extremely light with fuel? **Photo: Alan Dahl**

35. *Motor Sport* podcast with Jonathan Williams and Dickie Stanford, February 2018
36. Ayrtonsennavive blog
37. *How to Build a Car* by Adrian Newey (2017)
38. *Life at the Limit: Triumph and Tragedy in F1* by Sid Watkins (1996)

Chapter 4

The safety car eventually pulled off at the end of lap five and the race resumed. The only other person to have driven an identical FW16 car to Senna on that track in those conditions was Hill. "Certainly, my car was more difficult to drive than usual during those first few laps after the re-start," Hill said. "At Imola, there is a tight chicane just before the start/finish straight. When I slowed for the chicane, the brakes and the tyres were cold. I locked up my left front wheel and, for a terrible moment, I thought I was going to slide off the road before I had even started the first flying lap. That alerted me to the problem caused by the five slow laps behind the official car."[39]

At the restart, Senna tried his best to pull away from his younger rival but failed. What Senna didn't know was Schumacher wasn't planning the one-stop strategy his warm-up time suggested – that was probably a smokescreen. Instead, the German was planning a three-stop strategy with a very short first stint. Therefore in the opening stages of the race, Schumacher's car would have been much lighter than the Williams hence the reason the Benetton was able to stay with Senna. Perhaps Senna thought Schumacher was on the same two-stop strategy as him. Understandable given that it was the conventional route and Senna wouldn't have known beforehand what Benetton's strategy was.

Therefore the Brazilian would have been highly surprised to find the B194 hounding him as it did on lap six, given the inherent superior pace Williams had shown all weekend. Also, Senna didn't have time to work out Schumacher's strategy had been ruined by the five laps behind the safety car. So Senna didn't need to push so hard, instead, he just needed to hold Schumacher up in those opening laps and the race would have been his. Remember Senna was also convinced he was racing an illegal Benetton that day.

The pursuing Schumacher had the clearest view of what unfolded at Tamburello on lap seven. "I saw that Senna's car was touching the track at the back quite a lot on the lap before. It was very nervous in that corner, and he nearly lost it. Then on the next time through he did lose it. The car just touched the track with the rear skids, went a bit sideways, and then he just lost it." Senna's car left the circuit and hit a concrete wall at 135mph (217km/h). He had the misfortune to be struck by a piece of suspension inflicting a fatal head injury. Brazil lost an icon, and the sport lost one of its greatest ever drivers.

To this day, nobody knows for certain why Senna crashed. Many theories of varying credibility have been put forward. My personal view is that Senna, desperate to break free from the car behind, carried a bit too much speed into Tamburello the car went slightly offline onto a part of the track known to be extremely bumpy. The ride height was still too low after the safety car so it bottomed out. This also caused the peaky aerodynamics on the Williams to stall, resulting in a catastrophic loss of grip made worse by tyres not up to working pressures or temperatures. This view is shared by Hill who drove an identical car to Senna, and Schumacher, who had the clearest view of what started the crash. In my opinion, they are the two best people to judge the cause of the fatal crash.

We know Senna did 188mph through Tamburello on lap six and 193mph on lap seven. We also know from video footage that Senna took a faster but bumpier line. This sent huge sparks flying from the rear of his car – evidence of bottoming. The largest plume appears as he left the third dark strip of resurfaced tarmac in the middle of Tamburello. Throughout qualifying and practice, you can see Senna's car bottoming through Tamburello much more than others. The difference then was that he didn't have Schumacher right up behind him, his car wasn't fat with fuel and he wouldn't have had tyre temperature/pressure issues caused by an Opel Vectra.

In his autobiography, Hill said he applied greater caution than Senna through Tamburello after the safety car, instead preferring to wait for the optimal tyre temperatures. Hill also detailed the bumps at Tamburello explaining that he took a slower line than Senna to avoid the worst of them. Immediately following Senna's crash Patrick Head, Williams Technical Director, stated: "The car was set up the same as Hill's. The two were identical for springs and settings, but the underside of Hill's car is unmarked". Whereas there are suggestions the floor on Senna's car was heavily worn.

An unnamed driver told *Autosport* magazine at the time that Tamburello wasn't as easily flat out as people believed. Stating it was much more difficult with the passive suspension than the active ride used in 1993. Ex-F1 driver Jonathan Palmer added from his own experience of Tamburello: "If the car is right, it's actually not a real corner: it's flat, foot down, you don't really think about it... But if the car's set-up isn't right – which includes cases where the car is bottoming out too much – the picture changes considerably."[40]

Alternative reasons why Senna crashed include a partial/total steering column failure, and a slow puncture from debris from the Lehto/Lamy startline crash causing the car to bottom out, or the steering column getting ovaled enough in the bushing to seize in the bushing and prevent the driver from steering all are also highly

Ayrton Senna (1960 to 1994). **Photo: senna.org.br**

Senna was idolised in his native Brazil. When his coffin returned to São Paulo, half a million people followed it through the streets.
Photo: Károly Méhes

The wreckage of Senna's Williams being returned to the pits.
Photo: Alan Dahl

In a final act of horror, a loose wheel (circled in yellow) from Alboreto's car flew off as he departed his pitstop and injured four mechanics, but thankfully not seriously so. **Photo: Alan Dahl**

likely. While this book is not about what caused Senna's accident, I would like to debunk a popular myth against the tyre pressure/low ride height theory. It has been asked how Senna's tyres could set the third fastest lap time of the race on lap six and then be cold enough to be a possible cause on lap seven. The tyres can take two or three laps at racing speed to be up to optimum working temperature/pressure. During qualifying sessions at places like Monza or Monaco, you'll often see drivers needing more laps than that to get their tyres in the zone.

Following Senna's crash, the race was stopped and eventually restarted because the true gravity of Senna's condition wasn't yet known to the world at large. Hill set the overall fastest lap of the race a mere four laps after Senna's only flying lap, suggesting that after all the appalling crashes that weekend, drivers wouldn't have been risking everything to set blistering lap times. You can see drivers avoiding kerbs in the race and nobody appears to be driving flat out after the restart. Further evidence of this is the fastest lap of the race was 1.7sec slower than the fastest warm-up lap that morning set in identical conditions. As the name suggests, warm-up is usually a final indication of race pace. Indeed, one of the few battles in that race involved Wendlinger catching Hakkinen for fourth place, however, Karl has since admitted that normally he would have pushed to get by Mika, however that day he didn't feel up to it.[41]

Schumacher got wheelspin off the restart allowing Berger into the lead. If Williams was still filming the German's starts from the roof of the garages then it proved to be a waste of time. The Benetton driver also made his first pitstop seven laps after the restart,

The race was stopped and eventually restarted. However Senna's passing was only confirmed after it had finished. **Photo: Alan Dahl**

showing just how light his car would have been when hounding Senna, especially considering the first five laps were behind a slow safety car so at a much-reduced fuel consumption level. Schumacher's victory signalled the end to F1's darkest weekend since 1960. By that stage, everyone was just relieved the nightmare was over. The two fatalities during the weekend sent shockwaves across the world, making front page news. F1 was now under an intense media spotlight, for all the wrong reasons.

Due to the season-long allegations that some teams had been using banned driving aids such as traction control, the FIA seized the black boxes of the top three finishers at Imola (Benetton, Ferrari and McLaren). This was the first time any spotchecks like this had been made and to help the FIA find any irregularities they employed Liverpool Data Research Associates (LDRA). They were a company that worked in computer systems for military aircraft, nuclear power stations and safety-critical applications, so they could match the best IT experts within F1 teams. In addition, they had unlimited time to analyse teams' engine software. If anything illegal was hidden LDRA would find it. The teams concerned were also asked to surrender their systems' source code allowing LDRA to access the data.

Ferrari complied immediately following their lucky escape at Aida over the 'power reduction' controversy. Benetton and McLaren relied on external engine suppliers, Ford and Peugeot respectively, to provide this. However, the two car giants refused, claiming 'commercial reasons' as the reason why. While the black boxes in question were not their responsibility, Ford and Peugeot apparently encoded them with the same source codes used on their road cars, hence their reluctance. Benetton and McLaren, therefore, claimed they were stuck in the middle. Ferrari didn't have this issue because they built their own engines, so they didn't rely on third parties for source codes. Ironically, a large advert in *Autosport* at the time was for Ford Electronics and read: "Revealed at last: the secrets of the black magic box. This year Michael Schumacher has a distinct advantage." What were those secrets and was that advantage illegal? Those were the questions the FIA sought to find out. What they did eventually find would divide opinion even to this day.

39. *Damon Hill's Grand Prix Year: The Inside Story of an F1 Season* by Damon Hill (1994)
40. *Autosport*, 12 May 1994
41. *Motor Sport*, February 2016

MONACO

May 1994

"The cars are immediately less stable without the electronic suspension. As a consequence, they are harder to drive and we'll have more cars spinning and going off the track."

Ayrton Senna, Williams driver
(died during the San Marino Grand Prix)

"Several commentators said it was the elimination of driver aids [to blame for the accidents], a classic post hoc point. It was an intensely stupid inference but was nevertheless widely reported."

Max Mosley, FIA President

Despite the removal of driver aids, the 1994 cars proved quicker than their 1993 counterparts. For instance, the Monaco pole time was two seconds under the 1993 pole. *Photo: Willem Toet*

Standings before the 1994 Monaco Grand Prix

DRIVERS' CHAMPIONSHIP			CONSTRUCTORS' CHAMPIONSHIP		
Pos	**Driver**	**Points**	**Pos**	**Constructor**	**Points**
1	Michael Schumacher	30	*1*	Benetton-Ford	30
2	Damon Hill	7	*2*	Ferrari	16
3	Rubens Barrichello	7	*3*	Williams-Renault	7

Did a return to simpler cars in 1994 contribute to the accidents? *Photo: Alan Dahl*

Following the tragic San Marino Grand Prix, the world's glare remained firmly on the sport, waiting for its next move. The death of Ratzenberger had been profoundly shocking: however, Senna's passing was another order of magnitude. He had been the world's most famous racing driver and his fatal crash was broadcast live on television in front of millions. The loss was felt across the globe, but especially in his native Brazil, which declared three days of official mourning. With everyone on edge, fate would soon deal the sport another cruel blow, turning a volatile situation into perhaps the biggest crisis F1 had faced in recent times.

Predictably, a mass-media hysterically called for immediate repercussions following Imola, but couldn't agree on what action should be taken. Some suggestions were constructive, some obstructive, while most were little more than a thinly veiled attempt to turn tragedy into titillation. Generally, the less journalists knew about F1, the greater their mock outrage was. Mosley was at pains to avoid a kneejerk response. Privately, he felt that there wasn't a connection between the accidents, believing it was simply a coincidence that so many incidents happened in one weekend.[42] Mosley had to tread carefully though, as he would have been branded as irresponsible by a media baying for blood had he stated this opinion publicly at the time.

A top-level FIA meeting was held immediately after Imola to investigate the incidents and decide on what action was needed. This resulted in changes coming into effect at the following race, Monaco, which involved reducing pitlane speeds and limiting the number of people allowed in pitlanes. Measures to reduce the speed of cars and improve driver protection would now be urgently reviewed, although discussions with teams were still required to assess possibilities — this was scheduled to take place in Monaco. Opinion was divided whether these emergency proposals went far enough.

Another debate raged over whether the banning of driver aids and active suspension played any part in the accidents. Mosley expressed his view in his autobiography: "The small teams didn't have them last year and in 1991 virtually nobody had them. It is inconceivable that a driver of Senna's skill would be inconvenienced by a lack of driver aids." Senna himself had lobbied for a ban on driver aids during 1992 in the belief it would shift the emphasis in F1 back to driver's skill. Equally, active suspension systems of the time were prone to failures and had been the direct cause of two serious accidents in 1993, suggesting the technology could be a liability as well as a benefit. In my view, Mosley's point seemed a little disingenuous, given the small teams (like Simtek) had planned to use them for 1994 – until the goalposts changed.

Redesigning an F1 car at such notice doesn't seem ideal from a safety point of view. Part of the problem was the 1994 cars being faster and inherently more dangerous than their predecessors, especially as a result of mid-race refuelling. While changes had been made to safety regulations, these changes had arguably not kept up with the increasing speeds. F1 cars are a delicate balance between power, aerodynamic downforce and suspension, so each component is designed to work in harmony with the other. In F1, no allowance is made for excess tolerance, which only adds weight and therefore costs lap time.

42. *F1 and Beyond: The Autobiography* by Max Mosley

Chapter 5

Thus a change to one component in isolation – active suspension, in this case – would upset this balance. Especially if we add refuelling into that mix, which results in cars lapping several seconds quicker during races. The increases in horsepower for 1994 were not just from engine improvements, but also from new fuels specifically designed to take advantage of refuelling by disregarding economy in favour of performance. Thus power and, consequently, aerodynamic downforce had increased, while suspensions — and, therefore, the car's stability — had taken a retrograde step.

Perhaps these technical considerations and the resulting strain on certain components didn't form enough of the debate when outlawing active suspension. The rule change was in itself a laudable action – given that F1 needed to spice up the show and reduce costs. Moreover, a malfunction in active suspension is inherently more likely and dangerous than a passive suspension failure. In late 1993, Zanardi and Berger were involved in two major accidents caused by the active suspension suddenly collapsing, which illustrated how dangerous a failure in the system was. However, the active suspension ban being forced through for 1994

seems questionable, wherever the fault lies. It being finalised so late makes you wonder how much consideration was given to any knock-on effects.

For instance, two of the three circuits visited thus far were extremely bumpy, with Imola being especially bad, as various drivers confirmed. Bumpy surfaces were no issue for actively suspended cars because they maintained a consistent ride height and, therefore, grip level for the driver. However, bumps proved problematic for the 1994 cars. Yet little had been done to improve track surfaces and high kerbs to accommodate the backwards step in suspension systems before Imola. At the corner where Senna crashed, the stewards had earlier tried to grind away the bumps in the track surface, but they were largely unsuccessful, and only prompted by drivers' concerns 15 days before the grand prix.

Autosport quoted Schumacher: "They tried to improve it [the bumps] at Tamburello, but they made it worse. For example, the chicane where Rubens crashed I had a big spin just beforehand, it has a bump which we will need to have improved for next year." Another factor was certain teams' reliance on underfloor aerodynamics. At the time, cars had flat floors and no lower limit on ride height. Therefore, car floors were extremely sensitive to even the smallest ride height adjustments, much more so than when the 'plank' was introduced (explained later). This resulted in teams/drivers pushing these limits because of the lap time reward. The downside was that the whole floor had the potential to scrape over bumps on the track, meaning that the risk of bottoming, and the danger of the driver losing control of the car, was high. Racing teams had limited technology to help them understand the risks versus rewards of ride height changes, so they effectively had to take educated guesses while at the circuit. As demonstrated by the Williams/Senna example during Friday practice at Imola.

"Aerodynamic experimentation in those days wasn't sophisticated enough to understand the ride height sensitivity of aero," explained Paddy Lowe who was at the heart of developing Williams active suspension in the early 1990s. "In the wind tunnel now, we run ride height sweeps, steer sweeps, roll sweeps, and yaw sweeps, plus a load more. Back then, if a typical model was running different front and rear ride heights in a straight line, you were at the leading edge of sophistication. That would mean the impact of introducing a much wider range of ride heights on circuit (through not having active suspension) would be greater than people were perhaps able to deal with."[43] Meanwhile Benetton's Pat Symonds claimed "we didn't have aerodynamics that were super-critical on ride heights. Of course, they were critical, and always will be, but much less so than, say, the Williams."[44]

In addition, teams had moved to a far stiffer suspension set-up for 1994 to emulate the benefits of active ride, like a stable platform for the aerodynamics to work, resulting in cars becoming extremely sensitive to bumps, however small. Combine that with primitive suspensions because many teams had not developed passive suspension technology for a year, and you have a recipe for disaster. Williams designer, Adrian Newey, later eluded to another problem they faced. "We made a bloody awful cock-up," referring to the FW16 in 2004. "The rear-end grip problem was purely a set-up problem. We were learning about springs and dampers all

The Williams FW16 bottoming, as indicated by the sparks emanating from the rear of the car. *Photo: Alastair Ladd*

over again after concentrating on active suspension for two years, whereas most people had been away for just one."

Aside from Williams' set-up errors, how much was the active suspension ban being rushed in for 1994 a contributing factor towards Senna's accident? Especially considering Williams had a greater amount of work in comparison to others. Mosley argued it wasn't a factor because Senna "had been around there (Tamburello) countless times in practice and qualifying and knew how to set the car up accordingly... So far except for that weekend, we have been extremely successful [with safety]."[45] Whereas Newey recently admitted, "I messed up the transition from active suspension [in 1993] back to passive and designed a car that was aerodynamically unstable, in which Ayrton attempted to do things the car wasn't capable of doing. Whether he did or didn't get a puncture, his taking the inside, faster-but-bumpier line in a car that was aerodynamically unstable would have made the car difficult to control, even for him."[46]

It would be foolish to lay the blame for Senna's accident solely on the banning of active suspension, because there were many other factors involved, as detailed in the Imola chapter. In addition to them, Williams' Paddy Lowe believes "traction control brought qualities to the car the driver didn't really appreciate. Everybody had been running traction control for at least a year, if not two [by 1994], so going to a car that suddenly doesn't have it is going to be quite a handful."[47] Meanwhile, Damon Hill adds: "One thing that changed was the width of the tyres for 1993. The rears were narrowed (from 18 to 15in) and I don't think that was terribly good. That carried through to 1994, so maybe with active suspension, the effect of that change was masked a little in 1993. That meant there was less development on those tyres on passive suspension. When I first tested for Williams at Imola [in 1994] we had the much bigger rear tyre. It was very stable, lots of traction and great to drive. But when we went to the narrower rear tyre the car was a lot less comfortable."

Crashes happen when things are pushed to the limit and, in Senna's case, it seems a combination of extreme driving, together with other mitigating circumstances which didn't provide a safety net once on the bumps. In his autobiography, Mosley highlighted most F1 drivers acquired their skills in cars not equipped with electronic aids – true, however those cars were slower than the 1994 F1 cars at Imola for the reasons alluded to above. Furthermore, they would have originally been designed without active suspension, so perhaps their correlation between power, aerodynamic downforce and suspension, was more balanced than the 1994 F1 cars.

It was Senna's early experiences in the 1994 spec Williams which prompted him to claim "It's going to be a season with lots of accidents..." Furthermore, Brundle added: "Some of the cars still had aero optimised for all the goodies and suddenly all the goodies were not there, so you ended up with – in F1 terms – a slightly agricultural fix while you were getting the rest of it together. You certainly had less control of the car. I didn't have all the gizmos, but my Ligier was quite good in '93 because Williams was desperate for Benetton not to get the Renault engine, so they started sending us bits."[48]

Prost: "The cars are more difficult to drive [in 1994]. They are traumatising on the physical side."
Photo: Alastair Ladd

Senna had more Monaco wins than anyone else after his 1993 victory. He was sorely missed at the 1994 event. **Photo: Instituto Ayrton**

Senna's prophecy above was supported by the statistics. By the end of May 1994, F1 suffered nine serious accidents resulting in two fatalities, five major injuries and two very lucky escapes. In 1993 and 1995 there were five and three major accidents by June of those respective years. Fortunately, none of those accidents in 1993 and 1995 resulted in serious injuries or fatalities. Undoubtedly F1's luck ran out during that dark period in 1994 and whilst these statistics tell a story, one must remember accidents can happen at any time.

Likewise, there was no direct connection between those nine accidents in early 1994. However, in the majority of cases drivers had been pushing too hard in unfamiliar cars – as they tried learning their handling characteristics. The 1994, Williams was notoriously unpredictable to drive on the limit, which stemmed from a lack of appreciation of the challenges converting its car back to passive suspension and remarrying the aerodynamics accordingly. Hill applied caution in his driving until he became familiar with the car. Senna, rightly or wrongly, took greater risks. In Mosley's defence, had actively suspended cars continuing beyond 1993 it might have been a bigger ticking time bomb due to the increased speeds. Maybe a more considered implementation of the active suspension ban and aforementioned knock-on effects might have prevented at least one of those accidents.

The blame game was then directed to who had not pulled their weight on safety matters. "Dialogue between the sporting authority, teams and drivers over safety hasn't existed for a long time," Prost stated. When he was driving, Alain claims people within F1 had not listened to him on safety issues preferring to call him a 'coward' instead. The 1989 Australian Grand Prix was one such example – Prost was the only driver who refused to race because he felt the track was too wet and dangerous. Derek Warwick supported Prost stating: "The cowards are the rest of us drivers who raced that day and didn't stand by him." Brundle, who also raced that day, concurred.

43. *Autosport*, 7 August 2014
44. *Autosport*, 7 August 2014
45. *Autosport*, 12 May 1994

46. *How to Build a Car* by Adrian Newey (2017)
47. *Autosport*, 7 August 2014
48. *Autosport*, 7 August 2014

Chapter 5

Mosley disagreed that race stewards were at fault and blamed the drivers, "In the last six months only one driver – Gerhard Berger – has taken the trouble to speak to me... It's easy to be wise after the event, but nobody asked for extra tyres or protection at Imola. The suggestion that we don't listen to drivers is false and should never be made. It's been made by people seeking to make trouble."[49] Supporting Mosley's claim was how the track stewards tried to improve the bumps at Tamburello after the drivers raised concerns prior to the race.

There was a dreadful irony that Monaco was the next race given it was an event Senna made his own. His loss, coupled with Prost's retirement, meant no driver starting the 1994 event had previously won Monaco, illustrating the generational shift F1 was undergoing. Another tragedy of Senna's passing was being deprived of seeing him battle Schumacher for the 1994 championship.

Perversely, the tragedies had the side effect of raising trackside attendance figures while there was also an increase in TV viewing figures in the immediate aftermath of Senna's accident. Similarly the number of journalists at Monaco increased by 30 percent compared with recent years. But it was a sombre mood that weekend and several fun events at Monaco had been cancelled out of respect. Nevertheless it was hoped the chorus of wailing engines, particularly the distinctive sound of Ferrari's V12 bouncing off buildings at Monaco together with the inspiring sight of the world's most expensive cars hurtling around the famous street circuit, might inject some much-needed enthusiasm into proceedings.

Schumacher's engine failed during his first lap in the opening practice session – bad news for Benetton as they needed their star driver out on track. Towards the end of the session, his teammate, Lehto, was asked to sacrifice his car to enable the German to get some much-needed running. Within six laps, he lapped four seconds quicker than Lehto's best time. Does this story prove the performance difference between Schumacher and his teammate was down to the Finn's lack of fitness following his near-fatal testing accident? Or does it corroborate the theory that Benetton was secretly giving their main man an illegal driver aid that Lehto didn't have? Let's explore both theories, starting with the latter.

Respected F1 journalist, Nigel Roebuck, said during *Motor Sport* magazine's June 2011 podcast that "Somebody senior at Williams told me... Senna said to the Williams guys those two Benetton cars are two entirely different cars. With the one leading (at Aida) behaving differently from the one that wasn't leading." Similarly, in recent years Flavio Briatore, Benetton's managing director in 1994, said during an interview with Sky F1 "[in 1994] we had the best car with the best driver because the second car wasn't like the first car." Several years after leaving Benetton, Lehto said in an interview in 2004:

"The cars had traction control earlier, but it was no longer was permitted in 1994. You know, when you have something allowed and you suddenly ban it, people try to take advantage of that, as long as they don't get caught. I don't doubt for a second that there was something. Probably there were many experiments going on. Benetton was hardly the only team, other teams must have had cracks at it too. At that time, covering electronics was easier than today. There were odd things going on sometimes. A few buttons that were pushed in a completely different order in the team-mate's car. Difficult to be certain about what they meant. They [illegal driver aids] will be difficult to ever prove. It could very well be that there never were any."[50]

Lehto seemed to imply he had suspicions his car functioned differently to Schumacher's but didn't provide proof about possible irregularities (if they existed). Nevertheless, let's assume he was onto something, does that alone mean that one Benetton was illegal? Maybe those comments suggest Schumacher utilised functions like a brake bias adjuster, or engine fuel mixture setting, more than his teammates. These systems required the driver to alter settings within the cockpit and the Benetton star proved throughout his F1 career he had spare mental capacity when racing. For instance, Willem Toet of Benetton noted how Schumacher asked for additional speed displays within his cockpit. Unlike other drivers, he had a spare mental capacity to use them to analyse and improve his driving technique while racing at 200mph.

Toet added: "To the best of my knowledge, all drivers got the same software settings." In Monaco, Lehto was still learning the car, something other drivers struggled with all season given

Briatore: "[In 1994] We had the best car with the best driver because the second car was not like the first car." What did he mean? **Photo: Yvmv**

Schumacher dominated Monaco whilst Lehto struggled. Was foul play afoot? **Photo: Willem Toet**

Would Benetton have installed illegal driver aids in full view of everyone?
Photo: György Szundi

This and the opposite photos (from 1991 and 1994 respectively) shows teams working on cars beside the pitlane during Monaco practice sessions. **Photo: Antony John Dennis**

Briatore's policy of constantly rotating the second Benetton driver. For this reason, it is doubtful Lehto would have mastered all control functions within the B194's cockpit like Schumacher. Moreover, he was known to constantly change functions like brake bias in between corners to maximise lap time, or be constantly on the radio to engineers, all of which required the driver changing settings inside the cockpit. Perhaps these were the buttons referred to?

The alternative explanation is that, when Lehto stepped out of his car during that practice session, engineers plugged in a laptop and somehow activated illicit devices to help Schumacher lap faster than Lehto. Due to space limitations at Monaco, teams couldn't hide their cars within garages during practice sessions, meaning Benetton would have had to done all this by the side of the pitlane in full view of the FIA, rival teams, and the journalists in attendance that weekend. If you were in Benetton's position with Schumacher enjoying a massive 23-point lead, would you take that risk? If Benetton was stupid enough, then the evidence suggests even with a full and unhidden traction control the benefit would have been one second per lap.

Coincidentally Monaco the previous year was the first race Benetton used its 1993 spec traction control, because the 1993 rules permitted it the system was audible to any casual observer. Benetton needed to develop a bespoke fly-by-wire throttle for it hence why they had not brought it to earlier 1993 races. Frank Dernie, Benetton's chief engineer in 1993, added: "Cosworth back then were concerned that spark cuts and ignition timing fluctuation may hurt engine reliability, and their contract with Ford meant they would pay for any problems. McLaren was using their TAG management system and could do whatever they wanted since they were paying, and had an effective system straight away." Benetton found running with traction control at Monaco 1993 gave them a 1.2sec per lap improvement.[51]

If Schumacher had used a hidden and illegal traction control at Monaco 1994 then it is reasonable to assume the lap time gain would be slightly less than 1.2sec, because the system is likely to be less effective when it is hidden. Also, how did Benetton ensure it was no longer reliant on electronic throttles in such a short space of time? Fly-by-wire throttles were controversially banned for 1994 pre-season, so the FIA would have been ensuring the system wasn't

used. Similarly, why were there no reliability issues from the alleged hidden traction control complying with Benetton's new-for-1994 Ford Zetec R engine?

Evidence that the lap time difference between the two Benetton drivers was due to Lehto's not having fully recovered from his pre-season accident includes his own comments. In 2014, the Finn was asked about his 1994 comeback: "I couldn't feel my hands on the steering wheel at all, I had to keep looking to make sure they were in the right position. I was so physically weak: I didn't have any strength in my neck muscles. It takes a long time to build up good muscles and I'd only had two days back in the car. I should have had six months' rest (as advised by doctors) and then got physically fit and got all my muscles right, but you know, in F1, you don't have time. Flavio Briatore is a businessman. Benetton needed two strong cars scoring points, so I didn't have any choice."[52]

His 1994 drive with Benetton was supposed to be Lehto's big break in F1, but his enforced absence during the opening two races handed a golden opportunity to Verstappen – who was touted as the next big thing. Lehto later admitted he didn't want Verstappen stealing his position full-time, hence his rushed return: "I came back to racing at Imola," remember the Finn. "It was way too early and I wasn't fully fit, but nobody really said no and I desperately wanted to do it. I wasn't under pressure from Benetton to come back – I was under pressure from seeing Jos Verstappen racing the car when I knew it should be me. That pissed me off in a big way."[53]

Moreover, the Finn believed he could better Verstappen's results considering Schumacher had won the opening races in the other Benetton. "Imola was okay because it wasn't very bumpy, but Monaco was impossible," he later explained. "Lack of feeling was an issue but the pain was the other problem. It was so painful to drive."[54] Lehto also admitted his neck was so weak because doctors had to cut through the muscles when operating on it so he barely had any feeling in his legs.

49. *Autosport*, 12 May 2014
50. MTV Uutiset, 23 February 2004
51. Speed Channel's retrospective of the 1993 Monaco Grand Prix (aired in 2003)
52. *Autosport*, 7 August 2014
53. *Autosport*, 30 March 1995
54. *Autosport*, 7 August 2014

Chapter 5

Determined as he was, Lehto's performances progressively got worse throughout the weekend as his neck pain became less bearable. He crashed in the afternoon qualifying session and had to use Schumacher's car to set his best time, but dropped from 12th to 17th during Saturday's qualifying session. When journalists asked about his neck that weekend, Lehto grimaced "look at the lap time". Eddie Irvine, who was co-commentating for ESPN during its race coverage, remarked: "I was talking to JJ [Lehto] before the race and he told me he still had massive problems with his neck. I actually noticed he had a neck brace on and he was getting his helmet strapped to his shoulders on both sides... and he said this morning that the bumps are causing him problems because he just cannot focus on the corners because his head is just rolling around so much." Irvine and Lehto had been teammates in Formula 3000 in 1989.

As a comparison, Monaco also saw the return of Alesi following a neck injury, although his was less severe than Lehto's given the Frenchman needed half the time to recover. "It should have been an easy race for my injured neck," Jean later stated. "The circuit is not too physically demanding because it does not have any long corners. But I had no idea how much pain I'd feel from the bumps. The last few laps were hell, unbearable. So much so I had to give up chasing de Cesaris." Therefore one can only imagine the pain Lehto was going through that weekend. Even if he was 100 percent fit, you would still expect a significant gap between him and Schumacher. You only have to look at their respective achievements in F1 outside of 1994 to see why.

Steve Matchett, a Benetton mechanic, said they only changed the seat, seatbelt and pedals on the car for Schumacher which is standard procedure in those situations. He insisted: "Now, some drivers may have suffered a terribly bruised ego, having just received instructions from Ross Brawn to hand their car to a faster teammate but, quite honestly, I think JJ was more than happy to stand down: his neck was suffering from all the on/off throttle work and constant

Sauber withdrew from Monaco following Wendlinger's accident and arrived at the following race with higher cockpit sides for added driver protection. **Photo: Alastair Ladd**

left/right g-loads that Monaco induces. Undoubtedly, JJ's fitness was affecting his ability to perform: we couldn't consider the car at fault, the evidence of that was clear for all to see."[55]

Commentator Bob Varsha stated during ESPN's coverage of the race: "As you may know, traction control is illegal in F1 for 1994... and if we had any doubt it was on either the Benetton or McLaren we were disabused of that notion in qualifying. Brundle, Hakkinen, Schumacher, Lehto lighting up the rear tyres in that run up to the start and finish straightaway like a drag racer doing a burnout." Former F1 driver and multiple Le Mans race winner Derek Bell, who was co-commenting that day, agreed stating how wonderful it was. While Benetton was increasingly being built around its main bread winner, Schumacher, by 1994, there is however a world of difference between this and the team secretly installing banned devices on his car. Ask yourself logically what sounds like the most plausible reason why Schumacher was able to go four seconds quicker than Lehto at Monaco.

Hopes of an incident-free weekend were shattered during the final moments of opening practice when Karl Wendlinger suffered a life-threatening accident. Braking late into the notoriously bumpy Nouvelle Chicane, Wendlinger lost control of the skittish Sauber

Alesi, like Lehto, was recovering from a neck injury while competing in Monaco. The Frenchman later admitted the pain adversely affected his performance. **Photo: Károly Méhes**

Wendlinger's incident. By now the world's media questioned whether F1 should be banned. **Photo: Motorsport/LAT Images**

and slid sideways into the barrier, the impact was measured at 110mph. With nothing to protect it, his head struck the barriers with considerable force and the Austrian was knocked unconscious. Although Wendlinger was fortunate that the impact had not broken his neck, it left him in a coma for several weeks and, while he eventually recovered, the after effects would halt his F1 career. After being made aware of the severity of Karl's injuries, Sauber withdrew from the Monaco Grand Prix.

Mosley had tried avoiding a kneejerk response after Imola, but Wendlinger's accident was the final straw. Having been savaged in Italian and French newspapers for his conservative approach thus far, the FIA president realised immediate action was necessary otherwise there would have been a major outcry from the media if the sport appeared to be continuing as if nothing had happened. "First of all, people were not used to it," the under-fire FIA president later retorted. "But secondly things had moved on, and there was less tolerance for people getting killed [in F1] than there was for example in the 1970s when it happened all the time."[56] The following morning Mosley held a press conference announcing drastic changes to slow the cars, the detail of which will be discussed a little later. These modifications were unilaterally imposed and implemented in four phases throughout 1994 and 1995, beginning from the following race in two weeks' time.

While the necessity of improving safety was disputed by nobody, the participants were against rushing through these changes without their consideration; teams' designers even expressed doubts they would be successful. "They've [the FIA] gone around like a chicken with its head cut off, and made changes without looking at them or their implications deeply enough," fumed Jordan's chief engineer Gary Anderson. Meanwhile, team bosses were outraged at having to redesign cars which were only a few months old, especially given the extremely tight timescales afforded. Pacific team owner Keith Wiggins joked: "If my engines don't bankrupt me, this stands a pretty good chance..."

Mosley knew his proposals would upset teams because they contravened how new rules should be implemented under the Concorde Agreement, but claimed it was a *force majeure* situation. He was under intense pressure from outside the sport and believed there was no alternative as he explained a year later. "As far as the Monaco changes were concerned, those changes were the minimum needed to keep F1 at its present level in the sense of maintaining the participation of the big companies, both from the automobile business and outside. We got very, very close, once we had the next major accident, at Monaco, to seeing the elements on the boards of these companies who are against motorsport – and there always is such an element – gaining a majority. It was necessary to demonstrate that we were in control and to react very quickly.

55. *Life in the Fast Lane: The Story of the Benetton Grand Prix Year (1995)* by Steve Matchett
56. *Autosport*, 7 August 2014

Chapter 5

"Everyone was saying they were very anxious and were coming under pressure from other elements on their boards. From virtually all of them, the message was coming that this was beginning to be a very serious situation. Backed up by an interesting phenomenon which was that we started getting applications, on the Thursday evening in Monaco, from political journalists in Paris, Rome, places like that, who had no interest in the racing at all. It was becoming the great attack on F1. We had 80 MPs who signed a motion in the Italian Parliament that F1 should be banned in Italy. We had the beginnings of trouble in Brussels and similar reactions in other countries. A groundswell questioning whether F1 should be allowed. Whether we really knew what we were doing and were in control. Because although we all knew that such events could happen at any time and that the only odd thing was that we got so many in one weekend."[57]

Pressure was also being applied from within the sport as the drivers reformed their own safety committee, the Grand Prix Drivers' Association (GPDA), to throw light on safety shortcomings at circuits. Having been disbanded in 1982, the drivers begun discussing plans to revive the body before the tragic events of Imola brought things to a head. As a particularly ironic twist, Senna spent the morning before that race with Prost discussing ways of reviving the GPDA, with Senna offering to spearhead the body at its planned launch at Monaco.

Niki Lauda emerged as the GPDA spokesman at Monaco, at the time he also worked as a consultant to Ferrari. Journalists therefore questioned whether Niki's involvement, along with Ferrari driver Gerhard Berger as a co-director, gave Ferrari an unfair

Teams were required to reduce their diffusers (circled in red), which in turn decreased speeds. ***Photo: www.williamsdb.com***

advantage given the power the GPDA had to enforce new measures. Nevertheless, the GPDA wasted no time and immediately inspected the Monte Carlo circuit looking to improve its safety.

Elsewhere, F1 teams had no alternative but to put their reservations to one side and make the mandated FIA car changes, but this wouldn't be the end of the matter. Mosley also announced the formation of an Expert Advisory Group which looked at improving F1 safety in other areas. It was perhaps Mosley's greatest legacy to the sport because this group developed measures, like higher cockpit sides or the HANS device, both of which have undoubtedly saved many drivers since. This body was chaired by Sid Watkins, who knew nothing about his

The diffuser cuts are circled in red. The 'plank' (circled in yellow) was introduced a few races later and forced teams to raise their ride heights.
Photo: Motorsport/LAT Images

Wendlinger's accident forced teams to implement significant car modifications immediately, much to their dismay...
Photo: Alastair Ladd

Lamy crashed while testing these new FIA mandated modifications and sustained severe injuries. Fortunately his life was not in danger. **Photo: Alastair Ladd**

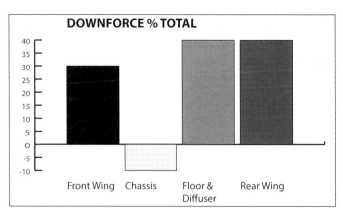

Toet estimated the 1994 floor and diffuser generated as much aerodynamic grip as the rear wing. Therefore the diffuser cuts were significant. **Image: Willem Toet**

appointment at the time it was announced, such was the speed which Mosley assembled the group.

Schumacher dominated the race itself, however, most were just thankful it passed without another accident. The possible exception being the additional 30 percent newshounds present at this race alone. After Monaco, the teams tested the first phase of the FIA's controversial safety modifications which included size restrictions on the front wing and diffuser which intended to slow the cars down by reducing downforce levels by 30 percent.

Unfortunately, some teams had begun using multiple stays that connected the rear wing end plates to the outer edge of the diffuser. Although primarily intended to enhance the interaction between the diffuser and the rear wing to improve the efficiency of the diffuser, these stays also provided a significant amount of support for the rear wing. Since the FIA reduced the size of the diffuser, teams had to remove many of these stays to ensure that the rear wing and diffuser remained legal. However, some had not realised the amount of support those stays had been providing to the rear wing, with sometimes catastrophic consequences.

During a test at Silverstone, held before the next race in Spain, Pedro Lamy was in a Lotus 107C which had been modified to satisfy the new regulations. Approaching Bridge corner at 150mph, the rear wing assembly suddenly collapsed under the loading imposed

on it. Spinning out of control, the car struck the barriers on the left hand side and began violently tumbling, throwing wreckage and spilling burning fuel across the track. Vaulting over a 10ft debris fence which would normally protect spectators, the survival cell slid along a pedestrian walkway and eventually came to rest inside a pedestrian access tunnel. Johnny Herbert, had been right behind the Lotus when the crash happened, was horrified by what he had seen and braced himself for the worst as he stopped his car and ran down the tunnel. An interesting side note is that Lamy started dating the nurse who attended to him afterwards.

Meanwhile, a fierce debate raged over the cause of the crash. Lotus claimed: "as a result of technical changes demanded for Barcelona… it is apparent that the rear wing structures are being subjected to new dynamic and aerodynamic forces. The accident was caused by a failure of the rear wing mounting system. The system has been used on the 107A and 107B over the past two seasons and has been proof tested to twice its design load without a single failure since its introduction."[58]

Lotus's claims were supported by other teams encountering problems with its rear wings during testing. Ligier had two wing failures, while Williams and Minardi suffering cracking on the wing supports. During the Spanish Grand Prix weekend, Lotus needed to re-engineer its rear wings again, while Gachot's rear wing collapsed during the race. Mosley disputed that Lamy's accident was a direct result of the FIA's Monaco safety initiative: "That is self-evidently nonsense because it was caused by the team failing properly to adapt their car to the new regulations. If they say they didn't have time to do it properly, then they shouldn't have run the car. It is up to them to take such steps as are necessary to make sure their cars are safe."

Rather than placating them, Mosley's response convinced certain team principles he was unfit to rule and needed to be replaced. Under the belief that Mosley was vulnerable, Benetton team bosses began taking steps to try and push Mosley out of his position. What they had not bargained for was Mosley was no pushover. The relationship between them was about to get very interesting indeed

The air box holes above the driver's head were another safety change because they reduced engine performance. **Photo: Martin Lee**

57. *Motor Sport*, February 1995
58. *Autosport*, 2 June 1994

SPAIN AND CANADA

May and June 1994

"It is our opinion that the ability of yourself [Max Mosley] and your advisers to judge technical and safety issues in F1 must be questioned."

Flavio Briatore, Benetton's Commercial Director

"I shouldn't really get involved, but the last paragraph of Mr Briatore's letter was very ill-advised and shows a lack of understanding about how regulations work and the FIA's role in safety."

Max Mosley, FIA President

Benetton's Walkinshaw (left) and Briatore both had separate personal feuds with Mosley and apparently saw F1's crisis as an opportunity to get rid of him.
Photo: Martin Lee

Standings before the 1994 Spanish Grand Prix

DRIVERS' CHAMPIONSHIP		
Pos	Driver	Points
1	Michael Schumacher	40
2	Gerhard Berger	10
3	Damon Hill	7

CONSTRUCTORS' CHAMPIONSHIP		
Pos	Constructor	Points
1	Benetton-Ford	40
2	Ferrari	16
3	McLaren-Peugeot	10

Spain, the first race where temporary chicanes were installed for safety. They also appeared in Canada and Belgium. **Photo: Motorsport Images/LAT**

The build-up to the Spanish Grand Prix summed up F1 in 1994. Teams were in an uproar over the cost, haste and knock-on effects of major car modifications imposed upon them a fortnight ago in the name of safety. Some felt Lamy's recent testing accident was a consequence of those changes and their tight timescales and as a result, teams openly criticised Mosley and took strike action. The FIA president responded by threatening the trouble-makers with race bans while publicly reminding teams they must either compete on his terms or not at all. Documents were leaked to the press and verbal pot-shots were exchanged, while drivers threatened their own boycott over safety. To the viewing public F1 was increasingly resembling a sport tearing itself apart and another serious crash that weekend only heightened fears and tension.

Following all the accidents in recent weeks, Schumacher met Spanish race organisers and requested a makeshift chicane before the high-speed Nissan corner. The Grand Prix Drivers' Association (GPDA), whom the German was acting on behalf of, felt a chicane was necessary because this was a dangerous area of the track where runoff was minimal. However, when the drivers arrived at the circuit and found nothing had been done, they threatened 'no chicane, no show'. Niki Lauda claimed to have called Mosley at 11pm that night to force the issue. The temporary safety measure was built out of a pile of tyres and nicknamed the 'Beirut Chicane' because it resembled a roadblock. It was a ridiculous solution, but the drivers felt it necessary to highlight a potential hazard with the track.

Little prior planning went into the 'Beirut Chicane', indeed it was opened up by two metres in between the Friday morning practice sessions. There were, however, a few comic moments to this affair, Berger's amusing mispronunciation of 'Chicane' as 'Schicken'

during various TV interviews. Eurosport commentator John Watson memorably shouted "Surprise SURPRISE!" when Bertrand Gachot clobbered the tyre stacked at the 'Beirut Chicane' on only his fourth lap of the weekend.

Spain saw the first phase of the car alterations which had caused so much controversy. Willem Toet, Benetton's Head of Aerodynamics in 1994, gave some insight into the amount of work required. "We were fortunate at Benetton because we had already prebooked a wind tunnel session starting on the Monday after Monaco. Back then, we only had about one week in every three (and only daytimes) in a rented wind tunnel in Farnborough. My boss, Rory Byrne, gave me simple, clear instructions: "War technology is all we can use – there would be no time to draw and make any fancy bits. Too true – same applied to the wind tunnel model.

"We started in the wind tunnel with a baseline run with the model as the car had raced in Monaco. Then we carefully marked up the place to make the first big cut, and using a hacksaw (literally) cut the front wing end plate extensions off the model. Test result – 17 percent less downforce, much of it off the front of the car. Then we took the hacksaw to the diffuser. A further 15 percent loss, much of it at the rear of the car. Balance pretty much back to normal. Thirty-two percent less downforce was going to mean *much* slower lap times. Then we got to work! By the Friday, we managed to recover from a 32 percent loss to 'just' a 15 percent loss. Probably 2sec per lap recovered in that week… Drawings were faxed from the wind tunnel and phone calls made to ensure we had the ability to make what we were inventing."[59]

59. Willem Toet LinkedIn blog, 28 October 2015

Stories soon emerged of other team personnel arriving to Barcelona completely exhausted after spending long nights regaining the lost grip mandated by these proposals whilst ensuring their cars were safe. By Spain, virtually every team had publicly expressed their anger over the changes and the timescales imposed. "It's far too early to say if the overall effect has been to make the cars safer," said a sceptical Harvey Postlethwaite, Tyrrell's respected Engineering Director. "The car handled pretty badly – especially in the slower corners – and the drivers reported difficulty in finding the limits. After discarding years of development, you'd expect that." Postlethwaite was part of Mosley's Expert Advisory Group and usually sided with the FIA president owing to their good relationship formed at March during the early 1970s so his words carried weight.

McLaren's Ron Dennis went a step further in a 'confidential' letter sent to Mosley which somehow found its way into the hands of certain newspapers and magazines. It read: "We, like the majority of teams in F1, consider the whole episode, and indeed the management of F1 by the FIA, to be unacceptable." The two men of Benetton went even further. Flavio Briatore and Tom Walkinshaw both had separate personal feuds with Mosley and apparently saw this as an opportunity to rid F1 of him.

Walkinshaw's rancour dated back to 1970, starting when he drove for Mosley's March team in Formula 3. The relationship ended badly after Walkinshaw struggled with the March 703 and his promised

Toet: "We had no planning time [adapting the cars to the FIA changes] because we had no idea if there would be [further] rule changes and, if so, how big they would be." *Photo: Willem Toet*

sponsorship never materialised. Relationships then soured further after Walkinshaw broke both his ankles during a big accident. Briatore, meanwhile, later claimed Mosley never liked him and the FIA (under Mosley) always handed his team unfair punishments, citing the 2006 mass damper affair as an example.[60]

Maybe it was a personality clash or perhaps Mosley had good reason to dislike Briatore as contemporary rumours suggest the flamboyant Italian had ambitions of running the FIA. If true, then Mosley, like anyone in his position, would have viewed Briatore as a threat considering how a former team owner had previously taken power from a former FISA president.[61] Briatore had also just taken control of a second F1 team (Ligier) so his power within the sport was increasing, furthermore he was friends with Ecclestone – the FIA vice president. Perhaps buoyed by this, Briatore felt confident enough to sign an open letter addressed to the FIA president which contained the following:

"Now the teams have had an opportunity to test and evaluate the Barcelona regulation changes, it has become apparent there are serious problems. The stability and consistency of the car has worsened. The cornering speed of the cars has been reduced, but the likelihood of an accident has increased. Several teams are experiencing structural failures attributable to the change. The loading on key components have moved outside the designed range. At the beginning of the year you campaigned and received my support to reduce costs in F1. These measures do the opposite, without the beneficial effect for which they were introduced.

In an FIA press release of 4 May, the following statements were made: 'Before firm decisions can be made, each proposed measure must be carefully considered with input from the teams, engine builders, outside consultants and medical experts. The modern F1 car cannot be safely regulated by snap judgements or panic measures... Despite these comments, you then proceeded to introduce the measures announced on 13 May... You continue to insist on these ill-conceived measures. It is our opinion that the

The Benetton almost remained unoccupied at Spain, following Briatore's open letter. *Photo: Ford*

Williams and others did not participate in first practice as they wanted to demonstrate their anger over the FIA's mandated changes. Ferrari did not join them. **Photo: Károly Méhes**

There have been contradictory reports over what was said during the Barcelona crisis meeting held in the Williams motorhome.
Photo: Károly Méhes

ability of yourself and your advisers to judge technical and safety issues in F1 must be questioned."[62]

The open letter explicitly stated should any serious accidents befall Benetton drivers (Schumacher and Lehto) then "it will be theirs and the FIA's responsibility" that they raced in these hastily modified cars. Interestingly, it was written in perfect English, even though Briatore is a man who speaks in broken English. This letter proved a catalyst for a public spat that almost resulted in the championship leaders missing the Spanish Grand Prix because:

■ Officials told Benetton they couldn't compete in the event until written confirmation was provided stating the team would take full responsibility for the safety of its cars.

■ Briatore countered that, as his cars had 'successfully passed' scrutineering, the race stewards had 'assured' Benetton were legal and safe by the race stewards.

■ Officials refused to accept that, reiterating their request for express written confirmation from Benetton acknowledging responsibility for their car's safety.

■ Ten minutes after the opening practice session, Benetton finally relented and their participation in the event was finally confirmed, the irony being the Benettons were as safe as any other cars.

■ Mosley held an informal press conference at Barcelona defending his position following recent events. "Benetton wrote me a long letter but Mr Briatore never bothered to pick up the phone. It's not surprising he doesn't know what's going on... It has now been demonstrated to him clearly what the true position is." When Mosley was asked why changes cannot be smooth, he replied: "A frank answer is that it's more personality problems than anything."[63]

The situation between the teams and Mosley came to a head during Friday morning practice when only Ferrari, Minardi, Tyrrell, Larrousse and Sauber took part. The other nine teams went on strike, to highlight their frustrations while their principals

forcibly engaged with Mosley. This latest crisis meeting was held in Williams' motorhome, so it must have been tempting for anyone sick of politics to jump in and drive it off the nearest cliff. Eventually, a thinly smiling Mosley emerged claiming after "Frank and open discussion the [race] meeting will continue in the usual way," ie with the cars running in the new Barcelona specification. Since many teams had not brought parts which would satisfy the old rules, in reality they was little alternative.

In return, the constructors obtained concessions such as an expansion of F1's Technical Working Group to include more team engineers and drivers and ensuring future reductions in downforce were equalised with a reduction in engine power, something that had not happened for Spain. Prior to which, teams found hacking off significant amounts of downforce but leaving the power untouched upset the delicate balance of the cars discussed earlier. Therefore future FIA phased alterations now allowed participants a greater say in how and when any requirements would be met.

For example, Mosley initially demanded teams removed air boxes which were situated above the drivers head, which encouraged air into the engine for better performance. However, aside from the performance benefits, the airbox was also a prominent area for sponsor decals, making it financially valuable to the teams. Following the Barcelona meeting this proposal changed so teams could retain this key bit of advertising space, provided they cut holes to reduce the ram effect of the airbox. Ironically, at the following race this concession provided something new to fight over (detailed shortly). Meanwhile, F1 folk had enough to argue over – not least the question of who emerged the winner from the Barcelona crisis meeting.

60. The FIA reinterpreted the rules during the middle of 2006 and banned a previously allowed technology, placing Renault's championship defence in jeopardy
61. Ecclestone wrestled commercial control of F1 from FISA president Jean Marie Balestre in 1982. Ironically Mosley drafted the legal documents
62. *Autosport*, 2 June 1994
63. *Autosport*, 2 June 1994

Chapter 6

FIA President, Max Mosley, found himself under attack during the Spanish weekend. However, he fought back.
Photo: Motorsport Images/LAT

Benetton's Ross Brawn made some interesting suggestions about the aftermath of the Mosley v Briatore/Walkinshaw 'war'.
Photo: fry_theonly

Toleman was the first to introduce ECUs to F1 in 1984. By 1994, they had become so sophisticated that policing them created unforeseen issues, like how to get engine manufacturers to surrender their highly confidential source codes. **Photo: senna.org.br**

After the sound of engines stopped following morning practice, paddock rumours revved loudly once more, with some declaring Mosley was forced to back down, others said the opposite occurred and some even labelled the conflict FISA v FOCA 2.[64] Subsequent press reports suggested Mosley's position had been undermined, while also portraying him in an unfavourable light. The following day Mosley felt compelled to issue a statement which read: "Suggestions that the FIA or any of its officers have made concessions or abandoned powers are wholly false. At no time did the teams seek concessions or threaten not to run in the qualifying session on Friday. Had such a threat been made, I would immediately have invited those concerned to carry it out. The FIA owns and runs the F1 World Championship, teams will participate on this basis or not at all." Mosley also sent an open letter addressed to Ecclestone on the Tuesday after the race which read:

"Last Friday, you invited me to a meeting with nine F1 teams... We had what I thought was a friendly and constructive meeting. The fact that the cars of those present were not running wasn't mentioned. No threats were made and no concessions were sought. You can imagine my astonishment when I read next day in the press that 'concessions' had been 'wrung' from me, that I had agreed to have no further say in F1 matters that henceforth all decisions would be taken by the teams, not by the FIA, and so on. Allegedly, these stories come from one of the team managers present. I cannot imagine why any of them should wish to fabricate these rather tiresome falsehoods but I should be grateful if, in your capacity as the official representative of the F1 Constructors on the World Council, you would let me have written confirmation of what really took place. This would help me explain the true situation to the FIA..."

Ecclestone replied, ensuring some magazines were copied in: "I am sorry these reports appeared in the press. They are entirely untrue and if they came from one of the teams, this is most regrettable... I am unable to offer any explanation to the statements which appeared in the press, particularly in Italy... It may be that, with the large number of journalists outside Frank's

motorhome, one of the team principals was unable to resist the temptation to seek publicity..."[65]

In his book *Total Competition*, Ross Brawn recalled Walkinshaw and Briatore came out of a meeting this weekend and announced "Max has resigned. He's gone. He's finished. We are going to have someone new." Brawn, knowing Mosley well, figured the fallout would be interesting. Lamentably, he was proved right because things got unpleasant between Benetton and the FIA afterwards. Benetton's Technical Director then noted after this 'war' started the black box from Schumacher's car at Imola was confiscated a second time.

You may recall that the FIA seized the ECUs from the top three finishers at Imola (Benetton, Ferrari and McLaren). This was due to allegations that teams were somehow circumventing the traction control ban. According to Brawn's book *Total Competition*, "the first time around they found nothing amiss, so we were given the black boxes back." In his autobiography, Mosley commented: "Unfortunately, in all the confusion and stress following that disastrous race weekend and its aftermath, I made the mistake of authorising their return to Benetton before they had been fully checked. Later in the season, we seized their electronic devices again..." Mosley added after confiscating Benetton's black boxes for a second time the FIA published its findings. Fig 5 shows an extract from those findings.

The "demonstration at Cosworth Engineering" was scheduled for 28 June (Tuesday before the French Grand Prix), what happened there will be discussed later. Meanwhile, let us analyse the FIA findings prior to 27 May, the date of Barcelona crisis meeting, to investigate Brawn's claim above. You may find the questions thrown up are in themselves interesting and telling and be able to draw conclusions based on the Occam's razor principle, which states that among competing hypotheses, the one with the fewest assumptions should be selected. Firstly, the case for Benetton being innocent...

The FIA report suggest that, between 15 May (Monaco race day) and 27 May (Friday at Barcelona), Benetton's black box was returned. Because the FIA accepted Benetton's "alternative suggestion" which presumably was allowing them to prove they were legal at Imola (ie satisfying Article 2.6). It seems the FIA couldn't verify this without the source codes and Ford was unwilling to provide this outside of their secure premises.

Engine Control Units (ECUs) had been introduced into F1 during the 1980s and the regulations on them had not kept pace with their development. Therefore in 1994, the rules were vague and there was no explicit regulation forcing engine manufacturers to surrender their highly confidential source codes. Months later, they would be updated to cover this point but at the time there was no precedent for this situation. The 'alternative suggestion' seems to be a 'demonstration at Cosworth Engineering'. In other words, the FIA authorised Ford/Cosworth[66] to unlock the black box data on its own premises to satisfy article 2.6.

Thus the FIA and their IT experts (LDRA) had possession of Benetton's black box for 14 days between 1 May (race day at Imola) and 15 May. Moreover, these dates correspond with Brawn's claim that Benetton's black box was confiscated a second time after the 'war' between Briatore/Walkinshaw and Mosley started. Because the catalyst for the 'war' was the open letter sent by Briatore to Mosley on the 25 May, ie after the FIA initially returned Benetton's black box.

Presumably, Briatore was assured the black box affair would shortly end in Benetton's favour otherwise why would he send the open letter to Mosley? Why would you unnecessarily provoke the rule enforcers if you knew you were cheating? The FIA findings state Benetton's black box was confiscated again in July (discussed later) and something would later be found which aroused suspicion. Because these suspicious items had not been deleted by Benetton prior to the second inspection, could that suggest they didn't know about them?

> Report by the FIA Formula One Technical Delegate on the investigations carried out on the electrical systems on Car Number 5 in the 1994 San Marino Grand Prix.
>
> An investigation into the software used in the computer systems of the cars finishing in the first three places at the 1994 San Marino Grand Prix was undertaken by Liverpool Data Research Associates Ltd. (LDRA).
>
> LDRA is a company which specializes in the analysis, validation and verification of highly complex computer software such as that used in modern civilian and military aircraft and a wide range of safety critical applications.
>
> On race day (1st May 1994), each of the teams was requested to supply the source code* for the software on board the car and schematic circuit diagrams of the electrical system. (Appendix 1)
>
> One team complied in full with this request and a demonstration of the complete electrical system was set up with entirely satisfactory results.
>
> Having received nothing from the other two teams, a fax was sent on 9th May (Appendix 2) asking for urgent action.
>
> An alternative suggestion was received from Benetton Formula Ltd. In this letter dated 10th May (Appendix 3), they stated the source codes could not be made available for commercial reasons.
>
> In a fax to Benetton Formula dated 15th May (Appendix 4), we accepted this proposal, on the condition that Article 2.6 of the Technical Regulations was satisfied.
>
> On 27th May we received a detailed program for the demonstration at Cosworth Engineering. (Appendix 5)

Fig 5. The FIA published its report into Benetton Ford's electronics. Why?
Image: www.motorsport.com

Ferrari and McLaren had their software investigated, but those findings were not made public. Why? *Photo: Martin Lee*

Let us now explore the alternative theory: that Briatore's open letter was to oust Mosley before he could expose Benetton's misdoings via the black box investigation. If that was Briatore's motive, his actions were a public way of eliminating Mosley. So there was the risk that Mosley's successor would have picked up the investigation themselves, particularly if Briatore was the cause of Mosley's (hypothetical) demise. Some believed Benetton knew its ECU contained illegal devices (not proven), so they fabricated the excuse of 'the source codes couldn't be made available for commercial reasons' to stall for time. However, McLaren also had its black box seized and used the same defence regarding source codes. So either Benetton colluded with their fierce rivals and agreed this common defence, or they rode their luck hoping McLaren would continue feeding the same excuse to the FIA.

McLaren and Benetton wanted to supply the source codes immediately, but both stated they had engine partners they needed permission from beforehand. It is claimed Ford was reluctant to hand them over because the source codes they used in their F1 programme were the same as their road cars, which also incorporated ECUs. So Ford (or Peugeot) didn't want them falling into the hands of rival manufacturers who would then be able to access their valuable road car data concerning engine settings etc.

For the purposes of exploring this hypothetical theory, let us assume the source code defence was fabricated. In this instance, Benetton was damaging Ford's reputation with this tactic and relying on its engine partner not protecting its image by exposing this. Ford was heavily promoting its brand within F1 throughout 1994, including sponsoring Eurosport's coverage and placing various adverts within *Motor Sport* magazine. So why would Ford want to take the blame for being uncooperative over source codes and risk damaging its brand? Especially as it was known at the time the Ford/Benetton relationship was unlikely to last beyond the end of the season, because the latter had been chasing Renault engines for 1995.

---

64. The FISA-FOCA war of the early '80s, where constructors demanded a bigger role in control of F1
65. *Autosport*, 22 September 2009
66. Cosworth built and serviced Benetton's F1 engines during 1994

Chapter 6

The data contained within the black box being investigated by the FIA was the sole responsibility of Benetton. Therefore an accusation against Benetton's software should in no way implicate Ford or Cosworth. In this hypothetical theory, the natural follow-on is Benetton proposed the 'alternative suggestion' to obtain its black box and delete any incriminating evidence. This assumption, however, relies on Benetton presuming the FIA would return their black box to them. Since it's commonly alleged that Benetton knew its black box was illegal, let's assume luck went their way on all the above to examine this theory further.

Assuming the black box was now in Benetton's possession, what is the likelihood of them being able to cover their tracks and provide the FIA with tampered evidence? LDRA's Steve Hennell indicated his feelings about this: "Telemetry in itself need not be conclusive. People talk about this sort of technology and dream up all sorts of models, but it's a lot harder to do than people think. Also, it is very dangerous to have a rogue code wandering about a system on something that travels at 200mph. It could work against the system very easily."[67] Assuming Benetton had better IT experts than LDRA and found a way of tampering with their evidence then why was something of interest found later on?

In summary, McLaren also sent a damaging letter to Mosley on the eve of Barcelona when their Imola black box was under investigation. Is that enough to suggest some form of collusion between them and their rivals Benetton to protect something from the FIA? Conversely, Mosley's autobiography does not state whether he returned McLaren's or Ferrari's black boxes earlier than he should have. Why, therefore, was Mosley singling out Benetton on that particular point? Ferrari had already been found guilty of using an illegal electronic device at Aida, while something compromising was eventually found on the McLaren (explained later). Was it a coincidence that the 'war' Brawn referred to started before Benetton's black box was seized a second time?

On Saturday morning at Barcelona, F1 had another rude awakening when Andrea Montermini, Ratzenberger's replacement at Simtek, slammed into a barrier at 140mph. As the car came to a stop the driver slumped motionless in his cockpit for a few awful moments. Fortunately, Montermini only suffered foot injuries, although onlookers were concerned his feet were visible from the smouldering wreck. In the race, Schumacher looked to be on another serene run to victory until his gearbox resolutely stuck itself in fifth gear (of the six available). Nevertheless, the German adapted his racing lines to the circumstances and drove two-thirds of the distance without any other gears, eventually finishing a remarkable second.

"He obviously slowed down for a little bit," said an astonished Pat Symonds of Benetton. "But after a couple of laps, we were thinking, 'What the hell is going on here?' We were in the early days of real-time telemetry then, the data was showing us he was always in fifth gear, but the lap times didn't suggest it. Afterwards, he said he had a think about it and referred back to his Mercedes [sports car] days. Michael had learned a lot about using long gears, and he just adapted so quickly to that situation."[68]

Initially, TV coverage equipped with live telemetry captured the moment the B194 became stuck in fifth gear. However, once they realised, Cosworth ensured their telemetry was stopped as they didn't want rivals learning about Benetton's problem. Schumacher was the only car to have this live telemetry data on TV during 1994, begging the question: if Schumacher used illegal traction control, why would Benetton have allowed the world to see his rpm, speed

Montermini's incident brought back painful memories of Ratzenberger's tragic accident. *Photo: Motorsport Images/LAT*

Some didn't believe Schumacher only had fifth gear despite it being obvious on TV. Benetton invited people to see the telemetry, prompting many requests from the public for free factory tours! *Photo: Alastair Ladd*

Hill won in Spain which gave Williams a morale lift. Most were happy to see someone other than Schumacher win. *Photo: Andrew-44-19*

and throttle data live on TV? It is likely other teams or the FIA analysed these graphics along with Schumacher's engine note to see if Benetton used any illegal traction control.

Some may feel these TV graphics were either inaccurate or contrived to fool viewers into believing Schumacher's Benetton was legal. Does that mean the gear problem at Spain, the onscreen graphics showing it, and Cosworth's aforementioned actions were all staged to assist in this elaborate cover-up plan? The data was supplied directly from engine telemetry and there is a clear correlation between the engine sound whenever Schumacher applies the throttle, and the acceleration bar increasing. This, along with the Schumacher being stuck in fifth gear incident and corresponding engine sounds underlined the accuracy of this on-screen display.

The next time it reappeared following Spain was during Friday qualifying in Canada, just as the German was negotiating the Old Pits Hairpin before the long back straight, a perfect example to judge whether he had illegal traction control or not. This footage can be found on the internet, and in it one can see Schumacher's acceleration graphic (the green bar) correspond with the engine note that can be heard. Both show Schumacher feeding in the power progressively on the exit of the hairpin. You even see the German have a small oversteer moment and the Ford telemetry graphic shows Schumacher holding the throttle position until it's corrected, before continuing to progressively feed in the power. With illegal traction control, he would have just immediately given it 100 percent throttle on the exit of the hairpin, and there wouldn't have been that oversteer moment.

If one pauses it at the correct moment, it shows Schumacher only applying about 80 percent throttle whilst the speed displayed is 56mph (90km/h) and he is in second gear. As a comparison, the Ford telemetry graphics also captured Schumacher exiting a similar corner (the Dequetteville Hairpin at Adelaide) in 1993, when he had traction control because the rules allowed it. Unfortunately, no screenshots can be displayed here due to licensing reasons, but the footage is available online.

If one pauses this at the correct moment, you'll see Schumacher on 100 percent throttle in 1st gear at 37mph (60km/h). This suggests that Schumacher didn't have traction control in Canada 1994, because he wasn't able to apply full throttle despite his

speed being 33 percent higher than the required level in 1993. The Adelaide circuit did require higher downforce levels, and their were diffuser cuts after Barcelona 1994 (circa 15 percent). But the effect of aerodynamics wouldn't have made a significant impact given the speeds involved in the above analysis, certainly nothing like 33 percent, particularly because the 1994 Benetton produced inherently more downforce than their 1993 car.

The 1994 Spanish Grand Prix ended with a feel-good story. Hill came into this event level on points with Barrichello but managed to secure Williams' first win of 1994. The situation mirrored that of his dad Graham who, following the death of Jim Clark in 1968, lifted a shattered Lotus team by winning that year's Spanish Grand Prix. Could Damon further emulate his dad by winning that year's world championship as well?

The Barcelona crisis meeting resulted in teams putting forward alternative plans for future car alterations and, the following day, Mosley announced his agreement to them. Finally, there was peace within F1, and it stayed that way – at least for a few days as constructors were busy transporting their cars to the next race in Canada. Once teams unpacked in Montreal, they found time for yet more arguing. One of the concessions from the Barcelona crisis meeting was teams could cut holes in air boxes instead of removing them completely. However, Ferrari upset rivals by placing their holes on the air box sides rather than behind the inlet, something others had done.

Mutterings of discontent grew when the top speeds of the two Ferraris were dramatically faster than anyone else during Friday's running. Whereas at Monaco and Barcelona the Ferrari's had been 6mph (10km/h) quicker in the speed traps than rivals, in Canada they had been 12mph (19km/h) quicker.

Having never got within 1.4sec of pole all season, Alesi topped Friday times by over half a second. The source of this dispute came from that old foe, vagueness in the rules following the hasty way they had been drawn up following a crisis meeting. Teams therefore came to Canada with different interpretations, because there were no specific ruling on where these holes should have been. Race officials had approved Ferrari's air box design in Canada.

67. *Motor Sport*, September 1994
68. *Autosport*, 7 August 2014

The air box holes (circled in red) proved another source of controversy. Williams' placing was typical of most teams… *Photo: Alastair Ladd*

…except Ferrari. "You don't need to be Einstein to understand the effect will not be the same," said a rival. *Photo: Martin Lee*

The following day, Ferrari boss Jean Todt stated: "As a gesture of goodwill, and under no obligation, we put another hole in the air box of the 412T1. And, as all could see, it made no difference."[69] It didn't escape people's attention that they were 8mph [13km/h] slower through the traps on Saturday than the day before, while Alesi was one of only four drivers not to better his Friday time. Ferrari maintained it was sour grapes against them doing well and no conclusions should be drawn from the speed trap figures. "When the Benetton laps two seconds faster than anybody else, it is said to be a miracle," Alesi fumed. "No questions are asked about its legality. So why is it that Ferrari is always a target?"[70] Despite this, by the time of the German Grand Prix, Ferrari would conform with others and cut a slit down the spine of their air box. Ligier was also required to place additional holes after they only cut the top of their airbox, however no suspicions were raised about Ligier's on-track performances at Canada. Accordingly to Joan Villadelprat, Benetton's Operations Director in 1994, teams then placed their air box holes in a position where their rear wing would stall and reduce drag in a straight line, thus increasing their speed.

"It's not elegant but it does the job," was Brundle's verdict on the newly installed chicane aimed at improving safety. It did, however, provide some great power sliding moments throughout the weekend as drivers, including Schumacher's Benetton, struggled with traction when exiting the chicane, the footage of which is available on the internet. Once again, the German dominated the race while teammate Lehto struggled, only qualifying in 20th position and finishing sixth. The Montreal circuit could hardly have been worse on his neck, with its bumpy nature, and heavy braking and acceleration requirements. It was similar to Monaco in this respect, which also proved troublesome for the Finn.

Paul West, a Williams mechanic in 1994, gave insight into the Montreal bumps. "I think that by 1994 we had the five-post rig operating which also helped with set-up. I remember watching the rig car do a 'lap' of Montreal when the temporary chicane was put in on the long straight back to the pits, I'm not sure if that was 1994 or '95, going through the chicane the rear springs were completely coil bound. I was quite shocked how violent the manoeuvre was." In Barcelona, a smoother track with few heavy braking zones where F1 cars peak in *g* loads, Lehto looked more competitive. Qualifying fourth and battling for a podium finish until his engine failed. Canada was also the first race Lehto didn't wear his neck brace.

The Ferraris proved competitive in Canada, unlike previous races. How much was due to their air box holes? *Photo: Alastair Ladd*

Lehto (towards the back) struggled in Canada, while Schumacher took another commanding win. **Photo: Alastair Ladd**

In the book, *Life in the Fast Lane*, Steve Matchett (Lehto's mechanic) detailed how, to no avail, Benetton changed everything on his set-up at Montreal. Having checked all of the components on the car and even the set-up equipment, eventually the spare car was raced in the belief the Finn's lack of performance might be down to the chassis. Lehto confirmed this to reporters during the weekend, adding the lap time improvement was only 0.1sec. His race engineer at the time, Christian Silk, believed Lehto was driving with trepidation in Montreal which was understandable given his horrific accident in preseason testing. "He was braking much earlier into turn one than Michael, so I asked him why? Lehto replied that there was a concrete wall in front of him." Mark Blundell, who himself suffered a massive accident in Indycars in 1996 at Rio, can relate to this, stating: "Once you've had a big one, it does put a little bit of an understanding into what the outtake could be."

After Canada, Lehto was replaced by the inexperienced Verstappen, the decision was reportedly reached by mutual agreement between Benetton and its struggling driver. In a press conference shortly afterwards, Lehto said: "My physical condition at the moment is not bad, but it's not 100 percent. I still have some problems, and there are still some things with my head that I need to straighten out... I wanted to come back as soon as I could, but I probably made a mistake to return that quickly. Then when I had the accident at Imola, it was difficult to pick up mentally."

The past year had seen Lehto experience considerable trauma, having witnessed the death of a close friend [Evan Demoulas]

first-hand during a road traffic accident when leaving the 1993 Canadian Grand Prix. About six months later in January 1994, Lehto was himself almost killed in his testing accident and subsequently went through hell to get back to F1 only to experience the horrors of Imola. The tragic events of that race was particularly personal for Lehto – having known Ratzenberger since competing together in Formula Ford 1600, he had been another close friend of Lehto. The two had even driven to that fateful race together, making it especially difficult for him to overcome.

Furthermore, as had been the case for many aspiring drivers of that era, Lehto had idolised Senna as he worked his way up the ranks into F1. It is often forgotten that Lehto suffered quite a shunt himself during the start which possibly aggravated his neck injury further, particularly as Lehto has since admitted he returned to racing at Imola well before his neck had healed. Some had suggested that the subsequent safety car might have contributed to Senna's own accident, so perhaps Lehto was carrying some kind of guilty about this, even though he was completely blameless. With Verstappen waiting in the wings, the races he drove afterwards were probably under a huge pressure and through a pain unimaginable to most. So it's little wonder Lehto needed to get himself straighten mentally after Canada. With Verstappen now stepping into the fore, would his performances shed any more light on whether Schumacher's Benetton was using an illegal driver aid?

69. Racefans, 12 June 2014
70. *Autosport*, 23 June 1994

Chapter 7

FRANCE AND BRITAIN

July 1994

"We could almost win the title in the middle of the year, and obviously for television and everything else, that's not very good... We messed up but then so did the stewards."

Joan Villadelprat, Benetton team manager

"It was a situation where the authority of the sport had been called into question. At that halfway point in the season, the future was wholly unpredictable and anything could have happened."

Max Mosley, FIA President

Williams now had the best car, so if the championship could be prolonged, Hill might close the points gap, possibly leading to a thrilling climax.

Photo: Alastair Ladd

Standings before the 1994 French Grand Prix

DRIVERS' CHAMPIONSHIP				CONSTRUCTORS' CHAMPIONSHIP		
Pos	Driver	Points		Pos	Constructor	Points
1	Michael Schumacher	56		1	Benetton-Ford	57
2	Damon Hill	23		2	Ferrari	32
3	Gerhard Berger	13		3	Williams-Renault	25

Mansell departed Williams and F1 on sour terms at the end of 1992, making his 1994 return to both all the more remarkable. *Photo: Alastair Ladd*

During the French Grand Prix build-up, F1's worst kept secret was finally confirmed – Nigel Mansell would return to Williams. Since winning the 1992 world championship, 'Our Nige' moved to Indycar and won that title at the first time of asking. However, 1994 proved harder and following Senna's fatal accident the press linked him with a return to his spiritual home. The Mansell/Williams deal was brokered by Bernie Ecclestone who realised Senna's passing left the sport without a former world champion and, by giving Schumacher a worthy rival, F1 would increase television viewers.

The deal worked for Williams Renault, because thus far its FW16 proved troublesome to set up, so it was hoped Mansell's vast experience might help identify that elusive sweet spot to exploit the car's potential. Furthermore, Hill would be pushed harder with Mansell alongside him while Renault, on home ground, enjoyed the additional crowds Nigel's 'guest appearance' pulled in. As observers were intrigued to see how Mansell compared with the new stars of F1, after almost two years away. Initially the Mansell/Williams arrangement was only for the French race, however it was later extended to the final three races of 1994.

Williams, bolstered by the arrival of the 1992 World Champion, started the weekend by locking out the front row ahead of Schumacher in third. During the race, Mansell was unable to take the fight to the Benetton star while Hill's challenge faded, thereby gifting the German his sixth dominant win in seven races. Coming into this event, suggestions that Schumacher's Benetton had run illegal traction control quietened down. Maybe some still had doubts but kept it to themselves after the recent tragedies. Alternatively, perhaps others got used to Schumacher and Benetton beating the previously almighty Williams Renault. Whatever, Schumacher's lighting getaway at France gave fresh impetus to these rumours, because without any hint of wheelspin, the Benetton shot past both Williams to lead from the start.

Hill, who had started from pole, later claimed he made the second-best start of his year, so was amazed to find Schumacher passing him at "a hell of a rate". While the championship leader suggested Hill "bogged down a little" and declared his own start as perfect before describing recent clutch improvements. Benetton's Technical Director, Ross Brawn, joked "I'd rather Michael not said anything (about the clutch), I'll have to give him a rollicking".

Nevertheless, questions remained over this start, particularly when Benetton's black box findings were publicly released weeks later, it forced Brawn to reveal more.

He claimed Schumacher's starting technique "causes a lot of distress" to the clutch, so Benetton developed a heavy-duty clutch which has a progressive feel to help Schumacher. "It's not a standard thing you buy off the shelf," Brawn said. "We modify it ourselves to give the ideal conditions for the start."[71] He later said: "The implication is that we are developing some system. We *are* developing a system and it is called a driver! Over the winter we initiated a programme with Michael where, at every test, he would practice the start three or four times a day. Like everything else, you cannot be good at something unless you practice and develop your technique."[72]

Benetton's Chief Engineer, Frank Dernie, added: "We did a lot of work on clutches back then. The difficulty was over compromise, a small diameter clutch allowed the whole engine and gearbox to be lowered but was prone to overheating and inconsistent engagement due to the combination of rapid heat expansion and sudden increase in friction coefficient at a certain temperature. My recollection was of Michael losing out often in starts in 1993 and I put a lot of start tests into the test plan late in the 1993 season and over winter reasoning that he was good at things we practiced and we were suffering from starts which we had rarely tested in the past since the old type clutches couldn't take it. The composite clutch could do a practice start at every test run, so we did. I actually think it was Michael getting really good at it that made more difference than any clutch development, we were doing maybe as many as hundreds of start tests more than the opposition back then."

Alesi and Berger were forced to practice their starts a few races into their Benetton tenure during 1996. Alesi, in particular, then made some explosive getaways throughout that summer, thus supporting Brawn's and Dernie's claims above. After Imola 1994, Lehto attended a shakedown where he told his helmet supplier "I'm at Santa Pod practicing starts". Perhaps his stall at Imola was due to a lack of practice given his limited time within the B194 prior to that tragic event.

71. *Autosport*, 7 July 1994
72. *F1 News*, 10 August 1994

Chapter 7

Alternatively, could the Finn's stall at Imola be a failure to engage a concealed and illegal launch control, so he was practicing that procedure during the subsequent shakedown? This theory is undermined by analysis of Lehto's race starts because until the French Grand Prix he never made great getaways, instead JJ usually held his grid position. So the second Benetton didn't dramatically make rocket starts after Santa Pod, indeed Verstappen also made a poor getaway upon his return in France.

Before Monaco, Schumacher tested at Silverstone following some soul searching after Imola. It is believed he also practiced starts – perhaps realising the importance it would play at the narrow Monte Carlo circuit – while trying clutch developments among other things. Prior to this test, the German had made poor starts in Brazil and at Imola after Senna's crash, so 50 percent of the time in race conditions.

However, from Monaco onwards, Benetton's star driver made good starts in four consecutive races. During the post French Grand Prix press conference Schumacher proudly exclaimed: "We have done a lot of development to our clutch which hasn't been very good in the beginning of the season. Since we raced this new clutch it's giving us a lot better performance in the start and that's what you see since then, we're doing always good starts." Clutch developments, along with Schumacher's willingness to practice his starting technique, is perhaps why he made good getaways from Monaco onwards.

Readers may wonder why start practice didn't seemly help Lehto like the Schumacher and Alesi examples above. According to Steve Matchett's book, *Life in the Fast Lane*, the Finn couldn't wait to leave the post-Imola shakedown, which was understandable given the trauma he had suffered in recent months (detailed earlier). So perhaps that, along with Lehto's lack of familiarisation to Benetton's unique clutch which had been developed for Schumacher's technique, explain this.

Weeks later, Brawn was asked to confirm Schumacher's French Grand Prix start wasn't assisted by electronic aids or a clever differential. "I can make that statement willingly," Brawn responded. "By his own admission, Michael was useless at starts last year. He has developed a technique of using the clutch and throttle in a way that, for a large percentage of the time, can eliminate wheelspin. Michael's view of Magny-Cours is that Damon was slow away from the lights and the TV coverage confirms that. Michael made an excellent start, Damon backed out and lost his bottle going into the first corner…"[73]

No post-race protests were made against Schumacher's French Grand Prix start, but you may recall Jordan submitted one against the winning Benetton after Brazil. This illustrates that teams were not averse to speculatively appealing results based on questionable grounds, provided the outcome benefited them. Nevertheless, the following week's *Autosport* magazine reported insiders within the sport "voiced private suspicions" that Benetton had used illicit traction control following Schumacher's start, however, none were prepared to be quoted. Interestingly, throughout pre-season various team personnel went "on record" accusing rivals of circumventing rules. In fact, it almost became a sport in itself as detailed in earlier chapters. Given rumours still persist today about Schumacher's start, let us analyse it in greater detail.

At Magny-Cours, the circuit hosting that race, the distance between the starting lights and first corner was short. Therefore questions were asked how could Schumacher pass two more powerful cars before the first corner without illegal traction control? Eddie Irvine did exactly that in 1997, coming up from fifth position to third, and fourth position to second during 1998 demonstrating it was possible. At the 1994 event, the drivers waited an unusually long time for the green light. Typically when this happens clutches drag, causing drivers to re-engage them and a delayed start should the lights change at that moment. While others might guess the start and are lucky, these two factors combined thus results in a greater variety of driver's starts. Someone making a good start can outdrag a more powerful car, as demonstrated by Irvine at France 1994 who initially overtook Berger's powerful Ferrari, only to be passed by the Austrian as they approached Estoril corner.

The early phase of a standing start places emphasis on engine torque over horsepower. In simple terms, torque is a better measurement of acceleration, while horsepower, relative to weight, is a better measurement of top speed. Schumacher's lighter V8 engine had superior torque characteristics over the V10 powering the Williams, and would thus be quicker in the initial phase of a start (all other things being equal). After reaching a certain speed, the horsepower advantage of the V10 becomes the defining factor. Remember Magny-Cours had a very short run to the first corner.

Schumacher made an unbelievable French Grand Prix start which many felt was proof of illegal driver aids. **Photo: Willem Toet**

The short pit straight at Magny-Cours. Note how close the grandstands are to the starting grid, meaning any sound of launch control should have been heard. **Photo: Cjp24**

Toet (in his hillclimb car) knows from first-hand experience more power doesn't automatically mean better starts. **Photo: Derek Hibbert/Richard Dunn**

The FIA investigation into Benetton's electronics was at a crucial stage when the rumours surrounding Schumacher's French GP start surfaced. **Photo: Morio**

Benetton's 1994 Ford V8 powerplant had particularly good torque, as demonstrated in Barcelona where Schumacher drove two-thirds of the race in fifth gear. A smaller V8 engine also had packaging advantages over a V10, allowing better weight distribution (ie a bit more weight on the rear) which assisted traction. These characteristics are partly why a Ford V8 won at all street circuits in 1993, because it was good at getting its power down. Furthermore, Mansell wouldn't have been used to standing starts in France, having just returned from Indy cars where rolling starts are used. Mansell clearly makes a poor start and is lucky to retain his third position.

The book *The Death of Ayrton Senna* claimed Schumacher made perfect starts by flooring the throttle and allowing his hidden and illegal electronics to do the work. Yet 25 years on, nobody has provided footage of this, despite there being a large grandstand alongside the Magny-Cours starting grid with many Renault employees/supporters keen to see a rival car disqualified. Nor is this apparent on TV footage, indeed legendary BBC commentator Murray Walker even mentioned how the engines were revving before the green light. Journalists later joked Mansell was whingeing so loudly about Schumacher's start that must have drowned out the sound any of illegal electronics. Moreover, Schumacher had a massive 33-point advantage over his nearest rival, Hill, coming into this race. So why would he and Benetton continue to run an outlawed electronics and risk severe consequences with that kind of advantage?

Interestingly, Schumacher made better starts during the first seven races of 1995 than the previous year. That period in 1994 saw him suffer two bad starts[74] compared to just one the following year. Despite this, no accusations of illicit electronics were made against Schumacher/Benetton regarding 1995, possibly because they used identical Renault engines and electronics as rivals Williams.

In 1994, the Magny-Cours start rumours couldn't have come at a worse time for Benetton because its black box investigation was approaching a crucial stage. The subsequent FIA report stated Benetton cancelled the demonstration scheduled for 28 June (the Tuesday before the French Grand Prix) "after some discussion between Ford and themselves concerning non-disclosure agreements". The FIA requested this test take place as soon as possible and it was eventually conducted on 6 July (the Wednesday after the French Grand Prix)... just when rumours surrounding Schumacher's Magny-Cours start were at their height. Afterwards, IT experts LDRA produced an inspection report which outlined its recommendations which the FIA would see on 11 July (the Monday after the British Grand Prix). Therefore, its findings shall be discussed a little later on.

Meanwhile, Silverstone was the mid-way point of 1994, and its second half was filled with controversy, with Schumacher right in the centre of it. Coming into this event, Benetton's star driver had accumulated such a lead in the drivers' championship that he only needed to finish second behind closest rival, Hill, in the remaining races to secure the title. Frankly, the chances of anyone stopping him taking the crown looked remote. Moreover, Schumacher's dominance since Senna's death had turned races into bore fests – precisely what the new-for-1994 regulations were designed to prevent. The majority of seasons since 1987 had seen one team generally dominate, hence the need by 1994 to spice things up.

In addition, the early 1990s saw an unprecedented number of big names depart the sport:
1991: Triple Champion, Piquet retired
1992: Newly crowned Champion, Mansell departed for Indycar
1993: Prost retired after winning his fourth championship
1994: Triple champion Senna crashed fatally

The lack of high profile drivers, the title fight virtually settled, and no exciting battles for lead positions were killing TV ratings and Ecclestone knew it. Gimmicks like bringing Mansell back were only a sticking plaster to the problem. Just when it was needed the sport got that vital injection of drama it had been longing for, and it all stemmed from a misdemeanour before the Silverstone race started.

73. *Autosport*, 9 March 2009
74. Defined as a start which resulted in a lost position

Chapter 7

During the pre-race formation lap, Schumacher overtook pole man Hill, thereby transgressing a little-known rule which stated cars must remain in grid order. The race start was aborted after Coulthard, who replaced Mansell in the second Williams, stalled his engine causing an additional formation lap. During which the runaway points leader committed the same offence in an identical manner as before. It is believed the German was trying to unsettle Hill in front of his home crowd. Remember, he did the same to Senna during the formation lap in Brazil. However, on that occasion no race stewards, TV commentators or press reporters pick up on the infringement, illustrating how little known this rule was at the time. For whatever reason, Schumacher escaped any penalty in Brazil over this infringement, which of course was incorrect. However, race officials were intent on punishing the German this time around.

The rules stated Schumacher should have started from the back of the grid, but this didn't happen – the first of many gaffes officialdom would make that day. Their next mistake was failing to notify Benetton within fifteen minutes of the incident about their intention to penalise them as stipulated in the rulebook, but confusingly it didn't state what should happen in this instance. Benetton team members later felt any penalty should have been disregarded, otherwise why have this fifteen-minute deadline? Whatever, twenty-seven minutes into the race the Enstone team was handed a note from officials stating "You are herewith advised that the stewards have decided to impose a penalty of five seconds on Michael Schumacher". The note unwisely didn't explain the infringement nor how the stewards expected the penalty to be administered.

It led to confusion within Benetton who later claimed they had not realised Schumacher's formation lap antics contravened the regulations. "We were told of the penalty," a livid Flavio Briatore added, "but the stop-go wasn't mentioned. Therefore we didn't ask Michael to come into the pits." Instead, the team incorrectly assumed the German would have five seconds added to his race time and informed their driver accordingly. Apart from this, Benetton took no further action – a crucial mistake – because race officials expected them to pit Schumacher for five seconds before resuming the race, a penalty of twenty-five seconds in reality.

The championship leaders didn't have good grounds to make their assumption because the rules stated a stop-go was intrinsic to a "time penalty" unless the incident occurred within the last 12 laps of a race. The FIA later claimed to have told Benetton verbally it was a stop-go when they handed them the note, and "officially via electronic information" three minutes later. Benetton's ignorance may have stemmed from stop-go penalties being a recent addition to F1 and having only being used a handful of times prior which does not excuse them, it merely explains things. It appears the rules were changed afterwards, so teams had to sign paperwork to acknowledge stop-go penalties whenever they were given.

Experienced F1 journalist Nigel Roebuck later remarked many of the press present at Silverstone were not initially aware a "time penalty" meant a stop-go either. While BBC commentator Jonathan Palmer, an experienced grand prix driver himself, incorrectly assumed teams were allowed to refuel and replace tyres during a stop-go penalty. Illustrating that, at the time, others were equally ill-informed of the rules surrounding stop-gos. Alternatively, perhaps Benetton knew these rules but was pleading

Schumacher always laid two black lines from his grid slot during formation laps to help race starts in 1994. Ironically at Silverstone, he made a poor getaway. *Photo: Motorsport Images/LAT*

Schumacher overtook pole man Hill during the formation lap. Barrichello committed the same offence by overtaking fifth place Hakkinen.

Photo: Motorsport Images/LAT

ignorance in order to take advantage of the mistakes race officials made when issuing the penalty, thereby hoping their tactics would change the stop-go to the lesser penalty of five seconds added onto Schumacher's race time?

As participants, Schumacher and Benetton are ultimately responsible for knowing the regulations themselves and should have known about the transgression of the rules on the formation lap and its consequences. So should they have needed their rule infringement explained to them on a note from race stewards? In reality, many didn't know the formation lap rule at the time as evidenced by Hakkinen and Barrichello both overtaking others during it at Silverstone 1994, thereby committing the same initial offence as Schumacher. Yet at the time few seemed to care about these breaches, unlike in the German's case. Read into that what you will.

Irvine commented afterwards: "Two people passed me [on the formation lap] at Silverstone, and I wasn't even slow away! So I can see why he's [Schumacher] seriously pissed off."[75] During his Eurosport commentary, John Watson, an experienced F1 racer himself, acknowledged Schumacher's actions on the formation laps but was clearly unaware it was against the rules. Thus Watson was equally confused about Schumacher's later penalty. Another former racing driver turned TV commentator, David Hobbs, said that during the 1970s it was common for cars to overtake on the formation lap. Therefore Silverstone 1994 was the first time he realised there was a rule against it. Again none of this excuses Benetton, it only adds context to those wishing to understand the full circumstances that day.

As Schumacher had not pitted to serve his five-second stop-go penalty, he was given the black flag on lap 21. The black flag is non-negotiable and requires the driver to stop on the next lap and vacate their car. Due to their alleged misunderstanding of how the

five-second penalty was to be administered, Benetton claimed to have been utterly shocked upon receiving the black flag. The team's management then entered into furious remonstrations with race officials while they reportedly instructed their driver to ignore the black flag.

Schumacher – seemingly under explicit orders from his team – therefore disregarded the black flag which had been shown to him on laps 22 and 23. On lap 24, the black flag was rescinded and Benetton was told it had been withdrawn provided they serve their original five-second stop-go penalty. Following the stewards' instructions, Schumacher did this on lap 27, which arguably cost him the race, thus gifting the win to home favourite Hill. It was a particularly special victory for the Hill family since Graham, Damon's illustrious father, had never won their home grand prix. British patriotism was at an all-time high when Princess Diana handed Damon the victor's trophy. Conversely, Schumacher's woes continued as Germany were knocked out of the football world cup by Bulgaria later that evening.

Despite the aforementioned comedy of errors, Coulthard came away with the most unbelievable tale to tell from the day. Midway through the race, he received interference in his radio from a local taxi company asking him to make a pick-up in Towcester, confusingly the taxi firm's driver was also called David. Although Schumacher ignored the black flag, a cardinal sin in F1, race stewards allowed him to keep his second position but fined Benetton US$25,000. The fine was "to formally reprimand the competitor Mild Seven Benetton Ford for a lack of a complete understanding of F1 rules and of the need for this to be corrected and for their meticulous application in the future."

75. *Autosport*, 11 August 1994

Benetton claimed it wasn't told of the 'stop-go' so carried on racing. **Photo: Martin Lee**

Coulthard stalled his engine causing a second formation lap, where Schumacher committed the same offence in an identical manner. **Photo: Martin Lee**

Having made a number of gaffes themselves, presumably race officials had not seen the irony in their wording. Benetton team manager Joan Villadelprat recalled: "We had the communication of that penalty late. The rules specified that you had a time when the communication had to come from the FIA – it was a piece of paper in those days – so I argued and said this is already out of the time. Then there was a lot of shit, in the end, we called him in, did everything that we were supposed to be doing, and we carried on and finished second."[76] This, however, wasn't an end to the matter.

In the days that followed, various press articles were devoted to how it was a scandal Schumacher should be allowed to keep his Silverstone points. Interestingly, none expressed any outrage whatsoever about Hakkinen or Barrichello not being punished for overtaking during the formation lap, despite it being reported in some publications. One rival team boss summed up the mood at the time: "The precedent is Mansell's ban. Forget the formation lap – Schumacher ignored the black flag. But of course, the rules won't be the same for everyone. Why? Because the German Grand Prix [the following race] has been sold out since March. Imagine telling 120,000 Germans that Lehto will be driving [instead]."[77] The Mansell precedent occurred during the 1989 Portuguese Grand Prix, after the Ferrari driver, ignored a black flag for three laps. He later

professed not to have seen it due to a low sun, and things were not helped after Mansell then collided with Senna, which severely dented the Brazilian's title chances that year. A furious Mansell was banned for the next race and his team was fined US$50,000, and the general mood after Silverstone 1994 was Schumacher should receive a similar penalty.

Following the shambles, the FIA summoned Schumacher and Benetton to the World Motor Sports Council in Paris on 26 July, to investigate the stop-go penalty affair. Prior to attending, Schumacher gave his thoughts to the press: "It is all a lot of hot air. I don't think it is right to interfere with the championship like this. All the theatre is rather stupid. Okay, I passed Damon and I wasn't supposed to. The thing is, I wasn't alone, I got a penalty and the misunderstanding was a mistake of the team. That was solved after a discussion with the stewards. I don't expect any more action than has already happened."[78] During the hearing, Benetton explained its confusion surrounding the note and how mistakes by race officials on the day added to this. They asked the FIA to consider extenuating circumstances like the black flag eventually being withdrawn, and how Benetton served their stop-go penalty immediately afterwards.

However, the FIA felt all of that was irrelevant and only wanted to know why the black flag was ignored. Schumacher used Mansell's defence from 1989, claiming not to have seen it due to a low sun, but the sport's governing body didn't accept this and soon announced their verdict. Those believing the FIA didn't have the guts to ban Schumacher from his home race were proved wrong, as

Mansell, the last driver to have been banned from a race prior to 1994, received a one-race ban for ignoring the black flag. **Photo: Stuart Seeger**

Schumacher: "The way Flavio Briatore dealt with it [the black flag] didn't really help either." Benetton reportedly instructed Schumacher to ignore the black flag while they argued it. **Photo: Alastair Ladd**

Benetton ignored a black flag while arguing the case. After three laps the black flag was rescinded because... **Photo: Martin Lee**

…officials allowed Schumacher to serve the original five-second stop-go instead. Afterwards, Benetton was fined US$25,000 for ignoring the black flag but was allowed to keep its second place. **Photo: Motorsport Images/LAT**

they did exactly that. Illustrating the powers-that-be were prepared to sacrifice any additional deutschmarks that Schumacher's presence at the German event might have achieved. In addition, the Benetton driver was excluded from the Hungarian Grand Prix and lost his second position from Silverstone. Furthermore, Benetton were fined an unprecedented US$500,000 for their failure to obey the stewards' orders at Silverstone. A twentyfold increase on the original Silverstone fine, and ten times the 1989 Mansell fine.

Many felt these penalties were extremely harsh and possible vengeance by Mosley for Briatore's and Walkinshaw's earlier attempts to oust the FIA president via the open letter at Barcelona. A few weeks later, Mosley was asked about the fine and retorted: "We intended the fine to be felt, and I think it *was* felt." When asked about the Mansell 1989 case and why a smaller penalty had applied there he responded: "In Mansell's case, having failed to stop for the black flag, he offered the excuse that the sun was directly behind the person holding the black flag, and that he would have seen only the sun. There was a video which supported his claim. On that basis, the World Council gave him a one -race suspension."[79]

"Now, Michael Schumacher said he didn't see the flag. We all saw what was seen on TV. If you watch the monitor from the car, you see not only the black flag that was shown on TV, but there was also the other black flag on the other side of the circuit. There were, in fact, *two* black flags. His offence was obviously graver than Mansell's. So… in reason and logic, you can say that Mansell got one, so Schumacher gets two. Maybe three would have been too harsh. But it had to be more than one: it just seemed rational. Now maybe it is all too harsh, but it seemed to me and, I think, unanimously to the other members of the World Council, that [the two-race ban[was right."

Schumacher probably saw the black flag because it has since been reported that Benetton instructed him to stay out while they

argued against it.[80] So the German's claim during the FIA hearing was likely a defence tactic to protect senior Benetton management which might explain why the German later declared "the way Flavio Briatore dealt with it didn't really help either". Perhaps senior Benetton management didn't want to be implicated, considering the open letter previously sent to Mosley, hence why they asked Schumacher to use this defence? Assuming that is correct, then this ploy didn't work and perhaps they should have just told the truth.

Years later, Schumacher fumed: "My impression at the time was that it was a set-up and I was the scapegoat. We had a big lead in the championship and a lot of people were happy about us getting this penalty. It turned into a real trend against us." Many would argue Schumacher had no right to feel scapegoated because he allegedly lied to officials afterwards. Nevertheless, past cases demonstrate other drivers in similar situations who also told fibs were still treated with greater leniency.

The most comparable situation to Schumacher's was Bruce Halford ignoring black flags for three laps, for no good reason at Nurburgring 1956. After finishing the race in fourth a colleague enquired "How are you?" Halford replied he was feeling a bit dodgy but essentially OK. "Well, for heaven's sake play it up a bit" was the colleague's reply. "You're in big trouble with the organisers so try and look as though you're really ill." Halford obliged and, after a modest fine and disqualification from his fourth position, that was that. Ah… but that was almost 40 years prior to 1994, and F1 was different then.

76. *Autosport,* 6 August 2014
77. *Autosport,* 14 July 1994
78. *Michael Schumacher: The Edge of Greatness* by James Allen (2007)
79. *Motor Sport,* 8 May 1994
80. *Autosport,* 7 August 2014

Chapter 7

Following Suzuka 1990, Senna claimed he had not purposely taken out his title rival, Prost, to clinch the championship, even though the video footage suggested otherwise. The following year, Senna admitted this was a lie, and ironically Mosley helped him word a confession. Perhaps because of Mosley's input, Senna received no penalties over that. In 2009, Hamilton and McLaren were disqualified from the Australian Grand Prix after stewards found they had provided deceptive information concerning Trulli passing him under the safety car. Other than losing his third position, no further action or fines were brought against McLaren or Hamilton.

In the 1986 Italian Grand Prix, Prost ignored a black flag for two laps following an illegal switch of cars, and for being silly enough to listen to the authorities who allowed him to start the race. Afterwards, he publicly bad-mouthed officials for allowing him to risk his life for half the race before disqualifying him. His penalty for that and ignoring the black flag eight years before Schumacher... a US$5000 fine and no race bans.

In Spain 1989 Senna was seen "running through eight black flags on the circuit, waved yellow flags at the scene of an accident and – most crucially – a red flag at the start-finish line. Senna counted himself exceedingly fortunate to only have received a US$20,000 fine and his times disallowed... The Brazilian rightfully accepted responsibility for the breach of the rules, but offered no justification..."[81] In this case along with the Prost 1986 example, handing them race bans would have immediately ended their championship chances and thus a thrilling climax for TV viewers.

Outside of F1 and days before the FIA hearing, England cricket Captain Michael Atherton was accused of ball tampering and subsequently lying during a test match with South Africa at Lord's. With irrefutable video evidence supporting the accusations, he was fined £2000, a fraction of the $500,000 punishment levied at Benetton after Silverstone. Indeed, adding the aforementioned cases together does not equal the Silverstone 1994 penalty. At the time, Mansell's 1989 punishment was seen as harsh because he collided with Senna after being disqualified. Also, there was no mitigating circumstances in 1989, unlike the confusion prior to the black flag at Silverstone. Should this have cancelled out Schumacher's alleged lie about not seeing the black flag, meaning these two penalties should have been comparable to one another?

The FIA headquarters, where it was decided Benetton's original fine from Silverstone should be increased twentyfold and Schumacher be banned/disqualified from three races. **Photo: Phanuruch8555**

During the Silverstone 1994 hearing, the FIA acknowledged errors made by race officials, although during a separate enquiry to Benetton's, the Clerk of the Course was given a suspension of one year on his super licence. The Race Director was banned from his post, though he did remain with the FIA. The Silverstone stewards were also required to "conduct a full investigation into the organisation of the 1994 British Grand Prix and implement the necessary measures to avoid the occurrence of such incidents in the future."

Interestingly, a similar shambles occurred four years later at the same track, albeit with a different outcome. Schumacher was given a time penalty, handed outside the 25-minute notice period stipulated by the rules and as in 1994, it wasn't clear whether the penalty was a stop-go. Nevertheless, Schumacher served it at the end of the final lap, thus winning the race in the pitlane while doing so. Afterwards, Schumacher was allowed to stand on the podium and his stop-go penalty was rescinded. Same driver but different championship situation, because in 1998 it was his title rival Hakkinen who was running away with things. Therefore not penalising Schumacher and Ferrari allowed the 1998 title fight to continue to the last race. A protest was lodged by McLaren who felt Ferrari cheated by not having Schumacher serve his penalty correctly, but this was rejected by the FIA. As a result, the three stewards involved handed in their licenses at an extraordinary meeting of the FIA World Council.[82]

Hill was also at the post-Silverstone 1994 hearing to answer a charge of stopping to pick up a Union Jack during his victory lap,

Schumacher's troubles gifted Hill victory at Silverstone. Given the German's looming race bans, the Englishman also had a golden opportunity to close the points defect. **Photo: Alastair Ladd**

Hill had to answer a charge of stopping to pick up a Union Jack following his Silverstone win. **Photo: Alastair Ladd**

Prost received a lesser penalty than Schumacher when he ignored a black flag during the 1986 Italian Grand Prix... **Photo: Martin Lee**

...As did Senna during the 1989 Spanish Grand Prix.
Photo: Instituto Ayrton Senna

Hakkinen (pictured) and Barrichello escaped significant punishment for overtaking during the formation lap, the same initial offence Schumacher committed.
Photo: Alastair Ladd

something he was later acquitted of. The Englishman later recalled "Although Michael's was clearly the gravest offence, by hauling up three teams Mosley could claim to be scrupulously fair by not appearing to be picking on Benetton, but the whole proceeding was a farce, as far as I can see... Bernie Ecclestone was there, which was expected as Commercial Rights Holder, the presence of Jean Todt, Ferrari's sporting director and a direct rival, was a sign of Ferrari's influence in the sport's administration, something we would become familiar with over the years. At the time, they had the right to sit in on court proceedings but didn't get a vote."[83]

Hakkinen and Barrichello were the others "hauled up" and both were found guilty of breaching Article 118: maintaining starting order on the formation lap. Along with Article 66: leaving the circuit without the consent of the stewards following their late-race collision, a rule Hill later admitted to not knowing about before this hearing. Neither Barrichello nor Hakkinen were given any penalties as the FIA citied "extenuating circumstances" in their press release, but didn't elaborate what they were. Instead the FIA press release effectively said they were keeping an eye on both for the next three races.

Roberto Causo was an FIA appointed observer and attended the 26 July hearing as an expert. *Autosport* magazine suggested thanks in part to Causo's report[84], Benetton's and Schumacher's penalty was increased significantly.[85] Interestingly, Causo was also Williams' lawyer in the Senna accident trial at the time. Bernie Ecclestone's biography recalled the aftermath of the hearing: "In his motorhome, Ecclestone was delighted about a tragedy with a happy ending. Schumacher's disqualification after Silverstone, he heard from Mosley, 'is a bonanza. Everyone's talking about it in the pub.' Germany versus Britain was guaranteed to score record television audiences."[86]

It was a clever political move from the FIA to ban Schumacher from the German event but allow him to race if he appealed. Thus should Schumacher miss his home race, the FIA could justifiably claim the decision was his because he had not appealed their ruling. Benetton, meanwhile, had incentives not to appeal – recent cases showed an unsuccessful appeal invited even stronger sanctions. For instance, Irvine's one-race ban following the

Brazilian Grand Prix was tripled on appeal. Moreover, the German track had many long straights, meaning top end horsepower was crucial to success. Benetton's Ford V8 engine was lacking in this, so they were not expected to beat the V12 Ferraris and the V10 Williams-Renaults. Thus should Benetton miss one race in 1994 they would have chosen Germany.

However, there were other factors at play. Upon hearing the FIA hearing verdict, some of the 120,000-plus fans attending the German Grand Prix took the prospect of Schumacher not racing very badly indeed. By now the 24-year-old had become a national sporting icon and was on the verge of becoming Germany's first ever world champion, indeed this event had been sold out since March because of him. Extreme fans threatened 'no Schumacher, no race' and erected a series of large wood piles within the dense forests surrounding the circuit. They threatened to burn the woodland thus forcing the event to be cancelled if Schumacher couldn't race. In the interests of public safety, the mayor of Hockenheim called out to the FIA to let Schumacher race.

According to Ross Brawn, the powers-that-be within F1 tried persuading Benetton to appeal Schumacher's race bans because that would avert this looming crisis. Brawn suggested any appeal submitted before the German Grand Prix would have been looked favourably upon,[87] but would the under-fire team play ball given their recent clashes with the FIA? Likewise, the on-going investigation into their black box gave the championship leaders more headaches, which only got worse. Because the FIA soon published its controversial findings to the world's press, the implication being the team might have somehow circumvented the driver aids ban all along. Predictably, this sent a media furore Benetton's way. The relationship between the Enstone team and the FIA was worsening by the day, and a near-fatal incident in Germany only added to this.

81. *Autocourse 1989/1990* by Alan Henry
82. *Grand Prix*, 3 August 1998
83. *Watching the Wheels: My Autobiography* by Damon Hill (2016)
84. *Autosport*, 6 August 2014
85. *Autosport*, 7 August 2014
86. *No Angel: The Secret Life of Bernie Ecclestone* by Tom Bower (2011)
87. *Motor Sport*, December 2004

GERMANY

July 1994

"In the circumstances, I am not satisfied that car number five [Michael Schumacher] complied with the regulations at all times during the San Marino Grand Prix."

Charlie Whiting, FIA Technical Delegate

"Data from the black boxes at Imola showed Michael making a normal start... It shows a large amount of wheelspin and Michael backing off the throttle then reapplying it when wheelspin stopped."

Ross Brawn, Benetton's Technical Director

The FIA discovered concealed launch control in Schumacher's car. Legal in 1993, but outlawed for 1994, Benetton claimed it was redundant. *Photo: Landmensch*

Standings before the 1994 German Grand Prix

DRIVERS' CHAMPIONSHIP		
Pos	Driver	Points
1	Michael Schumacher	66
2	Damon Hill	39
3	Jean Alesi	19

CONSTRUCTORS' CHAMPIONSHIP		
Pos	Constructor	Points
1	Benetton-Ford	67
2	Williams-Renault	43
3	Ferrari	42

Schumacher was a national icon in Germany. Upon hearing about his ban, extreme fans threaten 'no Schumacher, no race'. **Photo: Landmensch**

Fears of a riot among the 120,000-plus crowd attending were averted after Schumacher appealed his race bans. No doubt that pleased local police and fire crews. **Photo: Alastair Ladd**

As the grand prix circus rolled into Hockenheim, few could have foreseen the drama about to unfold. The race itself saw half the field wiped out on the first lap, a terrifying pitlane fire, and Ferrari finally winning their its grand prix in four years. However, the off-track politics proved just as eventful. The news Germany had been waiting for was announced shortly after teams arrived: Benetton would appeal Schumacher's two-race ban following Silverstone, and because the case couldn't be heard for weeks he could, therefore, race at his home event. Even so, additional security had to be laid on after his main rival, Hill, received a death threat. The recent stabbing of ladies tennis world number one Monica Seles during a match in Germany by a Steffi Graf fan played on everyone's mind. As things turned out, it was Benetton who came under fire in more ways than one.

You may recall IT experts, LDRA, carried out tests on Schumacher's Imola black box during 6 July to ensure Benetton had not used illegal driver aids, a crime many believed they were guilty of. On the Monday after Silverstone (11 July), LDRA

The FIA investigated Schumacher's car and made its findings public. As a result Benetton found itself under more scrutiny. **Photo: Ford**

reported a number of unanswered questions to the FIA. They also recommended a closer examination of the source code – the means to access the data contained in the ECU. The FIA later detailed what happened next: "In a letter to Benetton dated 13 July, we made it clear the demonstration had been unsatisfactory and we required the source code for the software. Following another exchange of letters on the 13 and 14 July a meeting was set up at the Benetton factory on 19 July, an agenda for which was received on 18 July which gave our advisors full access to all the source code, but only on Benetton's premises and subject to the instructions set out."[88]

Following this 19th July meeting Charlie Whiting, the FIA Technical Delegate, reported his findings to his bosses during the 26 July FIA hearing. Whiting's submission, which shall be reviewed shortly, outlined exactly what was found within Benetton's black box by LDRA. The FIA was therefore in possession of all the known facts when making its final decision on this matter. Below is part of its subsequent press release:

"The FIA World Motor Sport Council also considered the report of the FIA F1 Technical Delegate in respect of the electronic systems used on car number five [Michael Schumacher] at the 1994 San Marino Grand Prix. After hearing the representatives of Benetton Formula Ltd, the World Motor Sport Council reached the conclusion that, in common with the other two teams, Benetton's computer system contained a facility capable of breaching the regulations. In the absence of any evidence that the device was used and certain evidence that it wasn't, the World Council imposed no penalty involving the results of the event. The World Council imposed a fine of US$100,000 on Benetton Formula Ltd for failing to make their computer source codes available immediately. An identical fine was imposed on McLaren for the same reason subject to McLaren's right to demand a hearing in October."[89]

88. FIA, 8 May 1994
89. FIA, 8 May 1994

Chapter 8

Significantly, the FIA admitted software "capable of breaching the regulations" was found in all three teams whose black boxes were seized during Imola (Benetton, McLaren and Ferrari). We'll examine the Benetton case shortly. Meanwhile, it is believed the questionable software found in all three instances was disarmed driver aids. *Autosport* magazine reported most teams did this with their (now outlawed) 1993 electronic devices, rather than rewriting complex software which potentially created unforeseen errors. "It's a bit like trying to take a card out of a playing card pyramid," said McLaren team boss Ron Dennis. "As you take it out, if you are not careful, the whole lot is going to fall down..."[90]

In the book *The Death of Ayrton Senna* there is a quote from an unnamed computer specialist suggesting it took them two days to purge their team's software of 1993 driver aids which were deemed illegal for 1994. Likewise, during a 2006 interview, Williams' Patrick Head insisted: "We were able to remove anything [on the ECU] that we were not using [for 1994]."[91] But, according to another renowned F1 Technical Director, Frank Dernie: "When I was seconded from Benetton to Ligier [in July 1994] the guy responsible showed me the letter from Williams [to Ligier] explaining the update to the code they had been using which included a switched off section for the banned functions." Williams and Ligier shared Renault engines and Magneti Marelli electronics for 1994. Moreover, the former had assisted the latter in order to prevent Renault transferring its Ligier engines supply to Williams' direct rivals, Benetton, hence the letter Dernie referred to.

At this point in the season, having redundant 1993 software present within ECUs was no crime in itself, hence why no team lost points over this, although Benetton and McLaren were fined for providing their source codes late. The 1994 technical regulations merely stated "Traction control is forbidden" (article 9.5) or "Anti-lock brakes are forbidden" (article 11.3). So rightly or wrongly, it was impossible to condemn teams for only disarming these 1993 functions – the rulebook was simply too vague. Remember the in-fighting before the 1994 regulations came about? Did this contribute to the vagueness problem?

"Our software engineers never said to me that we had to leave our traction control code in place otherwise the software wouldn't work properly," insisted Patrick Head. **Photo: Stephen Lathamq**

"We've got active ride, traction control, power braking, and a whole range of other features [disabled within the McLaren]," claimed Ron Dennis.
Photo: Martin Lee

The policing of electronic driver aids was unprecedented and Imola had been its first ever spot check, therefore the FIA and teams had not foreseen these complexities. It is worth remembering this before apportioning blame. Given the FIA had published the findings into Benetton's investigation, this learning was now being conducted in public – with all the quirks and foibles that entailed. It is also worth noting that McLaren and Ferrari were F1's biggest teams, so had more staff and resources than Benetton (or anyone else) to rewrite their 1994 software, yet they were found with supposedly redundant 1993 software.

To police driver aids more effectively, the FIA issued a notice to all teams on 27 July ordering:

- Before the German Grand Prix, teams must "state whether or not the computer systems fitted to its cars contain any feature which might infringe the current technical or sporting regulations" (ie disarmed launch control etc).
- If teams do have such features disabled, they must provide full details and prove the offending programs cannot be enabled.
- Beginning with the Italian Grand Prix, if "we find such a system in one of your cars, we shall assume it is there to be used and the FIA will act accordingly."
- Teams will also be required to show that no such features are loaded into volatile memory that can be erased before any components are examined.
- Source codes must be made available and they themselves might be examined.
- From the Hungarian Grand Prix onwards, computer systems on cars must have an upload capability from which the FIA can inspect the software at any time.[92]

These new measures eliminated future cheating, but questions were soon asked whether Benetton played fair in earlier races. "To avoid speculation" the FIA published its Benetton black box investigation findings to the press on 29 July. It acknowledged the presence of a disarmed and concealed launch control facility, and highlighted a mechanism to arm the system which had not been disclosed by Benetton. However, it wasn't clear if that latter point was a genuine mistake, or an attempt to cheat.

The FIA report concluded "according to LDRA the best evidence is that Benetton wasn't using 'launch control' [an automatic start system] at the 1994 San Marino Grand Prix". Max Mosley later admitted because the FIA couldn't prove Benetton used launch

Ligier and Williams shared engine/electronic suppliers in 1994 and Frank Dernie saw a letter between them explaining how to disarm the banned 1994 functions. **Photo: Martin Lee**

control, they did the next best thing – publish their findings so the press would investigate further. Let us explore the key points of the FIA report along with Benetton's defence given by Ross Brawn during a press conference at Hockenheim. Perhaps you can draw your own conclusions?

FIA Report: "Analysis of this software, which had been used at the San Marino Grand Prix, revealed that it included a facility called 'launch control'. This is a system which, when armed, allows the driver to initiate a start with a single action. The system will control the clutch, gear shift and engine speed fully automatically to a predetermined pattern."

Brawn: "Benetton made the FIA aware of certain redundant facilities in the software. These were used in 1993. Some development had been carried out during the winter of 1993, which was due to the different characteristics of the new Ford Zetec engine. This work was only ever conducted on an engine dynamometer, and it never reached a stage whereby it could be used on a car. It didn't work. The system was based on ignition cut, an extremely audible effect. The project was abandoned when it became clear it wouldn't be legal in 1994. It was never deleted due to the amount of work necessary to reconstruct the software."

FIA Report: "Benetton stated the system can only be switched on by recompilation of the source code. Detailed analysis by LDRA revealed this statement was untrue. 'Launch control' could be switched on using a laptop computer connected to the gearbox unit. When confronted with this information Benetton conceded it was possible to switch on the 'launch control' using a laptop PC, but indicated the availability of this feature came as a surprise to them. In order to enable 'launch control', a particular menu with ten options, has to be selected on the PC screen. 'Launch control' is not visibly listed as an option. The menu was so arranged that, after ten items, nothing further appeared. If however, the operator scrolled down the menu beyond the tenth listed option, to option 13, launch control can be enabled, even though this is not visible on the screen. No satisfactory explanation was offered for this apparent attempt to conceal the feature.

Brawn: "There was a genuine belief by the engineer who had written the software that he had deleted references to it in that menu. So when he was asked the question: 'Can you access launch control via the menu?' He said: 'No, I've removed that from the menu.' Once we understood this feature wasn't going to be legal,

Revealed at last: the secret of the black magic box.

This year Michael Schumacher has a distinct advantage.

We've presented him with a new brain; our incredibly powerful EEC-V engine management computer.

Imagine. This magic black box can receive and interpret over 1.7 million electronic signals and relay its commands back to the engine every second.

Its purpose is to co-ordinate all the engine's vital functions. Thus maximising its performance and making it instantly responsive to the driver's commands.

It's enough to boggle the average person's mind. But then the people who designed it, Ford's electronic engineers, don't have average minds.

They are now transplanting their brain to our latest road cars, where it performs exactly the same functions. Maximising performance and responsiveness, and minimising fuel consumption and exhaust emissions.

And, having proved itself with more than 700 bhp in our Zetec racing engine on the track, we're sure it will manage our standard Zetec engines on the road.

So now that you know what it does, the only question is, how does it do it? Sorry. Even if we knew we couldn't tell you. That's Ford's secret.

 **Ford** ELECTRONICS
TECHNOLOGY WITH A PURPOSE®

The advert Ford was forced to withdraw following the launch control discovery. **Image: Ford**

it was removed from the menu so that other engineers wouldn't initiate it accidentally. It was never removed with the intent of trying to deceive anybody because all the software showed it was present. We had already let LDRA know that feature was present in the software, so why would we try to conceal it?

FIA Report: "Two conditions had to be satisfied before the computer would apply 'launch control': First, the software had to be enabled either by recompiling the code, which would take some minutes or by connecting the laptop PC as outlined above, which could be done in a matter of seconds. Secondly, the driver had to work through a particular sequence of up-down gearshift paddle positions, a specific gear position had to be selected and the clutch and throttle pedals had also to be in certain positions. Only if all these actions were carried out would the 'launch control' become available. Having thus initiated 'launch control', the driver would be able to make a fully automatic start. Such a start is clearly a driver aid as it operates the clutch, changes gear and uses traction control by modulating engine power (by changing ignition or fuel settings), in response to wheel speed.

90. *F1 News*, 10 August 1994
91. *Motor Sport*, January 2006
92. FIA, 27 July 1994

When asked why, if this system was only used in testing, such an elaborate procedure was necessary in order to switch it on, we were told it was to prevent it being switched on accidentally. In the circumstances, I am not satisfied that car number five (Schumacher) complied with the regulations at all times during the San Marino Grand Prix."

Brawn: "The facility is exactly as it was in 1993 when we had no need to conceal it. 'Launch control' was always initiated in that fashion."

Below are additional questions Brawn was asked during that press conference:

Q: *"Article 2.6 of the F1 technical regulations puts the onus on the competitor to prove his car is legal at all times. How can you prove you didn't use launch control?"*
Brawn: "The data from the black boxes at Imola showed Michael making a normal start. It shows a perfect correlation between engine revs and throttle. It shows a large amount of wheelspin and Michael backing off the throttle, then reapplying it when wheelspin stopped. All that data was taken and sealed by the LDRA and that is how we can substantiate what went on."

Q: *"Was Michael made aware that this system was still on the car and of the penalties that could fall on him?"*
Brawn: "He was aware it existed last year. We tried it for the first time at Spa with disastrous consequences and then we used it sporadically. He wouldn't necessarily have been aware of the deleted system this year, because it was irrelevant."

Q: *"Does the FIA's policing prevent all kinds of cheating?"*
Brawn: "I don't think anything is impossible – but I think the risk involved with being caught and eliminated from the championship is tremendous. If we were foolish enough to use such a system willingly and be caught, we would be putting 200 people and their family's futures at risk."

Q: *"Do you feel vindicated?"*
Brawn: "It's very difficult, these are complex issues. Our success has been gained by hard work and the talents of Michael Schumacher. Unfortunately, it is a cross we have to bear that some people look for easy reasons why we are successful."

Q: *"Why was Ferrari not called up before the beak, but you were?"*
Brawn: "Ferrari had the advantage that the company supplying the software code was owned by Fiat, so it was much easier for them to make the information available. We are partners of Cosworth and Ford and it was necessary for us all to consider how we were going to deal with this issue. I stress, we have been cleared of any offence other than being late in supplying the source codes."

Brawn has since implied Benetton could have deleted everything that aroused suspicion after the FIA had prematurely handed back their ECU. Benetton's Technical Director indicated this showed they didn't know what was hidden within their software.[93] Furthermore Brawn eluded to the FIA wanting to dock Benetton's Imola points following the black box investigation. However he and Rory Byrne would have left Benetton immediately had this happened, after feeling they had not done anything wrong.[94] It forced Benetton to fight this proposal.

Some believed recent events were the FIA's payback for the 'war' started by Benetton directors, Briatore and Walkinshaw

Like Benetton, McLaren claimed the delay in supplying ECU source codes was due to confidentially clauses with its engine supplier. *Photo: Martin Lee*

"I know Michael. He would not have used a system that was illegal with all the consequences it would have brought. I am categoric on that point," claimed Brawn.
Photo: Alastair Ladd

Tamper proof FIA seals, similar to that shown above, were used on team's black boxes along with technology which detected any non-approved software.
Photo: Antony John Dennis

Verstappen: "People think I'm looking for an excuse when I say this, but I just know that his [Schumacher's] car was different compared to my car."
Photo: Alastair Ladd

against Mosley in Barcelona. The FIA categorically dismissed this proposition, declaring it wouldn't look to damage its own championship to satisfy a personal vendetta. Whether intentional or not, the FIA's powers were reaffirmed amongst teams as a result of this affair. Given whenever someone was accused of cheating it inevitably caused them PR damage, irrespective of whether that team was innocent. For example, in the wake of the above saga, Ford were forced to pull an unfortunately phrased advert.

It is worth re-iterating this action should in no way implicate Ford, as its electronics were contained within a completely separate black box to the confiscated one. But the general public wouldn't have been aware of that intricacy, hence why Ford pulled its advert. The media attention over this affair was an unwelcome distraction for Benetton since it needed to implement the latest FIA-mandated safety changes (detailed shortly) to its B194.

Antony John Dennis worked for Vodac, a company contracted to Ford Electronics/Visteon from 1987 to 2000 as Race/Test Field Technician to Benetton in 1994. While he wasn't present at the LDRA/Benetton electronics audit, his task was to supply the means for them to interrogate the ECUs. So he would enable the communication between their different computers, and provide things like car looms, wiring boxes and generally assist as necessary. He states: "LDRA investigated all teams' software suppliers using checksum technology, approved software was locked into "black boxes with tamper-proof FIA seals. Checksum technology will detect a single bit variation from a known version of code, making it impossible to use non-approved software for racing." It seems, LDRA positively identified and validated both Benetton's black box data and the source codes against previous records, hence the reason they were satisfied afterwards nothing untoward was used.

Antony John Dennis also reinforced the claim that source codes used in F1 were also used within Ford's road cars at the time. "Quite possibly the non-disclosure clauses from Ford to Benetton [concerning source codes] was to ensure Ford's latest electronic developments, which would have been tested in F1, didn't fall into the hands of rival car companies." He has also suggested that, if 1993 software was present in 1994, disarming it would have been considerably cheaper and safer than removing it completely.

It's worth reiterating this whole affair was over launch control, which only provided assistance at the start of a race. So even if Benetton was guilty (not proven to date) the advantage is likely to be a one second gain over an almost two-hour race. Although it would have provided protection from overtakes during the most vulnerable time of a race, the start, in an era where passing was difficult. Furthermore, no irregularities were highlighted over any other Benetton function during the LDRA investigation. The traction control Benetton used in 1993 required wheel sensors to detect wheelspin and this hardware wasn't found by the FIA in 1994. Despite this, Schumacher's then teammate latter claimed Benetton wasn't being straight with him in 1994.

"You see, Michael also depends on machinery," Verstappen told Dutch magazine *NUsport* in 2011. "For most people, he was god, but he's not Superman, he never was When I went karting with him he never beat me. I know what happened when we were together at Benetton in 1994, there is a reason... I kept thinking that this cannot be done! I would brake on the limit and go as hard as I could into every corner. So what could I do when Schumacher was able to do that and not me? It just wasn't right. There were electronic aids. They will never admit it, but I am convinced of it. I later asked Flavio Briatore, who had brought me to Benetton and was then the team's manager. He said 'Let's not talk about it.' So I know enough now. I drove Michael's car a few times, at Hockenheim for example, but I spun off. There's no way that he could have been so fast with that set-up. But the system that Michael used wasn't in the car at that moment."[95]

93. *Auto Motor und Sport*, 21 December 2014
94. *Motor Sport*, April 2007
95. Crash.net, 9 December 2011

Chapter 8

When these comments were first published in 2011, it sparked various debates among F1 fans because some considered this conclusive proof Schumacher and Benetton cheated in 1994, so let's explore this belief. Christian Silk, Verstappen's race engineer during 1994, believes there was one occasion where the Dutchman drove Schumacher's car during a race weekend, which was the Friday qualifying session at Hockenheim. Silk claims: "Jos crashed his own car in the morning session because he spun on some oil which I had not told him about." The 21-year-old was then loaned Schumacher's car following the German's initial qualifying run. However, Verstappen failed to complete a single lap as he spun at the second chicane, thereby leaving the team with no usable cars for the remainder of Friday qualifying. Commentators joked he was the bravest man in Germany for returning to the Benetton pits to face the music.

In *Autosport* interviews during 1994 and 2014, Verstappen admitted crashing Schumacher's car at Hockenheim was his fault, even citing it as the most embarrassing moment of his career in the latter. During another interview in 1996, Verstappen admitted: "The [B194] car was too nervous for me. I cannot handle that style of car... At Benetton, I got on fine with the engineer but he couldn't do what I wanted because the other guy was winning races with the car as it was. At Arrows, I feel I have the whole team behind me. They do exactly what I want in terms of setting up the car. I didn't have that at Benetton. I was the second driver. They said: 'Here is the car. You drive it.' When I asked for something new, it took a long time to get it. The B194 was a good car for Schumacher – but it wasn't a good car for me..."

"I must have had the same driving style as Johnny [Herbert] because he said basically the same things about that car that I did and seems to have had the same feelings. It was a very difficult car. You couldn't feel the limit and so you were pushing and pushing and then suddenly it would have oversteer. Normally when you get oversteer you can control it but the Benetton would go very suddenly and so you ended up having a spin. I had big problems with that car."[96] These statements seemingly contradict Verstappen's 2011 comments. Nevertheless, because so many people believe his 2011 comments let us assume Verstappen was telling it how it was.

The Hockenheim circuit consisted mainly of straights, so it was the first time during 1994 teams ran minimal downforce, meaning the cars were difficult to drive through corners. Thus, Friday at Hockenheim was the first time during his short career Verstappen drove an F1 car in this configuration. Likewise, this was the first race the teams ran the FIA's latest safety modifications – a wooden plank bolted to the car's floor. The plank as it soon became known, forced teams to raise their ride heights. This along with other rear wing and diffuser changes reduced the car's grip and speed further.

Whether by design or coincidence, the plank played into Williams' hands because it forced all teams to run their cars higher. You may recall at Imola, Senna had a set-up dilemma where raising the ride height of his FW16's cured the aerodynamic instability but

Hockenheim was the debut of the 'plank' and teams ran minimal downforce. Could this explain Verstappen's 2011 comments? *Photo: Alastair Ladd*

Christian Silk (in the blue socks) was Verstappen's race engineer at Benetton and confirms Jos never raised any beliefs to him about illegal electronics aids on Schumacher's car during 1994.
Photo: Martin Lee

Verstappen assumed his Benetton teammate was given some kind of illegal advantage during 1994 because he beat Schumacher in karting.
Photo: Alastair Ladd

made it slower. Because the plank forced the same reduction in speed amongst other cars, it allowed Williams to run the optimal ride height which allowed its complicated aerodynamics to work. Conversely, Benetton was adversely affected by these changes because "the better optimised the cars were to the old rules, the more devastating the change," insisted Willem Toet.

At the time, Schumacher admitted: "The situation is probably a bit different for me, probably because my car worked quite well without the step. At Hockenheim the circuit was very bumpy, there was no downforce at all on the car, plus we were using a lot more ride height. So we had to run it very stiff to get the performance, and for me, it was like having my stomach turned over when I went over the bumps. I don't feel very comfortable with it."[97] While Lehto cited these car modifications as part of the reason he under performed in 1994. "The rules changed twice last year [in 1994] and I was turning up at races like a zombie and having to get in the car for practice just to learn about it. It was very difficult."[98]

Did Verstappen, a man with limited car racing experience before F1, adjust his driving sufficiently to allow for this reduced grip? Perhaps he found Schumacher's car difficult to drive because of the aforementioned car modifications and the suspension being too stiff for him? The video footage of him approaching and then spinning at the second chicane in Schumacher's car can be found on the internet. In it one can clearly see, as Verstappen approaches the second chicane, how little rear wing the Benetton is running, meaning his grip would have been minimal.

Prior to clipping the second apex, one can see the Benetton jumping over bumps, and the left front wheel actually hanging in the air as a result. This is evidence of how stiffly sprung the car is. Once the car has landed, Verstappen immediately unsettles it again by running over the high kerbs at the second apex whilst

simultaneously applying the power. This then pitches the car sideways and the start of his incident, yet amazingly it takes the Dutchman 0.5sec to apply the brakes. We know this because Verstappen's lap time counter reads 48.3sec when the car starts to spin. His application of the brakes can clearly be seen by the smoke emanating from his tyres and the tyre labels no longer spinning around, by which point his lap time counter reads 48.8sec. In F1 terms, 0.5sec is a long time to apply the brakes after a driver has lost control of his car.

The video footage supports driver error being the cause of Verstappen's Hockenheim spin rather than switched off driver aids. The launch control identified within the FIA report wouldn't have prevented this spin, because (if armed) it only worked off the startline. Thus, Verstappen's 2011 comments do not tally with the black box investigation findings. It is surprising the Dutchman never raised this issue before 2011 especially to his race engineer, Christian Silk, who drivers would usually confide such things to. Not least because Verstappen and Silk would have left no corner unturned in identifying why Schumacher, in the sister Benetton, was so much quicker.

Verstappen's 2011 comments are considered among the strongest evidence that Benetton used illegal driver aids that year. Although he made the grid the following day, Verstappen qualified in a lowly 19th position, whereas Schumacher qualified in fourth. Examples such as this are often cited as further proof that Schumacher was using illegal driver aids which had not been given to teammates.

96. Grand Prix
97. *F1 News*, 10 August 1994
98. *Autosport*, 30 March 1995

Chapter 8

However, Verstappen confessed afterwards: "On the Saturday [at Hockenheim] I took it easy because I really didn't want to go off again. I really didn't feel confident. That's why I ended up 19th on the grid."[99] Steve Matchett, Verstappen's mechanic in 1994, suggested he was caught off guard with the reduced downforce at Hockenheim, so was told to keep it steady and ensure he qualified for the race following his various incidents. Ex-F1 driver turned Eurosport commentator, John Watson, put it more bluntly stating Verstappen was "pussyfooting" around during Saturday's qualifying. Worth noting, an F1 team would prefer not to have two cars in different specifications as it doubles their workload. Moreover, Benetton was fighting for the Constructors' Championship so why would they purposely hamper one car, and therefore their chances? The Enstone team demonstrated how desperate they were for championship points by constantly rotating their second driver throughout 1994.

In the book *The Death of Ayrton Senna*, Richard Williams recalled a pre-season test during mid-March 1994 where he asked Benetton about the function of three coloured buttons on the car's steering wheel. Williams remembered: "they clammed up in unison. It was curious, but it didn't seem important at the time." The implication being these buttons may have activated an illegal driver aid. Assuming he was onto something, what illegal driver aid might it have activated? Not launch control, because the FIA report said the only way to activate that was the driver undertaking a sequence of commands using the throttle, clutch and gearshift levers.

It also cannot have been traction control or ABS, because they were never highlighted during the black box investigation. Also it defeats the purpose, having to press a button each time you want to use these devices, so what other illegal driver aids could those buttons have activated? Williams' aforementioned observation originates from an interview with the German[100] during which he states Schumacher "gives the powerful impression of straightforwardness."

Furthermore, the Williams article was generally benevolent and positive towards Schumacher and Benetton. For instance, Williams never discusses any suspicion over the car's legality, or indeed it making strange noises despite him being present while it was running during private testing. This seems surprising given some of the accusations Williams later makes in his book *The Death of Ayrton Senna*.

Di Spires worked with Benetton during 1994. She later recalled an interesting observation the night before the Hockenheim race: "I went into the garage to check that all the team had been for dinner. I was surprised to find that one person was still there and he was messing about with the fuel rig: in my naïveté I said, 'Well, what are you doing there then? It's a bit late to be messing about with that thing.' From the look I got I decided to go back to the motorhome."[101] Simon Morley was in charge of servicing and cleaning Benetton's refuelling equipment.

"The nitrogen supply to the rigs [to supply the pressure to transfer the fuel] was up to the team's discretion," Morley said. "Benetton used 'balanced nitrogen regulators'. These are designed to maintain

The Verstappen pitstop. Benetton's refueller, Simon Morley, is having difficulties inserting the nozzle. Consequently a small amount of fuel sprays out…
Photo: Motorsport Images/LAT

...It ignites and causes this frightening incident. Mercifully nobody is seriously injured. The sport was extremely lucky that day.
Photo: Motorsport Images/LAT

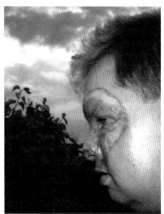

Simon Morley's injuries. He believes the pitlane fire marshals were slow to react and Greg Field (Benetton's team coordinator) saved him.
Photo: Simon Morley

a constant pressure throughout the flow cycle. We would spend hours on Saturday evenings adjusting these regulators to get the maximum pressure without them 'blowing off' at any point during the refuelling run. If the valve did blow off during the run, then we could lose a second or two during the pit stop.

"I do not know how the other team's nitrogen supply was set up, but I do believe that the valves we used and the hours of set-up allowed us to have consistently faster refuelling times than most of the other teams... I believe that most of the pre-Hockenheim pitstops went without any major issues. Occasionally, the nitrogen regulator on a rig would blow off before all the fuel was delivered which we would then turn it down a tiny amount before the next pit stop. We were always trying to get the maximum out of these regulators."

Schumacher made a poor start at Hockenheim, which to some cast more doubt over the launch control rumours, whereas to others this supported them. The (unproven) logic behind the former being after the LDRA/FIA investigation, something was allegedly taken off and Schumacher's bad starts here and at the previous race, Silverstone, was the result. Whatever the case, behind him all hell broke loose as approximately half the field was involved in first lap accidents. Benetton's cup of misery that weekend was full but on lap 15 it overflowed. When Verstappen pitted his team struggled to engage the refuelling equipment correctly and, as they tried a second time, fuel spilt out and ignited on the car's hot brakes.

The driver, some mechanics and the entire car became engulfed in a horrific ball of flames which billowed up towards onlookers above the garages. Thankfully the team was quick to react, extinguishing the blaze within seconds, thus restricting the injuries to Verstappen and six Benetton mechanics, most of whom had comparatively minor burns, although some needed to stay overnight in hospital after inhaling white extinguisher power. Considering what a potential catastrophe this could have been, the sport was very lucky that fateful day.

Morley came off worst, suffering serious burns to his face despite wearing a full face helmet. "I wouldn't say we were relaxed about the thought of having an accident and fire," Benetton's refueller recollected, "but in hindsight our protective gear was obviously inadequate. Only the driver and fueller wore full-face helmets along with their fire suits etc, the rest of the pitstop crew wore only nomex balaclavas and ski goggles. The ski goggles were fine to protect eyes for foreign debris but no match for a fire. I wore three-layer fire suit, Nomex underwear, Nomex shoes, Nomex gloves, open-face Nomex balaclava – I couldn't breathe well in a full face balaclava – and a full-face helmet.

"The full face helmet was fine except that quite often it would fog up inside the visor making visibility difficult. I would often have to leave the visor 'cracked open' until the last possible moment, then close it as the car was coming down pitlane to the box. This meant I had to take one hand off the nozzle to quickly close the visor then get my hand back into the correct position on the nozzle. One fault with my full face helmet was the visor didn't have a tight seal around its opening, there was always a small gap present which would prove to be an issue later.

"From a fuel rig standpoint, everything had been perfectly normal up until that pitstop. Jos Verstappen came into the box for his scheduled pit stop stopped on his marks as normal, I went to connect the nozzle to the car as done previously during the weekend at other events with no issue but this time I couldn't get the nozzle engaged. As I attempted to rotate and twist the nozzle it got slightly engaged on the outer lip of the car receptacle, with my rotating and twisting and this engagement it was just enough to distort the nozzle so as to break the seal on the fuel side, as the fuel is pressured a small amount of fuel was dispensed (I believe about 1.5 litres but someone else may know better).

"This fuel and subsequent vapour sprayed over the car, hit the engine cover and sprayed back over myself and others either side of me. It was mainly the vapours that ignited on the hot brake rotors, first the right rear and then the right front. These two fire balls then grew and met in the middle of the car where the majority of the sprayed fuel was. The large fireball then ensued. Some of the fuel that had splashed of the engine cover back onto myself had, unbeknown to me, got inside my helmet due to the small gap.

99. *Autosport*, 25 August 1994
100. *The Independent*, 20 March 1994
101. *I Just Made the Tea: Tales of 30 years inside Formula 1* by Bernard Ferguson and Di Spires (2012)

"This fuel then ignited inside my helmet. What do you do? Run right? I had nowhere to go, believe me I thought about running but to where? Two fuel rigs right behind me, nitrogen bottles either side of me for the wheel guns, colleagues either side of me also trying to figure out an escape and a burning race car in front of me. So I closed my eyes as tight as possible and waited hopefully for someone to put me out. Luckily for me and colleagues, we had Greg Field our Race Team Coordinator manning a very large (I think 25kg) Halon Extinguisher. He pulled the trigger and put the whole thing out in seconds. The fire was extinguished long before any of the assigned pitlane fire marshals had even started to move!

"I am very happy Greg was there in that position – he was and still is my hero. Some of the guys ran into the garage on fire, I think the hose holder had his hands on fire. One of the guys put them out only for them to reignite seconds later. Verstappen was extremely lucky. I believe that was the first race that he actually wore all of his fireproof underwear! He told me later that he couldn't figure out who was spraying water over him until he realised it was fuel. By then it was too late and he was engulfed. I think Verstappen escaped with some minor burns to his hands and face. After the fire was extinguished, we all gathered in the garages to check on each other and regroup but not for long as Michael Schumacher was due in for his pitstop within a few laps.

"Luckily or unluckily depending on how you want to look at it, Schumacher had an engine issue and had to retire just before his pitstop. Bad luck for us as a team both cars out, but glad we didn't have to try and service his car moments after what had just happened. While standing in the back of the garage, some of us could feel areas of our skin getting hot so we found water to pour over the affected areas, while I was doing this I could also feel a burning sensation very close to my groin area so I put my hand down to open the zipper and instantly burnt my fingers on the zipper handle it was that hot!

"I also had red lines down the back of my fire suit, these were from the vent hose, which had melted and stuck to my fire suit. Some of us went to the track medical centre where we continued to pour cool water over our affected areas. Myself, Paul Seaby and Dave Redding got a free helicopter ride to the local hospital for further treatment. I think Paul and Dave got released later that

The damage to Verstappen's helmet following the fire.
Photo: Mike Fairholme Designs

The start of the first-lap chaos in Germany. Hakkinen, who had been given a warning after Silverstone, was blamed for it and banned for the Hungarian Grand Prix. *Photo: Alastair Ladd*

evening but I had the pleasure of staying overnight. I was bandaged up around my head like the Invisible Man (remember that TV show?). Huub Rothengatter (Jos's manager) came to see me that evening, walked into my room pissed himself laughing, ran back to his car to get his camera came back in and took a photo of me all bandaged up. I thought it was funny."

"I flew back to UK the next day, went to see my doctor and the local hospital burns unit, and explained what had happened. They said 'oh you're from the grand prix fire, but the news stated no one was injured. These look like quite severe injuries to us.' I spent the next two weeks in and out of the local burns unit for dressing changes and to have dead skin pulled of my face, not allowed back to work for fear of getting an infection. Once I stopped having to go for dressings, my wife would continue at home for several weeks to pull dead skin of my face. After two weeks I was allowed by the doctor to resume work but not allowed to wear anything over my head/face so no refuelling for me. I missed the Hungarian Grand Prix, I think my first race back was the Belgian Grand Prix.

Kenny Handkammer, another mechanic caught in the inferno, said: "What was tough, though, was the fact Schumacher was due a stop soon after. Some of the guys had gone off to hospital already and I needed to find people, but some were saying they didn't know if they could do it. It wasn't needed in the end because Michael's car stopped with a fuel problem but in a way that was worse. It meant we had two weeks of downtime going through what happened, you were just asking: 'Do I really want to be stood in front of a car? Do I really want to be putting fuel in it?' If we had done that second pit stop straight away, it would have got it out of the system a bit."[102]

Despite the fire and a rapidly depleting field, the race carried on, with Ferrari eventually taking its first grand prix win since 1990. It was an unusual result after a strange weekend, in what was increasingly becoming a peculiar year. During an interview with *Sky Sports* in 2013, Schumacher professed Berger's victory was illegitimate because the wooden plank under his Ferrari had been worn by 60 percent, well over the 10 percent allowable wear,

"If you don't mind, I dedicate this win to me!" said Berger upon ending Ferrari's four-year winless streak. The sport needed them doing well.
Photo: Alastair Ladd

but nothing was done about it. When asked about this Mosley retorted, "The first race at which this regulation was imposed was Hockenheim, and if leniency was to be shown, you would expect it to have been shown there.

"Ferrari won that race, and according to my information, the winning car was impeccable. It had in fact probably been run a little too high, to be conservative. The two Ligiers which finished next, and all finishers down to one of the Footworks, were legal, according to the reports which I received. One of the Footworks had excessive wear, but some of the bolts (which held the skid block) were missing because of an accident. And that was the only car at Hockenheim which could have been contentious."[103] Another point of debate was whether mid-race refuelling should continue in light of the Verstappen/Benetton incident?

Two leading magazines, *Motor Sport* and *Autosport*, implored the FIA to stop the practice with immediate effect. The latter carried out a survey the following week among team bosses and drivers with the majority in favour of a ban. This strong depth of feeling was reiterated during a meeting between teams at the proceeding race in Hungary. However, Ferrari's support was required to initiate a ban. With the Italian team proving more competitive in 1994 and having just won its first race in four years, understandably it didn't want to see the back of refuelling, meaning others were stuck with it at least until 1995. Also, had it been discontinued after Hockenheim, the cars' fuel tanks sizes would have meant either the subsequent races had to be 50 percent their original distance, or the cars would have needed another major redesign. Persisting with refuelling avoided these headaches.

Bernie Ecclestone played down the Hockenheim fire: "The accident does not worry me any more than an accident happening on the circuit. We have not had any problems with it this season. It does not make me rethink refuelling. You saw how quickly the fire was put out."[104] The media backlash following Senna and Ratzenberger's deaths were still fresh in everybody's mind, so the powers-that-be wanted to avoid a similar occurrence after the

Hockenheim fire. The FIA did have powers under safety grounds to force through a ban on refuelling at any time, but would they?

If refuelling was banned for safety reasons after one year, this would reflect badly on the FIA for having allowed its reintroduction, especially in F1's new safety conscious world post-Imola. Furthermore, teams might see the FIA caving into their demands as a potential show of weakness by the governing body and exploit it to regain more control. Banning refuelling within F1, the pinnacle of motorsport, for safety reasons might also have implications for other categories like Indycar, sports cars etc because if consistency were applied they would also be forced to look at refuelling.

Conversely, if the FIA continued refuelling after Hockenheim and the fire was attributed to either human error or defective equipment, then the press might call them irresponsible for allowing questionable apparatus into F1. Other questions might also be asked: how much safer would the fuel rigs be in subsequent races? Seemingly, the ideal outcome for the FIA was the fire being attributable to something other than human error or equipment failure.

Benetton found itself in deep trouble after being blamed for the Hockenheim blaze because the FIA claimed it tampered with its refuelling equipment for quicker pitstops. The team were, therefore, facing fresh accusations of cheating and exclusion from the championship if found guilty. Benetton vigorously refuted these allegations, citing defective apparatus as the cause of the fire. It also insisted they had evidence of this as well as permission from the FIA to alter the equipment. Furthermore, it employed Britain's most successful libel lawyer in order to send a clear signal to the FIA: proceed with your accusations and exclude us from the championship at your peril. The stakes couldn't have been higher in this latest battle between the FIA and Benetton.

102. BBC Sport website, 25 September 2016
103. Max Mosley speaking on 9 September 1994
104. *Autosport*, 4 August 1994

HUNGARY AND BELGIUM

August 1994

"The Stewards decided to inflict to Competitor Mild Seven Benetton Ford the penalty of the exclusion of car number five, driver M Schumacher, from the Event."

FIA press release following the Belgian Grand Prix

"That incident at Spa was just so bizarre... So we appealed the decision. It just seemed that we could do nothing right that year."

Pat Symonds, Schumacher's race engineer

Following Spa, Schumacher had been banned/disqualified from a quarter of 1994 races due to various rule infringements. Politics or cheating?

Photo: Alastair Ladd

Standings before the 1994 Hungarian Grand Prix

DRIVERS' CHAMPIONSHIP		
Pos	Driver	Points
1	Michael Schumacher	66
2	Damon Hill	39
3	Gerhard Berger	27

CONSTRUCTORS' CHAMPIONSHIP		
Pos	Constructor	Points
1	Benetton-Ford	67
2	Ferrari	52
3	Williams-Renault	43

Benetton removed a filter from its refuelling equipment. The FIA claimed that was "the most likely cause" of the Hockenheim fire... **Photo: Nic Redhead**

...In response Benetton claimed its Operations Director, Joan Villadelprat (pictured in recent years) was given verbal permission by the FIA's Charlie Whiting to remove the filter.
Photo: Trapaga

Following the black flag incident at Silverstone and the horrific pitstop fire at Hockenheim, Benetton must have been praying that nothing else would go wrong in the next race. Its troubles, however, were only just beginning. The fire had everyone wondering what caused it, so on the Wednesday after the German Grand Prix (3 August) an inspection of Verstappen's refuelling rig was carried out by Intertechnique (the manufacturer), Benetton, and AFTA – an independent accident investigation company commissioned by the team. The equipment was dismantled and each component carefully checked and measured. AFTA asked to see Intertechnique's assembly drawings to check the size and tolerance of the components against those on the drawings. Intertechnique apparently refused to cooperate citing "confidentiality of design". After the inspection, Intertechnique took its apparatus away leaving Benetton and AFTA convinced the problem lay with the manufacturing tolerances between various components.

Once Intertechnique finished its own internal investigation, the FIA issued a press release on 10 August. It concluded the most likely cause of the fire was a foreign body (ie a speck of dirt) which became jammed in the fuel valve. Thus, the FIA deemed equipment failure or human error wasn't to blame, instead the fault laid with Benetton because they had removed an internal filter designed to eliminate this risk. It was claimed that doing so sped up fuel flow by 12.5 percent which saved around one second during a typical pitstop. For some, this explained why Benetton had faster pitstops, such as Brazil where Schumacher overtook Senna in the pits.

Benetton was therefore accused of deliberately cheating via tampering with their refuelling apparatus to gain an advantage. The inference being that Benetton had put the lives of their mechanics and everybody within the pitlane at risk over their actions. The regulations clearly stated the refuelling equipment "must not be modified in any way" therefore Benetton had to appear before an FIA hearing on 19 October to explain themselves. Within the FIA press release, it stated "A report has been submitted by the FIA

Observer, Mr R Causo" who, remember, was Williams' lawyer during the investigation into Senna's death at the time.

Later on, the 10 August, Benetton responded with its own press release which included part of AFTA's interim report. It stated: "No evidence was seen, during the examination, of scouring or of other effects which could have resulted from debris fouling any of the moving parts. A study of the layout of the fuel path and of the evidence surrounding the incident didn't suggest any way in which any feasible debris contamination from the fuel flow could have caused the failure of the nozzle to engage correctly." Benetton also said: "Given our concern over refuelling safety, we had hoped to be able to discuss this report with the FIA and undertake the necessary actions to reduce the risks involved in refuelling. A written request has now been placed with the FIA urgently requesting such a meeting. A copy of this report was immediately lodged with our legal advisors, Marriott Harrison of London, upon receipt of the FIA's press release.

"The filter mentioned was introduced part way through the year in response to problems teams were having with debris entering the valve and car. Benetton was able to eliminate this problem. The Benetton fuel rigs prior to Hockenheim had been thoroughly stripped and cleaned and there was no risk of debris entering the valve assembly. Benetton also pre-filter their fuel twice (through a much finer grade filter) before it is placed in the fuel rig. Benetton Formula concluded the filter was unnecessary and it was removed with the full knowledge and permission of the FIA F1 Technical Delegate, Mr Charlie Whiting. This permission was given on the afternoon of Thursday 28 July to Mr Joan Villadelprat in the presence of Mr Ross Brawn. The consequence of attributing, in Benetton Formula's view incorrectly, the cause of this fire to the lack of a filter, means that such an incident could happen again, possibly with far more serious consequences."[105]

105. Benetton press release, 8 May 1994

The refuelling equipment was vastly improved following lessons learnt after Hockenheim. ***Photo: Motorsport Images/LAT***

One question that confused many was why didn't Benetton refit the filters prior to Intertechnique's inspection on 3 August, thus covering its tracks? After the German Grand Prix, Benetton had two clear days to refit the filter to the refuelling equipment should they have felt inclined to do so. The only possible answer was the team genuinely believed they had permission to remove the filter and, according to them, that permission was granted six days before the Intertechnique inspection. The man who received that verbal permission from the FIA, Joan Villadelprat, revealed "there were parts of the fuel hose which the FIA allowed the teams to make minor adjustments for maintenance. Since they were parts with very small tolerances and could cause the fuel difficulty to exit the hose properly. Benetton eliminated one of the filters in one of the maintenance and found that the fuel was coming out faster from the hose. Those parts of the filters were included in the maintenance allowed by the FIA. That's why the FIA, when investigating, realised that many teams were making changes to the hose and that it could affect the safety of the mechanics."

Initially, the FIA refuted Benetton's claim that permission to remove the filter was granted, and so did Intertechnique via a press statement released on 11 August which added any such requests would be refused for "technical and safety reasons". However Max Mosley later admitted during a press conference that the FIA's Charlie Whiting told Benetton removing the fuel filter was "OK by me if it's OK by Intertechnique." According to Willem Toet, Benetton's Head of Aerodynamics in 1994:

"Benetton didn't have written permission to remove the filter – fact. However, the Ligier team did and team boss Flavio had bought into Ligier who were in financial trouble. So the team knew about permission to remove a filter. Did they gain an advantage from it – yes but less than the one second claimed by an "independent witness". Ligier (French and not at the front of the field) had been given permission by Intertechnique (also French) to remove the filter. If I was running Benetton I would also have used this communication technique to get the answer I wanted. As a winning team, you're much less likely to be granted a favour than if you are a backmarker. That was clever, but the information should have come out immediately when there was the fire... the team didn't want to immediately disclose that Ligier had a letter from Intertechnique as the team really didn't want the closeness of the working relationship to come out in full! That would have been another day in Paris to see the headmaster – and wouldn't have ended well for either team!"[106]

So according to Toet, Benetton had a dilemma. By showing evidence that Intertechinque granted Ligier written permission to remove their filter, Benetton might implicated themselves in another crime, namely working too closely with Ligier. If true, this explains why Benetton claimed they had proof that authorisation was given to remove the filter but were reluctant to provide it. What Benetton needed was to find another team who had also been granted permission. It later transpired that Larrousse, also French and a backmarker team, had received prior correspondence

Ron Dennis: "The filter has no relevance to the fire." Paul West, a Williams mechanic in 1994, concurred. **Photo: Stu Seeger**

The fire prompted McLaren to provide its refuellers with greater protection as illustrated by the yellow circle. Why would McLaren do this if they had not removed their fuel filter?
Photo: Andrew-44-19

from Intertechinque relating to the filter in question. Would that constitute the evidence needed? Benetton also supplied Larrousse with gearboxes in 1994 – would this be construed as working too closely with another team? We would find out shortly.

Interestingly, on 12 August (the Friday of the Hungarian Grand Prix), Intertechnique changed the components which Benetton and AFTA suspected to be the cause of the Hockenheim blaze. Every team's refuelling equipment was altered accordingly, so not just Benetton's, and Intertechnique did this without publicity or a corresponding explanation. However, a subsequent Benetton statement gave more details: "We believe the most likely cause of the Hockenheim fire was a faulty part in the Intertechnique refuelling valve...

"...Benetton was alerted to the problem when Intertechnique personnel arrived in Hungary and started to change parts of the refuelling valves they supply to the teams. When engineers inspected the parts being removed they discovered that these were a different size to the same component in Verstappen's fuel rig

The car's on-board valve. The middle section is pressed down by the fuel hose and should spring back immediately after it is removed.
Photo: www.finallap.net/Default.aspx

used in Hockenheim. All of the same parts removed from the fuel valves of six different F1 teams had been found to have five times the operating clearance of the same part removed from Verstappen's fuel rig. Benetton has concluded that the faulty part wasn't to the correct specification and this could have caused the valve to jam during the refuelling process."[107]

Ironically it appeared the Benetton equipment was incorrectly reassembled following the work Intertechnique carried out in Hungary. When Benetton practiced a refuelling pit stop the following day they suffered another leak. *F1 News* and *Motor Sport* magazines reported by the evening of 13 August the general feeling within the Hungaroring paddock was that Benetton tried to gain an advantage by removing the fuel filter but rivals believed Benetton genuinely felt they had the authorisation to do so. Whether they did or not is something we shall investigate shortly.

Both magazines reported the consensus among rivals was the removal of the filter didn't actually cause the Hockenheim fire. Paul West, a Williams team mechanic said: "With regard to the fire, I personally don't think the removal of the filter made any difference. I think it was down to the coupling not going on straight and causing the valve to stick open. The guy who did our refuelling had it happen a few times during pitstop practice but never with a 'live' rig."

Steve Matchett, one of the Benetton mechanics affected by the Hockenheim inferno, was adamant the removal of the filter didn't cause the fire. Matchett was convinced he wasn't alone in thinking this, by the huge concern shown towards the safety of the refuelling equipment afterwards, and the improved fire resistant overalls teams like McLaren had brought to Hungary. McLaren was a team not accused of removing its fuel filter. Matchett's views were supported by a Benetton commissioned report undertaken by AFTA. While it gave the caveat "the precise mechanism which enabled fuel spillage is not clear" it detailed how the nozzle could easily be misaligned when attempting to connect to the car's on-board valve.

106. Willem Toet LinkedIn blog, 5 April 2016
107. *Autosport*, 18 August 1994

Chapter 9

This appears to be what happened if you watch a replay of the Verstappen/Hockenheim pit stop closely. As the fuel sprayed Benetton's refueller (Simon Morley) appears to take evasive action with the nozzle, thus allowing the valve to close immediately as it is designed to do. This explains why a small amount of fuel escaped (around 1.5 litres) considering the typical fuel flow rate of the equipment was 12 litres per second. Had the valve been "slow to close due to the presence of a foreign body" as claimed by the FIA, wouldn't you expect more than just 0.12sec worth of fuel to have sprayed out?

Intertechnique had previously told teams it was impossible for fuel to spill before the nozzle was fully mated to the car's valve – a reassurance called into question following AFTA findings which highlighted the "low integrity of the connection". The recommendations made by AFTA to improve the equipment included a 'lock-on device' between the nozzle and car's valve before refuelling commenced, greater integrity nozzles and valves and, should the driver depart with the fuel hose still attached to the car, AFTA recommended a provision for a self-sealing 'weak link' to prevent a spillage in that occurrence. These proposals were passed to the FIA.

For the start of 1995, Intertechnique introduced extensively redesigned refuelling equipment which incorporated some of AFTA recommendations. Primarily the 'lock-on device' between the nozzle and valve before refuelling commenced, which may have prevented the Hockenheim inferno. In order to mitigate against a car departing with the nozzle still attached, Intertechnique incorporated a 'dead man's handle' which, if released, would immediately stop fuel flow. They also featured larger nozzles and a cover for the valves on the cars. During an interview in early 1995, Max Mosley defended the continuation of refuelling by admitting: "First of all, the 1995 refuelling equipment is very significantly better. A lot of thought and effort has gone in, both from the F1 teams and Intertechnique, in light of the experience, to make it safer and more foolproof."[108]

Despite these improvements, mechanics were advised to refuel the cars slowly and carefully. "Gives you a lot of confidence, that..." is the alleged sarcastic reply from one team member.[109] Interestingly, fuel valve problems continued. For example, McLaren had around ten kilos of fuel (almost three times the amount from Hockenheim 1994) leak during 1995 pre-season because their valve stuck open.

McLaren boss, Ron Dennis, revealed: "Our leak was on a cold engine with no electrics on the car [hence why it didn't ignite]... There was a retaining spring which had not been correctly fitted in the valve. But also, that area had not been designed to be idiotproof. Therefore, it was possible for it to be incorrectly fitted on all other valves."[110] Intertechinque ensured the part was redesigned and replaced in other team's fuel valves.

Despite this, Gachot's Pacific retired from the 1995 Spanish Grand Prix due to a pitstop fire and his boss, Keith Wiggins, explained the circumstances. "As the hose came off, the valve on the car didn't fully return and, as soon as he left the pits, fuel jumped back out on to the bodywork. When we brought the car back, the valve had returned, but we don't know when it did that. We've got the Intertechinque people looking into it."[111] Wiggins considered it 'fortunate' their fuel tank was only around 75 percent full. Had it been brimmed, more would have leaked out. Moreover, it was a cooler day than Hockenheim 1994, and their car had been moving when the fuel ignited thus helping to combat the blaze, hence why this wasn't as catastrophic as Benetton's incident.

Also at Spain 1995, Ligier mechanics were unable to mate the refuelling nozzle to the valve on Brundle's car losing him over thirty seconds. "The problem was due to the sensitivity of the refuelling probe of the rig," said Ligier's Director of Operations Tony Dowe.[112] Despite the rain at the 1995 Belgian Grand Prix, Irvine's Jordan ignited during a pit stop after his fuel valve stuck open.[113] Similarly, Diniz's Ligier burst into flames during the 1996 Argentine Grand Prix because his fuel valve jammed open following a pit stop, which spawned the memorable headline in the following day's *The Sun* newspaper "DINIZ IN THE OVEN". Fortunately, none of the above incidents resulted in any serious injuries.

Adrian Ward worked at Benetton during that era, within research and development, so was involved in the post-Verstappen fire testing to determine the cause of it. "The reason for the [Hockenheim] fire was a piece of tyre rubber was on the car valve face," argued Ward. "This was why all cars were fitted with hydraulically operated flaps over the valve [mandatory in 1998]." At Hungary 1994, some accused Benetton of using the AFTA findings to divert attention from its fuel rig tampering charge. Briatore

The fuel filter Benetton removed acted similar to a coffee filter, but was heavier duty and housed within teams' refuelling hoses.
Photo: Sarah Antar

Mosley admitted: "The 1995 refuelling equipment is very significantly better." This photo is from 1996 and shows the improvements to the fuel nozzle (circled in red). **Photo: Andrew-44-19**

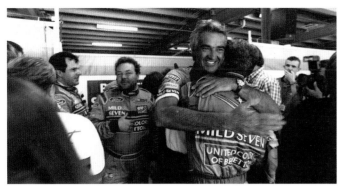

Benetton undertook five quick pitstops at the following race (Hungary) and finished first and third. The team felt this was the best answer it could give its critics. *Photo: Antony John Dennis*

responded: "I'm the one who has to take the calls from the wives and girlfriends who want to know why they are watching their husbands or boyfriends and the fathers of their children burning in front of their eyes on the television. I cannot rule out civil action and I will be having a meeting with Luciano Benetton next week."[114] Meanwhile, in the background, Benetton prepared its case for the looming FIA hearing.

For this book, extensive research has been undertaken to see if any Benetton employees claimed the fire was caused by the filter's removal. To date, none has stated that was the case... perhaps telling considering the Benetton mechanics engulfed by the blaze had their lives put at risk. Had I been in that situation and believed the inferno was due to colleagues' cheating which endangered my own life, then no amount of money would have kept me quiet over that. Would it do so for you?

Steve Matchett insisted all the Benetton mechanics affected by the fire volunteered to do pitstops at the following race,[115] except Simon Morley who was too badly injured. This was despite them overcoming the psychological effect of knowing another inferno could happen again, because the cause had not been established by that stage. If those mechanics believed the fire was due to Benetton cheating, would they have volunteered for future pitstops?

Tighter checks on refuelling rigs were carried out after Hockenheim. Because Benetton was accused of causing the fire by removing their filter, presumably the FIA ensured it was in place by Hungary, where Benetton made five very quick refuelling pitstops. Indeed, Schumacher's final stop was recorded at 6.8sec by the TV graphics, thereby demonstrating if their fuel filter was added then it made little gain to pitstop times. Thus begging the question why would Benetton risk the severe consequences of modifying the refuelling equipment for such little advantage? Unless Benetton believed it had sufficient permission to do so.

According to Morley: "The filter itself was quite a coarse mesh and was only there to catch 'large' particles, definitely not suitable for catching small particles. It would be the smallest of particles that could potentially interfere with the operation of the nozzle, as the clearances were very tight [note the valve clearances were different to those of the nozzle]. The filter mesh size was big enough that it would also have no impact on fuel flow it was just simply to coarse to have an impact. Therefore removing the filter was no

---

MEMORANDUM

To:	Ross Brawn
	Technical Director
From:	Simon Morley
Subject:	Hockenheim Grand Prix - Pit Stop Fire

Jos Verstappen came into the pit lane for his first fuel/tyre pit stop. Jos stopped on the marked out pit area.

I went to engage the refuelling nozzle as I normally do. The first attempt at aligning the nozzle was slightly too low so I realigned the nozzle by moving it up and engaged the nose of the nozzle onto the on-car connector.

I tried to push the nozzle further onto the on-car connector to fully engage the nozzle to the car connector, so as to start the fuel flowing into the car. As I tried pushing the nozzle it would not move and therefore the vapour sleeve would not slide back as is its normal operation. I then tried pushing the nozzle harder and twisting to try and engage it properly, but it still would not fully engage.

I then removed my right hand from the nozzle handle so as to grip the flange behind the sight glass. This is a normal operation which I have done at every race so far this season. The reason for this is twofold:

1   It enables me to feel the refuelling hose so I know when the fuel has stopped flowing.
2.   It makes the operation of removing the nozzle from the on-car connector easier.

I moved my hand to try and gain a bit more leverage to try to help insert the nozzle better, but as I did this the nozzle moved out slightly and at that instance the fuel sprayed out forcing the nozzle completely out of the on-car connector.

I am absolutely sure that at no time did the on -car connector open and allow any fuel into the car. After the fire was extinguished I went from the rear of the garage to the circuit medical centre and then by helicopter to hospital.

NOTE

Whilst attending a Fuel Rig service training session at the Intertechnique factory on the 14th March 1994, myself and others present were told by Mr J M TONNEAU that the filter in the nozzle was originally put in to catch the manufacturing debris that was left inside the fuel rigs. He also stated that once we were happy that the filter was no longer catching debris and therefore the fuel rigs where clean, the filter could be removed if so desired.

What an internal Benetton memo said about the Hockenheim fire. *Image: Simon Morley*

performance gain and due to the mesh size wouldn't make any difference to fuel filtration anyway. All of our fuel was filtered out of the drums, filtered again after the pump into the rig, the fuel was clean. The fuel rigs were clean and sealed."

Hungary was the third race in a row Schumacher made a poorer start than Hill. The Englishman joked: "I did three or four practice starts in testing and already I'm making better starts than him, Funny isn't it?"[116] Despite his poorer getaway, pole position man Schumacher braked later than Hill into the first corner so didn't relinquish his lead. The German then dominated the race, owed partly to his three-stop strategy which proved superior over the two-stops adopted by Hill. Schumacher's win was the best possible answer Benetton could give its critics following the recent scrutiny the team was under. An added bonus was its second driver, Verstappen, finished in third thanks in part to Schumacher's help. This was an especially welcome result since Verstappen was receiving a hard time in the press following his poor showings.

108. *Motor Sport*, February 1995
109. *Autosport*, 30 March 1995
110. *Autosport*, 30 March 1995
111. *Autosport*, 18 May 1995
112. *Grand Prix*, 15 May 1995
113. *Grand Prix*, 1995
114. *Autosport*, 18 August 1994
115. *Life in the Fast Lane: The Inside Story of Benetton's First World Championship* by Steve Matchett (1995)
116. *F1 News*, 24 August 1994

Chapter 9

Afterwards, Hill sportingly conceded Schumacher had beaten him fairly without any apparent illegalities. Moreover, Schumacher's black box was sealed immediately following the race and its contents were subjected to another LDRA/FIA examination, which it passed.[117] Attention was then turned to why Panis's blatant jumpstart was never penalised, a decision which undermined the FIA's creditability. Mosley later admitted this was due to one official's stubbornness who refused to acknowledge Panis's jump start despite clear video evidence. Furthermore, outdated regulations didn't allow the FIA to overrule said official, however, shortly afterwards the regulations were 'put right'.

Following Hungary, it was announced the FIA inquiry into the Hockenheim fire was brought forward from 19 October to 7 September. Benetton's rivals had pressed the FIA to resolve the controversy as soon as possible. With this black cloud hanging over the championship leaders, along with its Silverstone appeal (due to be settled shortly), the F1 fraternity travelled to the next race, Belgium. However, in keeping with the rest of 1994, this event didn't pass without controversy.

Alliot had been McLaren's test driver at the behest of new engine supplier Peugeot, and his backers went to great lengths to secure a race seat by ousting Brundle. Indeed, a previous comparison test between them was rigged so Alliot posted a faster time because a straw bale chicane had been removed during his run. McLaren soon realised, because its telemetry showed his steering input was minimal through that part of the track.

Although that deception failed, Alliot stood in for Hakkinen in Hungary following the Finn's race ban after Germany. Alliot then found himself in an uncompetitive Larrousse for Belgium and commented to journalists its gearbox didn't have an automatic upchange facility, like the McLaren. This caused a stir within the FIA who felt the McLaren device constituted an illegal driver aid. The FIA made enquiries and their judgement would be announced on 7 September.

Alliot was also lucky not to be penalised for jumping the start at Belgium because his car appeared to be rolling before the green light. Thus it was the second race in a row where officials, seemingly, did nothing about a jumpstart. Meanwhile, Belgian newcomer, Adams, mistakenly parked in the 27th position grid slot, having qualified 26th and last. Again, race stewards appeared not to notice this and signalled to start the race. Usually when this occurs

The FIA needed to resolve the fuel fire case immediately, otherwise Schumacher and Benetton could be crowned 1994 champions only to be disqualified. *Photo: Morio*

the driver is sent to the back of the grid, however clearly in Adams' case that wouldn't have been any penalty. Even so, the Belgian rookie does not appear to have received any fines or retrospective penalties for this misdemeanour. One can only speculate whether the leniency shown in this case, along with Panis's or Alliot's apparent jumpstarts examples, would have been applied had Schumacher's Benetton been the offender instead?

The race proved another event which Schumacher dominated. It was a particularly crushing blow to Hill's championship hopes since this track was thought to favour his more powerful V10 engine over Schumacher's V8. If the outstanding FIA hearings went his way, Schumacher could clinch the championship at the following event – round twelve of sixteen. Towards the end of their race coverage, Eurosport commentator John Watson twice made the joke: the only way to stop Schumacher winning was to disqualify him. Words which proved prophetic as, five hours later, race officials did just that, thereby awarding Hill a victory crucial for his championship chances. By now, Briatore must have wondered whether sending that open letter criticising the FIA president before Spain was such a good idea.

This fresh row related to the mandatory wooden 'plank' underneath the car. You may recall it was introduced in Germany during the final round of FIA safety changes to force teams to raise their cars' ride heights, thereby avoiding its underside touching

Schumacher won in Belgium but was later disqualified due to excessive plank wear. The fourth accusation levelled at Benetton within two months. *Photo: Alastair Ladd*

Panis (pictured) was accused of jumping the start in Hungary, while his teammate Bernard finished the race with an excessively worn plank. Neither was penalised. *Photo: Alastair Ladd*

Disputes raged over Schumacher's plank wear in the area marked in red. Whereas the damage to the plank in the area marked in yellow was accepted as wear from Schumacher's spin. **Photo: Morio**

An official (pictured in 2008) inspected the kerb Schumacher spun over and concluded Benetton's claim should be rejected because no missing plank fragments could be found on or beside the track. **Photo: ph-stop**

the ground (bottoming out). If a car's plank had worn by more than 10 percent (or 1mm), then the driver would risk exclusion from the race, as they may have gained an illegal aerodynamic advantage by running their car too low. After the Belgian Grand Prix, Schumacher's plank was worn by 26 percent in one specific area at the front of his plank (directly underneath the driver). Benetton argued this was down to "accident damage" caused when Schumacher spun over a kerb during the race.

The rules stated if the excessive wear was due to accident damage then the plank must be weighed. Should it be greater than 90 percent of its original weight then that plank would be legal, period. At Hungary, Eric Bernard's Ligier finished the race with a plank worn by more than 10 percent. According to Max Mosley: "[Bernard] had been off the road and had gone over several kerbs. It was quite clear that it [his plank] had sustained accidental damage".[118] Therefore the Ligier driver was allowed to keep his race result afterwards. Schumacher's plank was reportedly weighed after Spa and found to be within the 90 percent weight limit[119] because only a small section of it transgressed the 1mm depth limit. However, race stewards maintained some of the excessive wear had not been caused by the spin thus the plank couldn't be declared legal on account of its weight.

It had taken five hours to exclude Schumacher because the Clerk of the Course inspected the kerb which he had spun over during the race. Afterwards, race officials concluded the kerb was "flat" and because the missing fragment of wood from Schumacher's plank couldn't be found, Benetton's claim should be rejected. The Enstone team appealed, citing these findings as fatuous, while adding the missing element from their plank was only 2.6mm deep and such a small piece was never going to be found on the race track.

It was argued that either Schumacher's spin obliterated that particle of wood into dust given the friction and heat forces involved, or another car would have blown it away into the adjoining gravel trap, where it would be like trying to find a needle in a haystack. The German spun on lap 19 out of 44, meaning other cars passed the scene at racing speed at least 400 times. An F1's cars aerodynamics could easily suck up and spit out a fragment of wood that size. Benetton also disputed the kerb Schumacher spun

over was flat and gathered photographic evidence in preparation for the appeal hearing. However, race stewards felt they had a strong case also.

It later emerged that Schumacher had asked his team to raise his ride height by half a millimetre following his lap to the grid before the race, implying they could have unwittingly strayed beyond the limit by not raising it enough. The situation had been complicated by wet weather during practicing and qualifying, forcing everyone to take a blind guess on their ride height for the race (held in dry conditions). Some pointed out that no other cars were found to have excessive wear on their planks following the race, including Schumacher's own teammate. Benetton retorted by claiming Verstappen was running the same ride height as Schumacher. Hill rubbed salt into Schumacher's wounds by claiming "It would explain why I was unable to catch him during a race which was absolutely crucial to the championship".[120] This latest row over the world's most famous plank of wood would be settled on 7 September, the same date as Benetton's Hockenheim fire hearing and the McLaren gearbox case.

Had Schumacher's win in Belgium stood, he would have had an almost unassailable lead over Hill in the championship. After this disqualification, his lead was still 21 points – comfortable under normal circumstances. However, given the upcoming FIA v Benetton hearings, there was a distinct possibility of further race bans for the championship leader. Whether intentional or not, that would ensure a climatic end to the title battle, which involved a German and a British driver who were increasingly growing a disdain for one another – a sure-fire hit for TV audiences. Or would the FIA ignore this and throw Benetton out of the championship, which many felt was the only course of action if they were found guilty of tampering with the refuelling equipment without permission? Indeed, Mosley had reiterated pre-season "draconian penalties" would be enforced for any team deliberately cheating. The world was about to learn the verdict of these cases, which continue to divide opinion even to this day.

117. *F1 News*, 8 March 1995
118. Max Mosley speaking on 9 September 1994
119. *Motor Sport*, October 1994
120. *Autosport*, 1 September 1994

FIA HEARINGS

September 1994

"The team were blamed for causing the fire by removing a filter from the fuel filler system. That wasn't the reason for the fire."

Willem Toet, Benetton's Head of Aerodynamics

"If you go back a week or so, the theme was that I in particular, or the FIA in general, had a vendetta against Flavio Briatore. Now the suggestion is that we have gone too far the other way."

Max Mosley, FIA President

The entrance lobby to the FIA headquarters became a familiar sight to Benetton as their various cases were heard. ***Photo: Stefano Brivio***

Race bans and disqualifications handed out in 1994

DRIVERS		
Pos	Driver	Total number of bans/DSQs
1	Michael Schumacher	4
2	Eddie Irvine	3
1	Mika Hakkinen	1

CONSTRUCTORS		
Pos	Constructor	Total number of DSQs
1	Benetton-Ford	2
2	Arrows	1
3	Ligier	1

Schumacher needed 45 minutes to compose himself before facing reporters after the Silverstone appeal verdict. **Photo: Fry**

Brawn claims Benetton had incentives not to appeal Schumacher's post Silverstone race bans, given its Ford V8 engine did not suit the Hockenheim track. **Photo: Landmensch**

Two and half months ago, Schumacher's life was very different. The championship was a foregone conclusion and he was popular within the sport, but the tables had since turned with Schumacher and Benetton's ethics under constant questioning. Now it didn't matter whether either were innocent because any success in 1994 would always be tainted by these accusations. Benetton's Technical Director, Ross Brawn, felt compiled to respond. "This is my third season with Benetton. I don't think it has ever been guilty of any infringement. Why didn't we do any cheating last year? We don't suddenly start cheating, particularly with the performance advantage and driver we've got."[121] The next few days was going to determine how accurate his statement was.

On the Tuesday following the Belgian Grand Prix (30 August), the FIA met in Paris to decide the outcome of Benetton's appeal against its Silverstone penalty. You may recall they ignored a black flag which resulted in disqualification from second position at Silverstone and a further two-race ban. But prior to Hockenheim Benetton appealed, which then allowed Schumacher to race at his home event. During the appeal, Schumacher and Benetton's representative (Pat Symonds) put forward a similar defence to their original 26 July hearing. They explained mistakes made by race officials surrounding the stop-go penalty which added to confusion on the day. Schumacher claimed not to have seen the black flag and like others, wasn't aware that overtaking on the formation lap was forbidden.

However, the judges felt these arguments offered no defence so they upheld the sanctions handed down on 26 July, meaning Schumacher lost his six points from Silverstone and was banned from the next two races. If his chief rival, Hill, won those races then the championship gap between the two would reduce to one point, thus ensuring a thrilling conclusion to the season. The German is someone who never normally shows his emotions in public, but even he couldn't hide his disappointment when answering media questions about the verdict. This latest blow for Schumacher came

a mere two days after his Belgian Grand Prix disqualification and the German told reporters: "I think what happened at Spa didn't help me". Benetton team principal Flavio Briatore has always maintained the penalty, in his view, was too harsh.

Conversely, the FIA could have increased the punishment as had happened to Eddie Irvine after Brazil, so Benetton and Schumacher could count themselves lucky in that respect. According to Brawn, "We [Benetton] were not going to appeal the Silverstone decision [due to possible increased penalties and Hockenheim being their weakest track]. But then there was a huge uproar from the German public. We had pleas from lots of important people in F1 to appeal so we could at least race in Hockenheim and appease the fans. So we did because it was indicated that the appeal would be looked upon favourably. We raced at Hockenheim, where we blew up. Then we were completely stitched up – the appeal went through and nothing was done."[122]

During this hearing, the only point the FIA conceded was the notification of the stop-go penalty was communicated to Benetton later than it should have been. "But that does not mean a violation of the regulations didn't take place," they insisted. At the time, the rules didn't express whether a penalty was still valid or not under these circumstances, it merely stated any time penalty needed to be communicated to the offending team within 15 minutes of the offence. Arguably this implied the time penalty was no longer valid should the deadline be missed, otherwise why stipulate this deadline within the rules? Two weeks after the Silverstone appeal, the rule was amended so a time penalty was withdrawn if race stewards failed to notify an offending team within that deadline. One wonders what thoughts Schumacher and Benetton had upon learning of this clarification. Had it come a fortnight earlier, it would have significantly strengthened their Silverstone case.

121. *Autosport*, 1 September 1994
122. *Motor Sport*, December 2004

If Benetton felt 'stitched-up' they could repay the FIA by causing them severe embarrassment in a few days' time. Because the Hockenheim fuel filter case was looming and Benetton intended to prove defective refuelling apparatus was responsible for the fire. Prior to the hearing, *Autosport* reported Benetton had compiled a list of failures involving the refuelling equipment. This included a leak Ferrari experienced during pre-season testing at Imola and a valve failure Arrows suffered in Barcelona. Both incidents were confirmed by those teams, and there were other examples as detailed in the Pre-Season chapter.

FIA President Max Mosley's response to Benetton's evidence was: "They have not told us and the only team to have written a letter is McLaren."[123] This list of refuelling apparatus failures wasn't common knowledge outside of specialist motor racing publications. Therefore, if Benetton drew attention to them via the fuel filter case it would cause the FIA headaches when dealing with the ensuing media storm. Remember, after the Senna and Ratzenberger's tragedies, there was lots of mock outrage from tabloid newspapers which forced Mosley to take drastic and immediate action. Something similar might occur if Benetton proved the refuelling equipment was defective.

Furthermore highlighting rig failures would increase the pressure to ban refuelling which the majority of teams, including Benetton, wanted. This may also explain why other teams pushed for the fuel filter case to be settled on 7 September rather than the original 19 October, because if it came to light the equipment was at fault, then refuelling might be banned afterwards. The earlier date would also allow teams more time to alter their following year's design to incorporate a larger sized fuel tank. Just before the hearing, *Autosport* reported Benetton was intending to prove it had permission to remove the filter, something the FIA and Intertechnique had denied until this point. Joan Villadelprat was who Benetton claimed received that permission (verbally) from the FIA, and he highlights another tactic Benetton used to up the stakes. "After the [Hockenheim] accident, the FIA threatened to exclude Benetton from the F1 championship for modifying the

Briatore hired leading libel lawyer, George Carman, to represent Benetton. Apparently this was a warning to Mosley to not disqualify Benetton at the fuel fire hearing. *Photo: Alastair Ladd*

hose. That forced Benetton to gather its lawyers and talk with other teams about this issue. Benetton spoke with Ligier [which it owned] and other teams to abandon F1 and the championship if Benetton was excluded."

At the hearing, Benetton astonished everyone by changing its stance and pleading guilty all to the FIA charges. To say that was unexpected, would be a masterpiece of understatement. For instance, that week's *Autosport* detailed how Benetton was intending to fight its case with a seemly vast amount of evidence. Benetton's Willem Toet outlines what he believed happened:

"I remember at the time the engineers coming back from discussions with the rule makers which indicated that, if we claimed the refuelling rigs were unsafe [ie there was a design or manufacturing fault], then we would be charged with bringing the sport into disrepute. In Paris and the FIA hearing, the engineers, along with lawyers and bosses, went with all the facts laid out. A copy of the letter from Intertechnique to Ligier, an animation of

Briatore and Benetton were about to shed light on earlier refuelling equipment failures to defend themselves. Would the FIA have wanted these details to have surfaced in tabloid newspapers? *Photo: Alastair Ladd*

The location of the FIA HQ where Benetton pleaded guilty during the fuel fire hearing. Only days before it had been reported they were intending to fight the charges. *Photo: PHGCOM*

Toet: "A lot of what went on is cloaked in secrecy." Before the fuel fire hearing, Benetton faced expulsion from the championship if convicted. *Photo: Willem Toet*

Toet believes: "The cars did not have big enough fuel tanks to allow racing without refuelling so they [the FIA] were in a bit of a corner."
Photo: Alastair Ladd

the particle sizes that the filter would have stopped and the size of particle that caused the problem (about 1/40th of the size of that would have been stopped by the filter).

"Design information about the parts that jammed and precise inspection information that showed the part tolerances were really on the limit that would facilitate this particular pair of parts jamming. You can imagine that the hole in the outer tube was a bit too small and the inner part was a bit too big. Small details but very, very important. The team (engineers) never got their opportunity to present the information.

"On returning from Paris, the engineers told me the story that, during the evening before the hearing, the team boss got a call from someone very high up at the FIA. I know who of course but couldn't possibly mention any names. It was explained that, if the team went ahead with their defence, they would be found guilty and face harsh penalties. However, if they played along they would be given a slap on the wrist and allowed to continue to compete. The boss "did the deal" and the engineers were told in the morning. I asked myself at the time – why the hell didn't the team get the chance to present their case?

"I believe that the FIA didn't want word to get out that the rigs might be unsafe you can imagine it wouldn't have gone down well with other teams or with the public. Refuelling had been brought back in to spice up the show but the fire wasn't positive publicity for those that had pushed the rule change through. By the time of the Council meeting Intertechnique had figured out what the real reason for the fire was and there was time to check all rigs and put right any potential problems. So in a way, it was a bit of a cover-up. I'm convinced the FIA felt that was a better outcome than going public with what would become a real concern about future safety... Does not right a wrong but I learned a lot about politics that year!

"At the time though the team boss wasn't flavour of the month with the engineers who felt he'd rolled over too easily. I felt that way too. However, looking back now and knowing the power that the FIA have, the boss would have put the very existence of the

team at risk if he had let the technical people go ahead with their defence and effectively told the FIA to go and get stuffed (as they say). I guess he felt he was managing that risk – knowing that the team were likely to win the championship if he played ball with the rule makers."[124]

By changing its plea to guilty, Benetton went from facing expulsion from that year's championship to receiving no serious penalty whatsoever. Understandably, there was lots of cynicism and confusion over this verdict because many simply couldn't understand why the FIA was so lenient. Conspiracy theories included the FIA manipulating the championship owing to the financial benefits of having a German world champion in Schumacher.[125] However, no evidence exists to support this. Quite the contrary, in fact, considering the FIA initially banned Schumacher from the German Grand Prix, until Benetton appealed the decision. Similarly, the FIA upheld Schumacher's Silverstone disqualification and subsequent ban for two races and more was to follow (explained later). These are not the kind of actions one takes to ensure a German world champion for 1994.

It is more likely the FIA realised the Hockenheim fire wasn't due to Benetton removing their filter and foresaw the threat of legal action if they excluded them from championship over it. Benetton had leading libel barrister George Carman QC representing them, and his appointment had been considered a warning to FIA president, Max Mosley (a lawyer himself), because Carman had won several high-profile libel cases. Until this hearing, Benetton had vigorously refuted all the damaging claims the FIA and Intertechnique had made against them. Similarly, it seems the FIA was unable to accept responsibility for the fire given the media backlash reasons outlined above. What they needed, therefore, was a plea bargain that worked for both parties and Bernie Ecclestone was just the man who could broker such a deal.

123. *Autosport*, 1 September 1994
124. Willem Toat LinkedIn blog, 5 April 2016
125. F1 had never had a German World Champion before.

Chapter 10

According to his biography, Ecclestone "had arranged for Carman to arrive the night before the hearing and stay at the Crillon hotel. On that evening, Ecclestone called on Carman in his bedroom and, over two hours, explained to the lawyer how justice worked in F1. 'He's guilty, that's decided' said Ecclestone. 'We're not looking for any change to the verdict. All that's left is the press release. We're looking for changes to the words in Flavio's appeal for sympathy.' To reduce the punishment, continued Ecclestone, Briatore needed to admit his guilt. 'I see,' said Carman. 'I need a drink.' Going down to the bar, Ecclestone telephoned Mosley and suggested that he come down from his suite in the hotel...

"...As a fellow lawyer, Mosley was noticeably impressed and responded positively when Ecclestone suggested, 'I think they want to do a plea bargain,' Mosley was pleased. FIA's judicial status, he believed was weak, especially if Benetton later appealed to a national court. To avoid the mess, two members of the English Bar could amicably settle the case by agreeing that Benetton would plead guilty."[126]

The meeting between Mosley, Ecclestone and Benetton's lawyer the night before the hearing was also recalled in a book about Carman's life by his son, Dominic. It revealed: "The interplay between the two key players in F1 was intriguing. George was especially impressed by Ecclestone's command and control of events."[127] One wonders how common it was for the judge and a member of the jury to meet the defendant's lawyer, the night before a trial. What was clear, however, was that F1 was under pressure to settle the Benetton fuel filter case on 7 September.

The supposed plea bargain involved Benetton accepting the charge they had removed the filter without written authorisation from Intertechnique or the FIA. However, in return, the FIA ruled Benetton didn't cheat because they thought verbal permission along with the Larrousse/Ligier correspondence sufficiently allowed them to remove the filter. Benetton's team manager, Joan Villadelprat, added: "In the end, the FIA decided not to penalise Benetton since the used parts were allowed in the maintenance of the hose of all the equipment." Villadelprat also believed the FIA might also be held responsible for leaving teams to maintain such critical equipment.

After the hearing a Benetton press release read: "The Mild Seven Benetton Ford Formula 1 Team is very pleased with the result of today's hearing in Paris, which has completely cleared its good name from any allegations of cheating. The team were also completely cleared of the charge of removing the fuel filter illegally. This should put an end to unfounded and wild speculations in the press that the removal of the filter caused the fire at Hockenheim. Before the hearing, the FIA conceded that it wasn't alleging that the removal of the filter had caused the fire. In giving the World Council's decision, the President stated that its unanimous view was that the filter was removed in complete good faith and that it would be inappropriate to impose any penalty whatsoever."[128]

Because they had pleaded guilty, Benetton was therefore given a public lambasting for removing the filter, ostensibly good PR for the FIA, because it took the heat off them for allowing refuelling after the fire. It also avoided awkward media questions over the safety of Intertechnique's equipment, despite Benetton stating above, the removal of the filter didn't cause the fire. It seems the press were too astonished and confused over the lack of punishment to notice this small but crucial detail. More eyebrows were raised when the FIA's press release was circulated, because it stated their jury was told a junior Benetton employee had removed the filter without the knowledge of senior management. Few believed this to be a valid defence and it became a bit of a running joke in F1.

For example, a couple days later at the Italian Grand Prix weekend, Eddie Irvine ran one too many laps during Friday qualifying and lost his times as a result. "Perhaps if we tell the FIA it was a junior mechanic holding out the pit board we'll be OK..." Irvine joked. Whereas, in late 1995, the Toyota Rally team were found to have an illegal turbo restrictor on their car. They used the infamous Benetton defence that their management had not known about this, because it was someone at a "certain level". In this instance, however, the FIA didn't accept that because the regulations had been updated to ensure the management were responsible for the actions of anyone in their team. As such, Toyota lost its 1995 points and was banned from rallying in 1996.

The Hotel Crillon where Ecclestone and Mosley reportedly met with Benetton's lawyer, Carman, the night before the fuel fire hearing.
Photo: Britchi Mirela

The Toyota Rally team's defence in 1995 was similar to Benetton's during the fuel fire hearing. However, the outcome was very different.
Photo: Morio

During the fire hearing, it emerged Larrousse (pictured) had been given permission to remove its fuel filter accompanied by a drawing from Intertechinque. **Photo Alastair Ladd**

Simon Morley was Benetton's refueller during that fateful pitstop which occurred mere days after his 27th birthday. If his suffering the worst injuries from it wasn't bad enough, then after the 7 September hearing he was singled out as the "junior employee." Frustrated at being made a sacrificial lamb, he later left F1 and now works in America. An informed source said: "It was all politics and legal stuff. Benetton had proof they could take the filter out, they had proof the rig was shit but the person who lost out the most was Simon. Everyone in the pitlane knew it wasn't his fault but the general public didn't. He did fuck all wrong, got burnt and trashed by the press for doing his job. Benetton had two full days to refit the filter. I wonder how it would have played out if they had, who would be blamed then? That 7 September hearing wasn't a court case."

Morley added: "As for the FIA hearing concerning the fuel filter and excessive plank wear I wasn't too involved. I did go to Paris for the hearing, spent a night in Hotel Crillon, but was never called into the hearing to present any 'evidence'... Larrousse had a letter stating that they could remove the filter. We used that letter as part of our case at the FIA hearing. I can tell you that the filter would have made zero difference to the outcome. I was the refueller, therefore, it was my responsibility to service and maintain the rigs (for safety).

"All seals were replaced after every event regardless of use, obviously, safety was in my best interest and my teammates'. Talking with colleagues up and down pitlane we probably went above and beyond other teams. If it had not been for Greg Field [Benetton's Team Co-ordinator], the whole fire situation could have been a lot worse. He put the fire out single handily, the pitlane fire marshals were way too slow to react. He is most likely the biggest unsung hero."

The FIA press release following this verdict also case stated Benetton "undertook to make substantial management changes so as to ensure that a similar event could never happen again." However, the following week's *Autosport* claimed both Benetton's directors, Walkinshaw and Briatore, denied promising this. Nevertheless, soon afterwards Mosley's old nemesis Walkinshaw was moved over to the Ligier team. The FIA press release also noted how Benetton made no attempt to disguise the removal of the filter despite ample opportunity to do so.[129] A couple of days after the hearing, Mosley used his smooth talking skills to explain the verdict to confused press reporters. Overleaf is part of the transcript:

126. *No Angel: The Secret Life of Bernie Ecclestone* by Tom Bower (2011)
127. *No Ordinary Man, A Life of George Carman* by Dominic Carman (2002)
128. *Michael Schumacher: The Whole Story* by Christopher Hilton (2006)
129. FIA press release, 8 May 1994

Chapter 10

Q: Going back to Wednesday, it seems that Benetton was well prepared and had a good lawyer. But it also appears that there was nobody as well prepared on the other side to contradict what Benetton said. Should the World Council not be prepared, as one would be in a court of law?

Mosley: That's a perfectly valid point. What happens is this: if, for example, they had pleaded not guilty, or had they said they offered a defence, such as "Charlie [Whiting] said we could do it," we had a lawyer who in fact was available [to represent the World Council]. The Stewards presented their evidence and both sides had their lawyers.

A lawyer [representing the FIA] was present, and he had been briefed as far as the filter was concerned. But the moment that Benetton pleaded guilty, the situation changed. Instead of being out to [prosecute] Benetton, we listened to what they had to say [in mitigation]. Their argument was that a filter was necessary only to clear the manufacturing debris within the pipe and that once that debris had gone, and there was obviously nothing further to be found in the filter, it was unnecessary and the filter could be removed.

Now, this was allegedly said, at a low level, between Intertechnique and Larrousse. And [Benetton] *did* produce a letter from Larrousse saying this, and they also produced a drawing from Intertechnique showing how the filter could be removed. But you still had to leave the ring in, because the ring that held the filter was part of the assembly. Now, at that point, we could do one of two things. One thing, though, that we cannot do is to evoke something that may or may not have been said on TV, or in a publication. We either have to accept the facts as put to us, or we might say, "we don't accept what has been put to us," and adjourn the entire proceedings to, in this case, 19 October, to bring in Intertechnique or, if we could get him there, Mr Walkinshaw, then examine every detail of the Larrousse/Intertechnique relationship including the letter, etc, and we considered carefully what to do and thought that in the interests of the sport, and in fairness to the other teams who wanted a decision, fairness generally wouldn't be served by following that procedure.

Following an unsuccessful appeal, Irvine was handed a three-race ban for the multi-car pile-up in Brazil. Mosley. "I think perhaps Eddie was rather harshly dealt with". *Photo: Alastair Ladd*

And once you have taken that decision, all you can consider are the matters that are placed in front of you, by counsel, on behalf of the person making his plea in mitigation. This we did. And just taking those factors into account – being strictly legal and fair about it – we decided that they were guilty, but that on the basis of the facts in front of us it wouldn't be appropriate to impose a penalty. That was how it happened. This is certainly the case in England, and probably also in other courts. Then you listen to what they have to say, and nobody is out to get them.

As I have mentioned before, we could have said, "no, we don't accept all of this, we are going to adjourn it to 19 October," and have a full hearing then. For better or for worse, we felt that the best thing was to get it over and done with. This may have been excessively fair to them, but the moment they pleaded guilty there was nothing that our lawyer could then do. We didn't have witnesses there, people like Larrousse or Walkinshaw, we didn't have all sorts of people that we would normally have had there for a full enquiry. So we accepted what they said. And I think a similar procedure applies in European courts of law.

Q: Who sent a letter to whom?

Mosley: It was a letter from Larrousse to Benetton which Benetton put in on the day. We were a little surprised and irritated that Mr Larrousse didn't when he sent the letter send a copy to us or also send us a copy of the drawing. But it did reach us by various means. Accompanying Larrousse's letter, which said he had been told the filter could be taken out, was a drawing which was purported to come, and apparently did come, from an Intertechnique employee on Intertechnique paper to Larrousse. It showed how to substitute a ring for the filter so that the assembly would still go together but the filter would no longer be present.

Q: Was your lawyer Mr Roberto Causo?

Mosley: No, the lawyer for the FIA was Mr Ian Titchmarsh. If you remember from last year's FIA prizegiving, he shared the announcements with Murray Walker. He is also a very competent lawyer. He defended Eddie Irvine in front of the Review Board and... (widespread ironic laughter) and... I know he did an excellent job. I think perhaps Eddie was rather harshly dealt with, but that wasn't for want of any ability or endeavour on the part of Mr Titchmarsh. He did indeed such a good job that I was informed. And that is why I decided next time we needed a good lawyer, to have him on our side and not the other side.

Q: The members of the World Council must have known that the effect of removing the filter was to gain a performance advantage. And the rules clearly imply that all the refuelling rigs should be identical, so as not to provide a performance advantage. They did it, they got a performance advantage, and yet even then no action was taken. If I may follow my first question, I would like to ask if you did this in the interests of the sport.

Mosley: The point about getting an advantage is absolutely valid. But you see, what they were saying was that they thought they were allowed to do it. In other words, if you analyse what they were really saying was, 'we believe that the equipment was now without the filter.' You can argue about that, but that's what they were actually saying. Now the moment you accept that then they didn't have an advantage, because what they were doing was using the equipment. And the people who were using the wrong equipment would have a disadvantage. Now as soon as someone pleads not guilty, you get into that area. But we never had to consider the guilt or otherwise, because they pleaded guilty.

Q: Second point?

Mosley: As far as being in the interests of the sport, we thought it was definitely in the interests of the sport to resolve the Benetton filter issue, one way or the other, on 7 September. We thought that public opinion, and the interests of the sport, and certainly the teams, would have found it very difficult to accept that we had adjourned the whole thing for six weeks, to have another look at it. Perhaps the result would have been different if we had adjourned: we don't know. But it would certainly not have been the right thing to do... It may well have been that we would have been less lenient after an adjourned hearing, but we shall never know.

Q: Benetton claimed that the FIA's Technical Delegate [Charlie Whiting] had given permission for the filter to be removed. What is your feeling about this, and the decision of the 'junior employee' to remove it?

Mosley: Well, the thing is that as far as the 'junior employee' is concerned, and his removing the part, once you accept that he thought, at whatever level, that he could do that, then, immediately, the level of guilt changes. Now it was said by the team that Charlie said they could. What Charlie said he said was, "it's OK by me if it's OK by Intertechnique." In other words, [Whiting was saying] "go and ask Intertechnique, because it is not within my competence."

I think the junior employee thought, because of the Larrousse business, that Intertechnique had said it was alright. Or that was what was presented to us in Paris. And the whole confusion at that level   [that it was] unknown to Briatore and to Benetton Formula – was taking place. Now what was said at the beginning of the season was that if we caught somebody with ... it's always the same example: traction control... I distinctly remember saying that if they deliberately used it, then this means that it is a fraud, like painting a racehorse a different colour to disguise it.

It is analogous to that: if you deliberately change something on the car, with the intention of getting an advantage, you will be out of the championship. That's what we said, and it still remains the case. The problem we were faced with here is that it became apparent on the facts placed before us that this knowledge which is the essential element in deliberate cheating was missing. And from what we were told on 7 September, it undoubtedly was missing. And as I have already said, we could have had a huge enquiry, who knows? But that's what was there, that's what we decided on.

Q. Do you think mistakes were made by the FIA?

Mosley: Yes. Perhaps I didn't say this clearly enough earlier on. Number one, all our suppliers and consultants – companies like

Ecclestone allegedly told Carman: "He [Briatore] is guilty, that's decided. We're not looking for any change to the verdict. All that's left is the press release."
Photo: Habeed Hameed

Mosley (pictured in 1969): "The suggestion that we were lenient [at the fuel fire hearing] in the interests of the sport is incorrect, though. We were lenient because the facts in front of us drove us to be lenient."
Photo: Raimund Kommer

Intertechnique and the computer people at LDRA – will sign a contract requiring them to speak exclusively to the FIA, not to the individual teams or to the press.

That way, at least we will know exactly what has passed, and if anyone claims to have been told something, we will be able to disprove it. We also need, as I mentioned, a clear understanding with the teams that the top man is responsible, whether he knows or not. It will be up to him to know. We will also require the teams to ask us first about all technical matters where there might be any doubt or where the rules are unclear. That avoids these doubts.

But we failed to do that before all of this. It wasn't clear. And it is difficult, particularly when part of the fault was ours, as it was in this case, then to condemn people. Sometimes you have to admit that you didn't do something quite right and that you will do it correctly from this point on. Who knows? Maybe Benetton and McLaren were a bit lucky. But now the luck has run out – it has stopped. There won't be any excuse next time, or at least they're going to have to be extremely ingenious if they are to find an excuse.

Q. It comes across as a bit of a whitewash in a fairly boneless organisation. You didn't have to throw Benetton out of the championship but you could have applied any of a series of penalties, including throwing out individual employees. Yet nothing was done. Why?

Mosley: Firstly, we don't have any power to throw out individual employees for life. We had a look and we don't have such a power. If you go back a week or so, the theme was that I in particular, or the FIA in general, had a vendetta against Briatore. Now, the suggestion is that we have gone too far the other way. I certainly didn't have a vendetta and I don't think we've gone too far the other way.

Chapter 10

A scale of penalties undoubtedly exists, but you sit there given all the facts and wonder what is appropriate. If you believe that they were misled and that it was done at a certain level in the company and compare it with Silverstone [the black flag incident] where there was an apparent deliberate failure to follow the instructions of the stewards at all levels at the top of the team. It is different. If you accept what George Carman said, it wouldn't be appropriate to fine them US$1million and when you go all the way down you ask "why bother".

Q: Is that not a shocking precedent?
Mosley: I don't think it is a precedent. What we have said is that we are going to have to start from now on the assumption that everyone in the team knows what is going on. If they have any doubt about anything they must ask us.

Q: Didn't Intertechnique put out a statement on 11 August saying that a request to remove the filter would have been refused?
Mosley: It's a valid point, but before one can criticise Intertechnique, one would really like to ask them what was going on. That we have not yet done.

Mosley's autobiography referred to the fuel filter case: "Benetton got away with it [just] so far as we were concerned by claiming that a junior employee had removed the filter and that someone from the fuel rig manufacturer had given permission for this. To our considerable surprise, a representative from the fuel rig manufacture had confirmed the story." Therefore instrumental in saving Benetton was the Larrousse letter. Some believed it didn't constitute permission to remove the filter instead, it along with the drawings, merely provided an explanation what to do if the filter was removed. However, two people who saw the correspondence, Mosley and Morley, appear to disagree based on the above.

Questions were then asked about the links between Benetton and Larrousse, and exactly why the latter came to the aid of the former during the hearing? Could it have anything to do with Benetton

The Larrousse permission to remove their fuel filter seemed to contradict Intertechnique's own statement on 11 August stating that any such request would have been refused. **Photo: Martin Lee**

supplying gearboxes to Larrousse in 1994? The relationship between the two was borne out of necessity because in late 1993 Larrousse was dreaming of Peugeot engines for the following season. However, Peugeot joined McLaren which in turn drove Larrousse's 1993 engine supplier, Lamborghini, out of F1 after becoming dismayed from McLaren's rejection. Larrousse was therefore left with no choice but to purchase customer Ford engines for 1994.

In 1993, Lamborghini had provided Larrousse with the electronic systems that made the engine and gearbox work in harmony. Also, Larrousse was one of the few teams still using an old stick shift gearbox rather than a paddleshift. So they couldn't simply bolt in the new-for-1994 customer Ford engine and have everything work straight away. Because their engine switch was confirmed at a late stage (15 December), Larrousse had no alternative other than to buy Benetton's 1993 gearbox as that was guaranteed to work with their customer Ford engines.[130] There simply was no time for Larrousse to develop its own gearbox and associated electronics.

Consequently, Larrousse's 1994 challenger went from concept to car in a record 80 days. In reality, it was only a modified version of their 1993 chassis, re-engineered to fit the smaller Ford V8 and modified for refuelling. But could their association with Benetton have been the impetus for Larrousse sending the letter and drawings which saved the Enstone team during the fuel filter hearing? Unlikely seems to be the answer because Larrousse had not come to Benetton's rescue during any of their previous allegations/hearings.

Moreover, there were several times during 1994 races when a Larrousse was distinctly unhelpful to a Benetton when being lapped. One example was Monaco when the Larrousse of Beretta held up Schumacher, the race leader, for several laps. Similarly, during the Hungarian race, Verstappen was held up by Beretta on lap 43 prompting Eurosport commentator, John Watson, to have a James Hunt style rant about it. If Benetton had influence over Larrousse, then it is unlikely these incidents would have occurred.

Although both Benetton and Larrousse used Ford engines for 1994, Larrousse was merely a customer of Ford (like Arrows, Minardi and Simtek), so it is doubtful Benetton could pull special

Did Ligier and Larrousse also remove their fuel filter? **Photo: Martin Lee**

Larrousse used Benetton gearboxes during 1994 and both had Ford engines. Is this why they came to the aid of Benetton during the fuel filter hearing?
Photo: Martin Lee

favours from them via their Ford relationship either. Particularly as a fortnight before the fuel fire hearing Benetton announced they were ditching Ford engines for 1995 in favour of Renaults. McLaren supplied Footwork with electronic assistance in 1993, while Williams supplied Ligier with gearboxes that same year, so the Benetton/Larrousse deal wasn't uncommon at the time. Furthermore, at the time of the fuel filter hearing Larrousse was so short of money it was rotating unrated pay-drivers in order to continue racing. In the midst of this fight for survival, it is questionable how high saving Benetton would be on Larrousse's priority list.

Interestingly, few cared whether Larrousse or Ligier also removed their fuel filter like Benetton. According to Morley "Larrousse obviously removed their fuel filter, how many other teams got wind of this through the grapevine and subsequently removed their filters? I guess we will never know!" However, there was no subsequent FIA hearing into them or Ligier and it seems things were quietly forgotten. At the time, one of Larrousse's co-directors was Robin Herd, who established March Engineering with Mosley and two others in 1969. Herd and Mosley worked together until 1977, and weeks after the fuel fire hearing Mosley attended a party to celebrate the 25th anniversary of March being founded, which was hosted by Herd.

Interestingly, Williams received an official reprimand from the FIA in 1994 for modifying its refuelling equipment to make it safer. During the Italian Grand Prix weekend, Patrick Head admitted his

Benetton mechanics felt their victories were being unfairly tarnished by the constant allegations. *Photo: Pete Hennessy*

team revised the fuel coupling on the FW16 to prevent the seals from leaking due to vibration from the car's engine. "I do remember that the fuel couplings leaked fuel when the car was about three-quarters full or more," said Paul West of Williams. "I don't think it was a large amount it just used to leave streaks on the side of the car... I think that at the start of the year the coupling was in the car from the start of practice but once we had this leaking problem we used to run a blanking cover and only fitted the coupling for the race."

Because no solution had been forthcoming from Intertechnique, Williams asked if they could manufacture a certain part to cure this problem. Intertechnique faxed Williams giving both its and the FIA's authorisation to do so. However Head said, "It seems the mistake we made wasn't to have it on FIA headed paper."[131] Williams first ran the revised part at Montreal until it was replaced by an Intertechnique manufactured component which was identical. Benetton's Joan Villadelprat added "Benetton internally may have had reports in Canada that they [Williams] were modifying the fuel coupling to improve things, but the truth is that many teams had problems with hoses at the [pit] stops and that could be seen on TV."

Returning to the 7 September hearing, the FIA was not quite as lenient towards Benetton in its other case: the appeal against Schumacher's Belgian Grand Prix disqualification. The previous chapter detailed Schumacher's plank being excessively worn, which is normally against the rules hence the disqualification. However, Benetton appealed because they were convinced the excessive wear was due to Schumacher spinning across the kerbs during the race. If Benetton could successfully prove the plank wear was due to accident damage, Schumacher would keep his Belgian Grand Prix victory. During the appeal, Benetton showed photographic evidence that the kerb Schumacher spun over wasn't flat, as had been claimed by the Clerk of the Course previously. Benetton's photos showed the kerbs were serrated and around four inches high – well in excess of the suspension travel of an F1 car.

130. The same specification as Benetton's pre-Silverstone 1993 engine
131. *Autosport*, 15 September 1994

Benetton also produced Schumacher's telemetry readout during the spin. It showed the rear wheels were lifted off the ground and hanging in the air as the plank underneath the car scraped across the kerb. Consequently, the front of the B194 was pushed into the tarmac and Benetton's telemetry showed the front suspension was subjected to compression in excess of full load as the back of the car hung in the air. Benetton felt this explained why the plank was excessively worn over an isolated area at the front (underneath the driver), whilst there were also gouge marks along its back (by the rear wheels). In other words, both ends of the plank had been damaged because of the way the car bounced back onto the tarmac during the spin.

Despite the above, the FIA maintained the excessive wear at the front of the plank was nothing to do with the spin. They believed its appearance was consistent with rubbing away rather than a one-off incident. In his book, *Life in the Fast Lane*, Steve Matchett disagreed, instead arguing the wear pattern didn't correspond with normal running on track. Nevertheless, the FIA upheld Schumacher's Belgian disqualification, but acknowledged the rear damage on the plank was due to Schumacher's spin. The subsequent FIA press release was quick to point out that it didn't feel Benetton intended to cheat at Belgium, instead, the infringement was an honest mistake as Benetton incorrectly guessed its ride height. Perhaps George Carman's presence might have prompted that clarification?

Joan Villadelprat added: "At Spa, there was a lot of talk about Schumacher but very little about Coulthard's loose rear wing. Since it could have caused an accident or be considered a movable aerodynamic device [not allowed in F1] to get less drag on the straights. But it was more important or it was more relevant to the FIA to focus on Benetton's problem with the plank."

"Benetton was angry about the continued sanctions and, because of that, a team member found a picture of the plank wear in one of the trucks and leaked it to the press to show the spin was the cause of the wear. The car was inspected and measured for quite some time by the FIA and was eventually disqualified." Villadelprat added: "Benetton used a higher rake on the car so would rarely get any wear on the rear of their plank. "This contradicts the images of scratches and scrapes at the rear of the plank (see Fig 7) indicating it was caused by spin damage."

Every Benetton interviewee I spoke to insisted the Spa disqualification was a peculiar decision, but they simply had no choice but to accept it. Would they have been given the benefit of doubt, were it not for the other allegations? It's an interesting thought to ponder, as is whether Hill would have been disqualified had it been his plank, and the exclusion would have effectively ended the Englishman's championship chances? At least Benetton was able to split the taxi fare to the airport with McLaren who were at the FIA headquarters defending their automatic gearbox facility from accusations of being a driver aid.

The McLaren gearbox case was unusual, since it exploited some ambiguity within the rules regarding gear selection. Article 9.2 of the technical regulations stated: "Semi-automatic gearboxes driven by automatic control are permitted and may, for the purpose of changing a gear ratio only, momentarily take control of the propulsion system away from the driver."[132] McLaren's gearbox used a questionable method of gear pre-selection: the driver still pressed the lever to change gear, but the car essentially optimised the gear shift.

It was particularly useful when downshifting, because it stopped the driver from doing this too quickly as the change wouldn't occur until a certain rpm threshold was reached. This, in theory, gave

McLaren escaped punishment for having exploited ambiguity within the gearbox rules. The FIA closed off this loophole afterwards. *Photo: Alastair Ladd*

Alliot told reporters the Larrousse gearbox wasn't as automatic as the McLaren's, which prompted the FIA investigation. **Photo: Károly Méhes**

McLaren drivers an advantage in braking zones, since its system maximised engine braking while eliminating any risk of locking the rear wheels. Technically, it was still a semi-automatic gearbox since the driver activated the lever to shift gears. But the mechanism itself was clearly intended to be an electronic driver assist by automating the process of shifting gears at the ideal time.

At the hearing the FIA ruled this was a 'driver aid' and, despite clear evidence McLaren used it during the San Marino Grand Prix (unlike the Benetton launch control case), the FIA didn't punish them. Because the FIA accepted McLaren had not intended to cheat, they merely interpreted the rules differently: the same verdict as the Ferrari Aida case. Following the McLaren case, a rule clarification was immediately sent to teams declaring these upchange facilities had to be removed prior to the Italian Grand Prix, while downchange systems had to be removed before the Portuguese Grand Prix. McLaren boss, Ron Dennis, revealed: "I'd say nearly 50 percent (of the grid) had upshift facilities and ran them up until the Italian Grand Prix. Three of those teams approached us before the hearing and offered to attend it and state that they were using similar systems. It was surprising because two were prominent teams who had something to lose."[133]

Months later, Mosley shed more light on the verdict during an interview: "In McLaren's case we had not clearly told them that an automatic upchange was outside the rules. In our minds, it was obviously outside."[134] Mosley also stated the regulations were clarified as a result of this, so teams now had to ask the FIA about any technical matters where either doubt existed or the rules were unclear. "We've now, I think, nailed it down so it starts to be very difficult [to use McLaren's excuse], but it was only really at Monza," said the FIA president. When referring to the Benetton fuel filter and McLaren gearbox cases elsewhere, Mosley commented "...here we had a situation where some teams had done things that were dubious, but it was difficult to prove they had cheated. So although we were criticised for not imposing harsher penalties, I believe we acted fairly in the circumstances."

Following the hearing, McLaren was also fined US$100,000 for failing to release its black box source codes when the FIA initially requested them. Like Benetton, McLaren claimed the reason for this delay was confidentially clauses with its external engine supplier (Peugeot). The FIA's subsequent press release stated: "The World Council recognised that the delay wasn't due to any intention by McLaren deliberately to conceal any feature in its software." Out of the three teams which had their black boxes examined after Imola, McLaren was the last to hand over its source codes.

Fig 7. The leaked photo of Schumacher's plank. Officials argued the wear closest to the camera was light and longitudinal so not consistent with a one-off incident. However they accepted the gouges furthest from camera was caused by Schumacher's spin. **Photo: Motorsport Images/LAT**

During their investigation into McLaren's gearbox, LDRA (the FIA's IT experts) discovered a fault which they claimed was producing a power loss with their engine. They advised McLaren accordingly which was thoroughly decent of them, and after this software bug was highlighted McLaren's reliability seemly improved. Indeed, they then scored podium finishes in all the remaining races of 1994, except Japan. Afterwards, Ron Dennis asserted: "I think the message, and it is positively taken, is that the FIA was trying to convey to the team is: we do have the capability of understanding your software."

The implication being LDRA understood team's software better than anyone, thereby suggesting teams were playing with fire if anything illegal was contained within it. The McLaren verdict was largely forgotten because their hearing was on the same day as the Benetton fuel filter case. In the fuss over Benetton escaping punishment, few cared about the McLaren ruling. Would this now spell an end to all the controversy in 1994? No chance.

132. 1994 Formula One technical regulations
133. *Autosport*, 15 September 1994
134. *Motor Sport*, February 1995

ITALY AND PORTUGAL

September 1994

"I'm surprised I couldn't go any quicker and I really don't know what to say, I'm suffering from a lack of testing."

JJ Lehto, Benetton driver

"In truth, there was little sign of the flair [from Lehto] we once took for granted."

Nigel Roebuck, Autosport journalist

Lehto qualified in 20th at Monza. Was that because Schumacher's chassis had been not made available to him. ***Photo: Alastair Ladd***

Standings before the 1994 Italian Grand Prix

DRIVERS' CHAMPIONSHIP			CONSTRUCTORS' CHAMPIONSHIP		
Pos	Driver	Points	Pos	Constructor	Points
1	Michael Schumacher	76	1	Benetton-Ford	85
2	Damon Hill	55	2	Williams-Renault	62
3	Gerhard Berger	27	3	Ferrari	52

Monza mainly consisted of straights which did not suit Benetton's Ford V8 engine. **Photo: Fabio Alessandro Locati**

With painful memories of Imola still fresh in everyone's mind, F1 made its return to the country of that tragic race. However, the Italian Grand Prix almost didn't happen in 1994. In the wake of Imola, several circuits needed improvements to their safety facilities which included extending run-off areas. At Monza, home of the Italian Grand Prix, this meant having to cut down a number of trees which local ecologists and politicians objected to on environmental grounds. The FIA called their bluff and cancelled the race as a result. However, the event was eventually saved by the intervention of Italian Prime Minister Silvio Berlusconi. Restoring the event at the eleventh hour did mean some safety improvements requested by the Grand Prix Drivers' Association (GPDA) were ignored for that year's race. The weekend itself saw more safety concerns and Benetton really struggling without Schumacher, who was now serving his two-race ban.

This latter point would be of interest to conspiracy theorists because Schumacher's car wasn't made available to either the returning Lehto (Schumacher's replacement) or Verstappen at Monza. Interestingly the two Benettons looked like mid-field runners throughout the weekend, whereas Schumacher had dominated races. Observers soon wondered why. Moreover, Monza is considered a 'car track' so driver skill (or the lack of it) shouldn't make a significant difference to lap time. Conspiracy theorists, therefore, felt this was evidence Benetton had been running illegal driver aids in Schumacher's car all along. Why else would they be so off the pace and make a special effort to keep Schumacher's car back at the factory? According to Benetton, it was because Schumacher's was the newest chassis the team had available, having only raced in Hungary and Belgium.

They claimed newer tubs were preferable as they were stiffer and more consistent, so easier to set up. Thus Benetton wanted to save its freshest chassis (08) for Schumacher's return. Sound logic, saving the best equipment for the driver fighting for the championship. But did it matter if the team kept chassis 08 at the factory because surely any illegal driver aids (if used) could have been installed into those tubs at Monza. The chassis is only the car's structure, so the engine and its black boxes were bolted onto them afterwards.

Benetton didn't make any more chassis after 08 because, by this stage, the focus for every team was their 1995 cars. Major modifications enforced in the name of safety meant the following year's cars required a significant amount of work by teams. Benetton also had to integrate a new engine (the Renault V10) into its 1995 car, which added to their workload. Hence why the team had to manage its existing allocation of 1994 chassis even though they were in short supply. Matters had not been helped by Verstappen writing off two tubs early in their respective lifespans. One was destroyed after the multi-car pile-up at Brazil, while another was written-off by Verstappen's qualifying crash in France having done a mere 126 miles (203km) of running.

Benetton's remaining usable chassis needed to do up to 25 percent more mileage than anticipated in order to compensate for these losses. Because they were not in contention for the championship, Lehto and Verstappen were understandably forced to use older tubs during their remaining races with the team. In addition, another chassis (03) had to be forced out of retirement in order to make up the emergency spare car at Monza. Higher mileage chassis also lose their rigidity thus making their aerodynamics less consistent, which in turn can create handling problems. Furthermore, they inevitably take knocks during events by running over kerbs etc which require ongoing repairs.

For example, Verstappen damaged his original race chassis during Friday at Monza by running over a kerb, meaning the team had to make overnight repairs to keep it running for Saturday. Willem Toet, Benetton's Head of Aerodynamics, explained: "The main problem with a repaired chassis was weight. If a chassis was damaged, weight had to be added to repair the damaged areas. The team would always try to repair damage as best they could (secure repair for the minimum added weight)." Keeping the weight down was critical to a quick lap time.

Verstappen had never been to Monza and, in addition to learning the track, he was effectively leading the Benetton team. While Lehto had only done three days of F1 testing since his last race three months ago, and part of that was in a Ligier. Not only was Lehto rusty but like Verstappen at Hockenheim, the Finn struggled with the lack of grip the Benetton offered in low downforce configuration. The reduced diffusers and raised floors, imposed on teams since Hockenheim, had eroded Benetton's early season advantage.

In Lehto's case, he qualified in 20th position and there was another reason for his lack of speed. According to Toet, "after Monaco [where Wendlinger was knocked out – and the events of Imola] JJ [Lehto] never gave races a full 100 percent in the opinion of the team. JJ's girlfriend was pregnant with their first child (I remember this from being at Monaco) and he just wasn't going to risk 100 percent anymore. He didn't find the full limit of the car." Lehto's first child, Julia, was delivered on the morning of the race at Monza. Cynics might say many racing drivers have had children without it adversely affecting their speed, so why was Lehto any different? To understand the answer, we must consider what happened to him fifteen months prior.

An earlier chapter mentioned that Lehto witnessed the death of his good friend Evan Demoulas immediately after the 1993 Canadian

Grand Prix. The two drove back from the circuit to downtown Montreal in convoy only for someone to run a red light and smash into Demoulas's vehicle, killing him at the scene. The two friends were actually going to meet Evan's pregnant wife, and it was left to Lehto to break the awful news to her.[135] Afterwards, Lehto retained contact with Evan Demoulas' widow and family, so would have seen the child grow up without her dad.

Lehto's girlfriend then became pregnant only days before he suffered his near-fatal accident at Silverstone on 21 January. So one can imagine thoughts of not wanting his unborn child to grow up without him would have been in Lehto's head as he laid in hospital recovering, especially after seeing first-hand what happened to Evan's widow and child seven months prior. "I've never thought about how far I could have got had I not had the [Silverstone testing] accident," said the Finn. "You could have the same accident again and wind up dead, so I feel lucky."[136]

This, combined with all the other F1 tragedies occurring throughout 1994 and Lehto's closeness to Ratzenberger and Wendlinger (his 1993 teammate), must have affected his subsequent approach. Furthermore, many believed the ensuing safety car at Imola played a part in Senna's fatal crash, which Lehto's stall prompted. This is not to suggest Lehto was in anyway responsible for Senna's accident, but perhaps the Finn was burdened by some kind of guilt afterwards?

All this, together with an apparent fallout with Benetton's management, may explain why Lehto allegedly was no longer willing to give 100 percent at the team anymore. If you do believe Lehto and Verstappen were not given the same illegal traction control that Schumacher was afforded, hence their lack of pace at Italy, then ask yourself how much lap time gain would you expect from a concealed traction control at Monza? The circuit is primarily made up of long straights, and there are only three corners where traction control might benefit a driver.

Despite being an Italian company, the locals enjoyed seeing Benetton struggle because they only had eyes for one team. The Tifosi are passionate about Ferrari, and they came to Monza fully expecting to see their first win on home soil since 1988. Unlike the British based teams, Ferrari had an extra advantage at their home track, the week before the race they had been testing at Monza for days honing their cars' set-ups and reliability.

After qualifying, it seemed their extensive efforts paid off as Alesi claimed his first ever pole position after five years in F1. How the Tifosi loved it! Hill promised "to spoil the party" from third on the grid. Race day didn't begin well for Ferrari as Berger crashed heavily during the morning warm-up because he forgot the car was full of fuel. It was a major crash which Berger was lucky to escape relatively unharmed, however what happened next alarmed observers.

Race officials showed their ineptitude by treating Berger in the run-off area close to where he crashed rather than moving him to a position of safety first. The approach to that section of track was 200mph, and race stewards felt it unnecessary to stop the session whilst Berger was receiving medical attention. "I don't know who was responsible for allowing that to happen," said Berger afterwards, "but I don't think it was acceptable. If they'd moved me

Alesi headed an all-Ferrari front row for the first time in Italy since 1975.
Photo: Károly Méhes

Portugal was Coulthard's final race in 1994. The Williams had now become the best car and was closing the points deficit to Benetton. ***Photo: Martin Lee***

behind the barrier, OK, carry on with the session – but not when I'm lying there in the run-off area with other people all around me, can you imagine if someone had a brake failure?"[137]

Almost 10 minutes later, the session was eventually stopped to allow the ambulance carrying Berger back onto the track. Reportedly the Clerk of the Course was 82 years old. It was ironic these questionable practices should occur in Italy not only because of the fierce debate surrounding the circuit's safety prior to the event, but also the Italian courts were looking to prosecute key Williams team members over the death of Senna, following his fatal crash at Imola.

Fortunately, Berger was fit enough to race, albeit in the spare Ferrari which had a less powerful engine than his now destroyed race car. During the grand prix, Alesi in the other Ferrari suffered a mechanical failure, robbing him of a fairy tale first win. The French-Sicilian was so furious he stormed straight out of the Ferrari garage, jumped into his road car and set off for his hometown of Avignon at breakneck speed. After half an hour, Jean's brother and only passenger during this legendary journey suggested if the car was going to maintain its current speed then he no longer wished to travel in it.

On the subject of luckless drivers and teams, Johnny Herbert and Lotus also fell into that category at Monza. Lotus had been on the brink of financial crisis all season long, while Herbert had been demoralised by how badly the car had performed. However, they had a new engine especially for this race, gifting both a real chance of scoring a podium for the first time in years. Reputedly such a result would have secured them more financial support thereby saving Lotus from financial collapse. Off the start, Herbert passed Hill and was eyeing up second position into the first corner, when he was rammed from behind by Irvine. This caused chaos at the first corner and forced the race to be restarted. Unfortunately for Herbert and Lotus, they had to take the restart from the pitlane and in a car with an older specification engine. Had it not been for that incident, Herbert claimed he would have won the Italian Grand Prix.

Having received a three-race ban for the pile-up at Brazil, Irvine must have been relieved to have only been sent to the back of the

grid for his Monza start misdemeanour. Perhaps he successfully blamed his rash move on a 'junior employee'. Lotus team boss, Peter Collins, was furious over the lack of serious punishment towards Irvine, because the incident was effectively the last nail in Lotus's coffin and the team officially went into administration the following day. The original Team Lotus, which carries so much affection for F1 fans, folded before the 1995 season.

These problems, along with a slow pitstop for Berger, gifted the victory to Hill who exploited a golden opportunity to cut into Schumacher's championship lead. Hill also asserted his authority within Williams that weekend. Because he demanded David Brown, the engineer who assisted Mansell and Prost to their championships, worked on his car rather than Coulthard's. It was a clever move by Hill, because Mansell was due to return to Williams for the final three races of 1994 and Brown had a special relationship with Nigel from 1992. So Hill's move helped ensure Mansell wouldn't outperform him upon his return. There had been concern whether Mansell would help or hinder Hill's title chances because Nigel needed to win races to improve his chances of securing the 1995 Williams drive.

Throughout his enforced absence, Schumacher stayed away from races, preferring to spend his time fitness training instead. As a result, the media speculated about his future with Benetton, particularly as the various allegations had tarnished Schumacher's name. His manager took advantage by renegotiating Schumacher's contract with the team on more favourable financial terms. He managed to double his retainer while ensuring Schumacher's Benetton contract ended by 1996, a year earlier than originally planned. This proved a masterstroke because it allowed Schumacher to double his salary again when he joined Ferrari. These successful contract renegotiations followed public comments made by Schumacher's manager about his client's status being undermined by the 1994 allegations, so he needed to be compensated accordingly.

The next race, in Portugal, was one Ferrari came close to withdrawing from following an altercation with officials. At around 10pm on the Friday evening, some mechanics tried leaving the circuit following a long day, Andrew Reedie explained what happened. "It was a late night for us at Pacific and for Ferrari too. The hire cars were parked outside the track behind the pit straight stand. Three of us had gone to wash up and so we were a few minutes later than the rest of the boys leaving. We walked through the tunnel under the track as the track staff closed the gates. We had an argument with them but they refused to open the gate again. With that, the Ferrari boys arrived and it all got a bit Italian. Realising we were going to get nowhere and worried we would get left behind, we started to go back when the boys in red started kicking the doors in.

"Then the police arrived and they have guns so we legged it and ran across the track and jumped the fence. The Ferrari lads broke the gate down and streamed out of the tunnel. The next day all hell broke loose but we just denied everything even though we started the argument. That's when the fine was handed down after an investigation." For breaking down a locked door, Ferrari was fined $50,000. In addition, Ferrari would be banned from a race should a similar incident occur during a subsequent event. If you are beginning to wonder whether the sport lost its marbles in 1994, you wouldn't be alone. Ferrari was livid at the excessiveness of this penalty for something they described as an "insignificant incident".

The Italian team's anger was evident within its subsequent press release. "Ferrari has been subjected to a ridiculous and unacceptable penalty by the stewards of the Portuguese Grand Prix. An appeal has already been lodged against the decision, but in the meantime, Ferrari would point out that the stewards' action definitely shows a total lack of credibility and seriousness

Panis was disqualified from Portugal for an excessively worn plank. It was the second breach of this newly introduced rule in four races.
Photo: Alastair Ladd

in Formula 1, which has been evident since the start of the season. The right thing to do would be to withdraw its drivers and cars from the event and return immediately to Maranello. Ferrari will not do this only out of respect for its motorsport enthusiasts around the world."[138]

F1 News joked the FIA might have been more lenient if Ferrari had blamed the incident on a 'junior employee', or produced a letter from the door manufacturer showing drawings of how to kick the door down. Ferrari eventually withdrew its appeal in the "interests of F1" and raced at Portugal with Berger achieving their third pole position of the season. However, both scarlet cars retired from the race, thus paving the way for Hill to claim another crucial victory

The rubbing strips and predetermined measuring holes (indicated by the red arrows) which were used to measure plank wear after Portugal 1994.
Photo: Morio

Paul Tracy (pictured in 1991) tested the Benetton and was 2.5sec slower than Schumacher. He later alluded to why Schumacher was so quick.
Photo: Stuart Seeger

to bring him within a point of Schumacher. With the German returning for the next race, the stage was set for a rousing climax between the championship contenders.

According to *F1 News*, Hill crept forward on his grid slot while the red lights were still on, an offence that should have seen a 10sec stop-go penalty handed out during the race. Had the stewards applied this then Hill would have likely finished in third rather than first, meaning he would have left Portugal with a seven-point deficit to Schumacher, a difference which in view of later events would have been significant. After Panis escaped punishment for his apparent jump start in Hungary, Mosley had promised electronic light beams would be installed by Portugal. Such technology would have detected Hill's misdemeanour and immediately flagged it to stewards. Ironically, they were not installed in Portugal and luckily for Hill, he remained unpunished which was convenient for the championship climax. Hill later admitted: "I crept a little bit up to the line where the front wheels should be, but I didn't actually manage to go over it!"[139] Interestingly, the sensors installed for 1995 would have detected this as a jumpstart.

Ligier once again finished a race with an excessively worn plank, this time it was Panis's car and there had been no reason to claim accident damage so the Frenchman was disqualified from ninth. Since Schumacher's controversial Belgium disqualification for the same offence, the majority of teams had wanted to amend this rule. Ron Dennis summed up the problem: "It's unfair to place on the technical delegate a responsibility for interpreting a rule that in some areas is grey."[140] One of the problems the teams were finding was the edges of the planks were grinding on the ground under braking and acceleration, causing it to wear. This is because under such conditions the *g* forces involved were in excess of 5*g* meaning plank movement and distortion was significant.

Teams discussed introducing a technical innovation onto the plank which would clarify matters. This was introduced in Japan (a few weeks after Portugal) after extensive testing. In addition, new plank measuring techniques were introduced for 1995 whereby a depth gauge was used to determine the wear by six holes set at pre-determined points. On the basis of these rules, it is thought unlikely Schumacher would have been disqualified at Belgium. Since Portugal 1994, no violations against the plank rule have been upheld after appeal, despite the rule still being in existence 25 years later, meaning Schumacher after Belgium 1994 remains the only driver to have lost points over it, despite others having finished races with excessively worn planks since.

In Portugal, Benetton once again struggled with Lehto qualifying a distant 14th before spinning out of the race, the Finn having complained of set-up issues all weekend. Recently, Lehto admitted that in 1994 he never fully recovered from his neck breaking pre-season accident: "When I came back I was sick and in pain: Flavio [Benetton's boss] didn't give me any testing, so I cannot say the car was so different I couldn't drive it. Truth is, I never got the chance. I did some races after the accident but I was in so much pain I couldn't drive."[141] Unsurprisingly, Benetton dropped Lehto after this race due to him under performing. Lehto then realised his neck injury spelt the end of his F1 career and, after 1994, drove less physically demanding cars. He later admitted Le Mans 1995 was "the first time I felt 100 per cent again after the accident."[142] That was more than a year after his F1 comeback.

138. *Autosport*, 29 September 1994
139. *F1 News*, 5 October 1994
140. *Autosport*, 29 September 1994
141. *Motor Sport*, April 2017
142. *Autosport*, 7 August 2014

Chapter 11

Verstappen fared better in Portugal, qualifying in his average spot of 10th before finishing the race in fifth. Once again, the two Benetton drivers chassis were not the best available because the team was understandably saving the freshest equipment for Schumacher's title challenge. Their freshest tub, chassis 08, was however used as the spare car in Portugal. Proving the team would run either Lehto or Verstappen in it should the circumstances have arisen. It also demonstrated how low Benetton was on useable tubs because they had hoped to save chassis 08 for Schumacher's return.

Benetton's lack of pace since Italy prompted some to wonder whether Lehto and Verstappen were really that bad. Or was the performance of the B194 adversely affected by the recent rule implemented in Italy demanding no traces of driver aids (redundant or otherwise) were left within the black boxes? In other words, had Benetton somehow circumvented the rules prior to Italy, and now they were forced to play fairly their car didn't look so competitive. Interested observers didn't have to wait long to find out because two days after the Portuguese Grand Prix, the circuit hosted a major F1 testing session involving many teams. It was also Schumacher's first time back in the Benetton since Belgium.

Within seven laps of the first morning of testing, Schumacher lapped within 0.1sec of Berger's pole position time. Verstappen immediately lapped 0.65sec quicker than he had throughout the race weekend. It would have put Verstappen fifth on the Portuguese Grand Prix grid, and the Dutchman ended the test with an even quicker time. Indycar star, Paul Tracy, was also in the Benetton. Bernie Ecclestone organised the test and helped Tracy overcome some legal wrangling involving Briatore who had tried to tie Tracy into a long-term contract before allowing him in the car.

Autosport covered Tracy's Benetton test at Estoril in detail, including transcribing all the in-car radio communication between him and Benetton during the first full day. At one point during a run, Tracy complained of wheelspin when the tyres started degrading, which wouldn't have been possible had illegal traction control been used. Afterwards, Tracy described the car as being on a 'knife-edge' compared to Indycars. "Having confidence in what the car will do is the tough thing," insisted the Canadian. "Schumacher is killing me on speed through turn two and Verstappen is quicker too, although there's not much in it. The car didn't feel too comfortable through there, and I know there is a lot more to come."[143]

Turn two in Portugal is extremely fast and Tracy's comments about confidence echo those of John Watson and David Coulthard during Eurosport's coverage of Friday's qualifying session at the French Grand Prix. In his commentary, Watson revealed he was at a recent Silverstone test involving most teams and what impressed him about Schumacher was his confidence to go through fast corners like Becketts completely flat when other drivers were lifting the accelerator. "What he is doing is understanding how to make the car work best," Watson sais. "He uses a lot of left-foot braking. He keeps the attitude of the car as constant as possible. For other people who come into Becketts and come off the throttle, they induce minor amounts of pitch change. How do you [have the confidence to] make yourself do what he's doing?"

When asked if he left-foot braked Coulthard responded: "I slight left-foot brake in the first part of the corner. But unlike Michael I'm not able to go flat into the second part, I need to

Schumacher, unlike many of his peers, had the confidence to utilise left-foot braking according to Eurosport commentator John Watson.
Photo: Ford

Dernie (middle) revealed: "Michael also used a smooth transition from throttle to brake to minimise the aero effect of pitch change."
Photo: Antony John Dennis

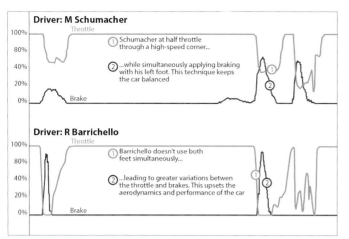

Fig 8. Schumacher's telemetry shows him using the throttle and brake simultaneously to balance the car... *Image: www.neilwhitedesign.co.uk*

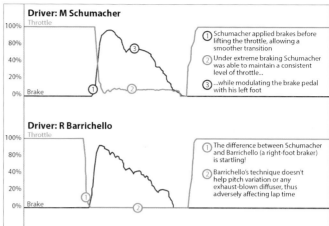

Fig 9. ...while his teammate Rubens Barrichello has a more traditional driving style. *Image: www.neilwhitedesign.co.uk*

change down [gear] for that part. At high speed [staying flat] it's a very useful way of keeping the flat bottom of the car, which is the most sensitive part of the car, as consistent as possible." Reducing pitch change and keeping the floor of the car as stable as possible not only to maximises its aerodynamics, but it also keeps the handling balance consistent, which in turn inspires confidence in the driver resulting in them performing better.

In 2004, telemetry traces were published of Schumacher's driving style against Barrichello. These traces looked similar to Figs 8 and 9.

The traces showed Schumacher simultaneously using the throttle and brakes to balance a car through a corner, compared to Barrichello (his 2000 to 2005 teammate) who used a more traditional style. Schumacher's precise driving enabled him to work to the car's strengths better than teammates, as demonstrated in Barcelona 1994 when he was stuck in fifth gear. Would Lehto or Verstappen have finished second given that gearbox problem? Schumacher also demonstrated his precise driving whenever there were changeable weather conditions during a race, for instance driving on slick tyres in wet conditions.

Moreover, Schumacher worked out what was needed to be successful and adapted himself accordingly. A case in point was the sprint style of driving in between pitstops required by the new refuelling era. Schumacher, therefore, ensured his fitness allowed him to consistently perform at a high level throughout races. Indeed, at the start of the year several magazines acknowledged the German as the fittest driver in F1, which proved a major benefit given the speed and unpredictability of the 1994 cars. Schumacher's rivals were slower on the uptake so their lap times during races proved more inconsistent as a result. A perfect illustration of this is during the 1994 French Grand Prix post-race press conference where Schumacher looked evidently fresher than either Hill or Berger. Hill later commented in his autobiography: "Having won the race, Michael got out of the car showing not a bead of sweat. That's when I began to think, 'This guy is different.'"

During Eurosport's coverage of the 1994 Portuguese Grand Prix warm-up, John Watson, a multiple race winner himself,

gave another example of Schumacher's driving exploiting the car better than teammates. Benetton ran an exhaust blown diffuser throughout 1994 which was a system of using the exhaust gases to interact with the diffuser to create additional grip. Watson explained how Schumacher's left-foot braking into corners, while maintaining some throttle ensured the exhaust blown diffuser produced additional grip for him. Watson claimed this element was a "considerable contribution to the downforce of the car...and the exhaust gases affected up to 70 percent of the rear downforce of a Jordan". The Eurosport commentator also believed Verstappen and Lehto were losing out by not having mastered this technique, which was another reason why they struggled in the B194.

Willem Toet explained that, unlike the 2011 to 2013 versions, the 1994 blown diffusers had not developed mechanical means to manage aero balance changes when off throttle. "Moves to manage exhaust airflow when off throttle started back then," Toet added. "Certainly, exhaust sensitivity was something we discussed a lot back then during the development of the car. Michael had a level of precision and repeatability [with the throttle] that other drivers I'd worked with couldn't match [except perhaps Ayrton]. That precision meant he could get close to the limit without overstepping the mark. Certainly applied to the exhausts."

An informed source confirmed the 1993 Benetton had an exhaust blown diffuser, but it wasn't fully utilised until 1994. Therefore, Schumacher would have had much greater experience at exploiting its benefits than either Lehto or Verstappen. This informed source added: "Blown diffusers are a part of the key to good rear stability and grip. When you get them right they are immense, but if the floor is not working correctly and air flow not attached well, it is worse than not blowing." Benetton was leading the way in this area during the mid-1990s as confirmed by Vincent Gaillardot of Renault.[144] Although Williams and Ferrari had their own versions, they placed their exhaust exits in an area which didn't maximise downforce but consequently was easier to handle for their drivers.

143. *Autosport*, 6 October 1994
144. *Sport Auto*

Chapter 11

Paul West, a Williams mechanic, believes they stopped experimenting with the exhaust blown diffuser in late 1995 because it made the car too nervous for their drivers. Similarly, Ferrari didn't use theirs at heavy braking circuits like Imola in 1995, because the larger the throttle movements the greater the fluctuations in downforce levels.[145] While Benetton's extreme version offered more downforce, consequently their drivers had to deal with a greater shift in the car's balance whenever the throttle was adjusted.[146] In 1995, Verstappen admitted "He [Schumacher] was unbelievable in fast corners and under braking. When I tried to drive the car like he did I had oversteer... My problem was that it was my first year and I didn't know how the car should feel, whereas now the Simtek is how I want it and I can play with it. Last year, I felt under pressure at Benetton and I was having to drive really hard just to get within a second or a second and a half of Michael. Maybe if I drove the car again now, I would be quicker."[147]

Recently Lehto admitted looking back on 1994, "Michael and I always had identical machinery. I never doubted that. His advantage came from his talent but also the fact the car was designed for him and his style of driving. He liked it edgy: it was quite strange to drive and I never really got the chance to get on top of it."[148] It's worth noting the majority of Lehto's and Verstappen's 1994 crashes occurred when the rear of the car broke away from them, rather than them understeering wide or braking too late and locking up tyres etc.

Schumacher appeared fresher than others while sitting in the post-race press conferences. **Photo: Károly Méhes**

Schumacher's other teammate during 1994, Johnny Herbert, declared: "I've tried to do what Michael does with our car but I just cannot. I've just had to come away from that and go my own way... One place Michael is very good is under braking..."[149] Mark Blundell added: "I think some of it would have been physicality because obviously Johnny had a huge accident in F3000 and that's one of the other issues with left-foot braking.

Benetton's 1995 exhausts blew under the central diffuser (yellow arrow) which offered more grip but made the car harder to drive compared to Williams' and Ferrari's solution (red arrow). **Photo: Morio**

Herbert: "I like to go into a corner braking and changing down, but Michael seems to be able to balance the car on the throttle and keep on the power".
Photo: Rick Dikeman

"If you're a right-foot braker, that's where your power output was on the brake pedal and you would use your left leg as a brace in the cockpit. To then try and achieve the same physical power output on the brake pedal using your left leg (while carrying some throttle with your right foot) and still get the right feel in modulating both pedals that's quite a difficult process to learn and your body's got to learn that as well." F1 drivers applied 930kg of (brake) pedal load per lap around the Montreal circuit and experienced up to 5g of force when decelerating.

Herbert admitted in 2016: "Everything was broken inside and the suppleness was gone [after his F3000 accident]. From then on everything I did had to be visual. Going into a corner, I wasn't relying on feel or sensation. I was looking at the speed instead. The other change was the pain. There was always pain there."[150] Similarly, during a recent podcast,[151] Martin Brundle cited his leg injuries sustained during the 1984 Dallas Grand Prix weekend as the reason he was unable to left-foot brake with any kind of finesse.

"So I was still right foot braking," Brundle admitted while acknowledging what a hindrance it was. Indeed, the Englishman's single-seater career was a perfect illustration. Brundle almost beat Senna to the Formula 3 title in apparently equal cars during 1983, and was the closest teammate Schumacher had in F1 when their 1992 Benetton had a three-pedal layout. However, in 1994 Hakkinen, a left-foot braker, annihilated Brundle when they were teammates in the two-pedal McLaren that year.

Over the course of their 15 races together, Hakkinen out-qualified Brundle by an average of 4.73 places per race. Whereas in 1992, Schumacher out qualified Martin by an average of 2.69 places per race. Brundle stated: "Then when I had to compete with Michael and Mika, it [right foot braking] was a hindrance because they could rotate the car into the slow corners and use their left foot on the brake and pick up the throttle and transfer between the two pedals in a way that I just couldn't do. So unfortunately that crash in Dallas was probably the key reason I underperformed [in F1]."[152]

At the post-Portuguese F1 test, Tracy matched Verstappen's best time, despite Tracy having no prior F1 experience and only spending two days within the Benetton. This supports the view Verstappen had not been extracting the most out of his Benetton, and perhaps the Dutchman's confidence had been eroded from all the accidents and poor results. Meanwhile, Schumacher was 2.5sec quicker than both Tracy and Verstappen and ended the test quickest overall. Schumacher and Hill were clearly engaged in psychological warfare throughout the test as they traded fastest laps. With Schumacher now back, and Hill buoyed by his recent wins, together with an ever-improving Williams, the fight for the championship between the two rivals was well and truly on. Before the next race, they tried out-psyching one another with public war of words. Things were about to get personal.

145. *Autosport*, 4 May 1995
146. *Autosport*, 11 May 1995
147. *Autosport*, 11 May 1995
148. *Motor Sport*, March 2017
149. *Autosport*, 11 May 1995
150. *The Telegraph*, 25 November 2016
151. *Beyond The Grid* podcast
152. *Beyond The Grid* podcast

EUROPE AND JAPAN

October 1994

"I do not have as much respect for him [Hill] as I do others. I wouldn't have been in this position if Ayrton had been alive. He would have driven circles around me. That doesn't say much for Hill."

Michael Schumacher, Benetton Driver

"I was surprised to hear some of the things Michael said about Damon because I know him well. The problem is the situation is tense and there are many pressures from the media, from everybody."

Alain Prost, 1993 F1 World Champion

Did Schumacher see this photo before making his outburst towards Hill? *Photo: Motorsport Images/LAT*

Standings before the 1994 European Grand Prix

DRIVERS' CHAMPIONSHIP		
Pos	Driver	Points
1	Michael Schumacher	76
2	Damon Hill	75
3	Gerhard Berger	33

CONSTRUCTORS' CHAMPIONSHIP		
Pos	Constructor	Points
1	Williams-Renault	89
2	Benetton-Ford	87
3	Ferrari	58

Was Schumacher lashing out after all the recent pain he'd endured? **Photo: Károly Méhes**

The press lapped up the F1 pantomime. Hill was portrayed as the good guy and Schumacher the villain. **Photo: Ann64**

Schumacher's scathing attack on his championship rival was just one of a number of comments he made during the build-up to the European Grand Prix. His comments were more than a contrived attempt at psychological warfare to undermine Hill; Schumacher was outraged to be level on points with someone who had not beaten him in a straight fight all year. To him, the FIA was manipulating the championship and he felt like a mere pawn sacrificed in a bigger political game. Despite being absolved of blame for the launch control and fuel filter allegations, Schumacher's image would forever be tarnished. The media quickly dubbed him F1's new villain. This, despite the brilliant driving Schumacher had shown which few gave him credit for precisely because of the rumours.

But, worst of all, Schumacher was deeply offended by his rival. "There were a lot of stories from Hill's direction about the 'cheating car' and that sort of thing," claimed the German. "Every time we proved that we never cheated, they twisted it around and said there was something else to answer. He always seemed the English gentleman but when you are in trouble you get to know people."[153] He'd earlier stated: "Other competitors, like Alesi, have always been fair. He could have said the same things as Damon, but he never did... I don't expect him to stand up for me, but I don't expect that somebody should make it worse than it already is. He would have been better saying nothing at all."[154]

Days after Schumacher's lighting start in France, Hill was quoted as saying the following in a national UK newspaper. "The Benetton seems to be able to go flat-out immediately and yet change direction without spinning its wheels under full power." These comments added to the rumours Schumacher's Benetton was assisted by illegal traction control. During an *Autosport* magazine interview, Hill remarked: "All I can say is since Magny-Cours his starts haven't been so good, have they? We have to be honest about that. He's made a lot of practice starts here in testing. I've seen smoke pouring off his tyres when he's been doing them and I never saw one bit of smoke in the first eight races of the season."[155]

When asked about Schumacher's Silverstone formation lap antics, Hill added "...he brought it on himself, that one."

Furthermore, Hill publicly accused Schumacher of being a bad sport for not handing over the winner's trophy after Belgium: it later transpired Williams had it all along. There were other examples of coded comments made by Hill towards Schumacher's recent plight.

Earlier in the year, Hill arranged a photo of him giving Schumacher two V-signs whilst the German drove past his Williams pits. Schumacher likely saw this before making made his outburst prior to Jerez (host of the European Grand Prix), which may partly explain it. Hill reacted coolly to the tirade against him: "I'd rather not drag the championship down by trying to diminish the reputation of the opposition. I think that's sad."[156] That was a PR masterstroke by Hill because it gave him the image of a gentleman driver being attacked by a ruthless competitor. Since the public at large wasn't aware of Hill's earlier insinuations against his rival, or the aforementioned V-sign photo, Schumacher's sudden animosity towards Hill at Jerez therefore appeared unprovoked to most, causing them to feel little sympathy for the German. For this reason, Schumacher's comments backfired and a few weeks later he publicly apologised for them.

Hill was also involved in the mind games at the time but was subtler in his approach. For instance, Schumacher rarely indulged in emotional language during interviews and, generally, his manner was that of a cold professional. Therefore, the press gave him a 'robot' image. According to one journalist who covered F1 at the time, much of that came from things Hill said and propagated during media briefings, especially with reporters close to him. Hill was very articulate, so usually would have very interesting replies and come across as 'human'.

As a result, some journalists spun events in Hill's favour, particularly as Schumacher was increasingly guarded during interviews following the scrutiny he and Benetton were now under. This might explain why Hill wasn't lambasted in the press over his V-sign photo yet Schumacher was over his Jerez comments.

153. *Schumacher: The Edge of Greatness* by James Allen (2007)
154. *F1 News*, 26 October 1994
155. *Autosport*, 25 August 1994
156. *Autosport*, 10 October 1994

Furthermore, Hill had also acquired the support of Senna fans, including the Brazilian national football team, because he was fighting Ayrton's nemesis. By lifting Williams following Senna's death, Hill emulated his father during 1968 who had carried Lotus in identical circumstances following Jim Clark's death. Damon winning the 1994 championship for his fallen teammate, like his father Graham in 1968, created a feel-good story for the media. Likewise, it would make Damon the first ever son of an F1 world champion who went on to become world champion himself, a unique achievement at the time.

This added to Hill's hero status among the press, which he seemingly used to his advantage. For instance, he tried influencing who his 1995 Williams teammate should be via a British newspaper. "If I can give some advice to Nigel [Mansell] it would probably be: knock it on the head and play golf." Mansell had qualified within 0.077sec of Hill during his only 1994 F1 race to date, while Coulthard was on average 0.9sec away from Damon during his previous eight races. Usually F1 drivers prefer a slower teammate, because it makes them look better. Moreover, one can only imagine the headlines in the British tabloids had Schumacher made such a comment: "CHEAT TELLS MANSELL 'YOU'RE TOO OLD'".

Hill later referred to events within his autobiography "...as a convenient PR rivalry between Michael Schumacher and me. Part of me thought it was good fun playing the Good Guy v Bad Guy game, but looking back I had picked a fight with the wrong guy." This F1 pantomime was enticed by Bernie Ecclestone who was responsible for ensuring the sport entertained, thus keeping sponsors and TV companies happy. Ecclestone engineered a photo of the two bitter rivals to promote the championship showdown to the world's media. Hill later revealed "So, we sat on the pit wall and did our bit. I said to Michael 'come on, let's forget all this bullshit and attempts at psychological warfare.' He said: 'Yes after the championship.'

The photoshoot, arranged by Ecclestone, with Schumacher and Hill.
Photo: Motorsport Images/LAT

So I said 'fine' – and squeezed a little harder when I shook his hand."[157] The animosity between the two was also evident during qualifying where Schumacher just edged Hill to claim pole position by a mere 0.13sec.

Meanwhile Verstappen, not having learnt his lesson from Hockenheim, destroyed his car during Friday qualifying before setting a time. Had it rained the following day, the 22-year-old wouldn't start the race and, unlike Hockenheim, Benetton were unwilling to give him Schumacher's car to also crash. Fortunately Saturday was dry allowing Verstappen to make the race... only for him to spin out on lap sixteen. Afterwards, few were surprised when the team dropped him for the final two races. Benetton was in a colossal fight with Williams for the all-important Constructors' Championship which determined team's prize money, and the Dutchman was clearly underperforming.

Indeed, the nickname 'Vercrashen' was given to him around this time because he had retired from 50 percent of his races due to errors. This statistic doesn't include his various incidents during qualifying or practice, all of which undoubtedly sapped Verstappen's confidence throughout 1994. As evidenced by his qualifying position in Jerez of 12th, whereas his average was 10th throughout the season. Usually with an upcoming rookie, you expect a steady improvement in performances as they gain experience, certainly after half a season's racing. However, that had not happened with Verstappen. It was a similar story with Andretti in 1993 who qualified closer to Senna during the first half of his rookie season than the second half, because his confidence was gradually eroded by the Brazilian's speed. Verstappen initially signed as a Benetton test driver to gain more experience, racing for them wasn't originally the plan. After he was thrust into Lehto's vacant seat following the Finn's accident, the 22-year-old suddenly found himself under huge pressure, yet had little car racing experience to draw upon.

Moreover, Verstappen had a fast but edgy car to drive, one of F1's greatest drivers as a teammate, and he was unsure how long his golden opportunity within a top F1 team would last. That is a potent mix to either make or break a driver even before the question of illegal driver aids arises. Flavio Briatore originally signed the Dutchman under McLaren's nose for a vast sum of money, it therefore seems unlikely Briatore would then devalue Verstappen's worth by giving Schumacher an illicit car advantage. One cannot deny Verstappen and Lehto got second treatment within the team, in comparison to Schumacher, but the question is to what extent?

Lehto's engine was reportedly 10bhp down on Schumacher's[158] who was given a special qualifying specification at Imola. This equated to approximately 0.2sec in lap time whereas Lehto qualified 0.8sec from Schumacher in reality. Afterwards Lehto commented, "Michael had the latest evolution engine for qualifying, but I don't actually need that last little bit at the moment, because there's still a lot more in me."[159] This appears to be the only time Benetton gave their second driver a lesser engine, yet it was the closest Lehto got to Schumacher during qualifying. Benetton was not alone in employing these tactics as Berger was also given a qualifying specification engine at Imola which reportedly had 20bhp more than his teammate's.[160]

Verstappen: "I think it [1994] was too early. I should have gained more experience in a lower team instead of going straight away into a top team next to Schumacher." **Photo: Alastair Ladd**

Dernie: "The idea of drivers being good (or bad) at setting up cars is a myth." **Photo: Alastair Ladd**

Likewise at Monza, Herbert received a special engine while his teammate, Zanardi, used an older, heavier engine despite Italy being his home race. Unless Schumacher regularly received better engines than his teammates (not proven), then the aforementioned Imola example above was not uncommon. Whenever teams only bring one new car/engine development to a race due to time constraints, the quicker driver will always get said improvements, it's a fact of life.

In February 1995, Lehto was interviewed for *CITY-Magazine* Finland and said at Benetton he couldn't choose his own set-ups. If he wanted to change something on the car, the mechanics would refuse and insist on a certain set-up. These comments echoed those made by Verstappen (see Germany chapter). Frank Dernie, Benetton's chief engineer, gave his thoughts: "We had a set-up system based on an early version of the simulation packages used by everybody nowadays, though it didn't always predict things that well! The idea was to not go down a blind alley with a set-up which threw away downforce or produced excessive bottoming – it saved time. Within the limitations of the bits we had available and the various adjustments, there were not that many limitations – just not doing something which would turn out to be a mistake. As practice sessions have got shorter, mileage limited and no testing this sort of approach has become more and more important over the years.

"There were differences between the cars to match differences in driver style, so I think the comments you have seen may well be simply drivers trying to find a reason for being slower than a teammate which isn't them not being as good... A very common thing in my estimation. Also, whenever I have worked with two equally quick drivers their set-up always ended up almost identical. I have never met a driver who understands the physics of how cars work, so how could they?

"Some have a superb memory and can help set up their car by saying something like – this feels just like what we had at the Jerez test, what did we do to fix it then? Which saves time, Schumacher was like this, he also studied the data with the engineers a lot which previous generations of driver didn't have. Others have a very good way of explaining what the car is doing which an

experienced race engineer or designer can use to deduce why and fix it, Jones and Piquet are good examples of this type of driver.

"In 1994, I did a lot of pre-season testing using the simulation data as a start point and came up with two set-ups, one soft for bumpy/slow circuits, and one stiff for high-speed stability. We used these with small adjustments until the huge influence of the changes rightly applied after Senna's crash. When I had to re-do them as quickly as possible in tests and then we used those for the rest of the year. In my estimation, if the car is good, once it is dialled-in with a set-up which suits it only tiny trims are needed from circuit to circuit – ride heights for example but the same settings are used everywhere. If the car isn't good, or cannot be adjusted to suit the tyres (which is rarer nowadays), there is pretty well nothing you can do with the set-up which will make it quick."

Paul West of Williams adds: "I think that we would have done a similar process with a baseline set-up and just small adjustments, either way, to dial in the car." There were times when the second Benetton driver took Schumacher's set-up after failing to find their own, like Lehto in Canada. In that instance, the Finn was given every opportunity to find his own set-up, yet he only qualified 20th and believed there was something wrong with his chassis. So Benetton gave him the spare car for the race which resulted in no significant improvements, hence why they dropped him afterwards.

In Jerez, Schumacher was questioned about being given a fresher chassis than his teammates and responded: "It is quite normal that you would save such a chassis [the freshest one] for the number one driver. I tested JJ's race car at Estoril and, generally, the cars are all the same."[161] Paul West of Williams concurs: "Normally the number one driver would get the new tub. All of the FW16s were modified for the shorter side pods prior to Germany, so there are no original tubs left. As to what difference if any a new tub made to lap times I couldn't say, it could be psychological with some drivers that a new car is going to be faster than their old one."

157. *Damon Hill 1994 Grand Prix Year: The Inside Story of a F1 Season*
158. *Quattroruote*, December 1994
159. *Autosport*, 5 May 1994
160. *Quattroruote*, December 1994
161. *Autosport*, 20 October 1994

Japan has settled many championships previously, and the 1994 race proved memorable owing to the weather. **Photo: Morio**

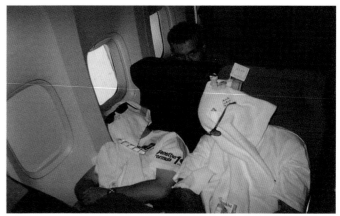

Two flyaway races concluded a gruelling season for mechanics. Despite this, they never lost their humour. **Photo: Antony John Dennis**

Willem Toet adds "the drivers had favourite chassis sometimes. After a bad result, drivers would develop a dislike to a chassis and 'demand' a new one (which of course takes time and money), which the team would try to accommodate but the team believed that mostly the differences were more psychological than real." Schumacher also proved a superior chassis wasn't behind his additional speed during that first practice session in Monaco. Because he stepped into Lehto's car and immediately went four seconds a lap quicker than the Finn, which was consistently the gap between the teammates all weekend. Likewise, Lehto drove Schumacher's car after he crashed his own during Thursday qualifying at Monaco, yet the Finn didn't improve his times as a result. Throughout F1 history similar situations have occurred.

During the 1950s, Alberto Ascari famously used Ferrari 500 chassis five exclusively, and refused to allow his team mates to use it.

Does the above, together with other aforementioned issues like Lehto's injury and Schumacher's left-foot braking technique, explain the significant gaps between the Benetton drivers in 1994? Or did something more sinister also play a part in those gaps? Lehto and Verstappen were certainly better drivers than they appeared in 1994, and it is likely they were not given adequate psychological support from Briatore. Equally, it seems the car didn't suit their driving styles. However, Benetton's approach of focusing on Schumacher, perhaps to the detriment of their second driver, put them in the 1994 championship fight. It is therefore very hard to fault this strategy.

Mansell replaced Coulthard in the second Williams for the final three races of 1994. In response, Benetton replaced Verstappen with Herbert.
Photo: Alastair Ladd

Herbert: "[The Benetton was] completely different from the Lotus, another world almost. Also aerodynamically it's another stage on."
Photo: Alastair Ladd

De Cesaris would have filled in for Wendlinger in Japan and Australia, but he was uncontactable. It gave Lehto a final opportunity at F1.
Photo: Károly Méhes

Jerez saw many driver changes since the previous race including Mansell's Williams return. Once the red lights turned to green, the 1992 world champion again showed his rustiness at standing starts by losing three places off the line. Indeed, Mansell never got a clean getaway during all of his 1994 F1 races which underlined the importance of regular practice. At Jerez, Schumacher's clutch started to drag and as he re-adjusted it the race started, causing the German to falter from pole position. Hill, meanwhile, took off perfectly and shot into the lead. The race was initially a tense duel between the two but steadily Schumacher pulled away, eventually emerging a commanding winner. However, this race flattered the Benetton's performance.

It later transpired Williams suffered a problem with its fuel rig meaning Hill was called in early for his second stop and took on more fuel than required. *Autosport* magazine studied the lap times the following week and suggested Schumacher had won the race by the time Hill encountered his problem. Although disappointed, Hill's championship chances remained excellent. The Williams was now considered the best car in the field and Mansell was assisting him. In another show of ineptitude by race officials, Hakkinen wasn't penalised despite speeding in the pitlane during the race. *F1 News* magazine reported this was because the stewards responsible for spotting this were busy in conversation. When they eventually glanced at their equipment to see a speeding crime had been committed, neither could agree with race control who the culprit was. You couldn't make it up!

Following the race, Herbert was confirmed as Verstappen's replacement at Benetton. He would become the third driver to partner Schumacher during 1994. He arrived from Lotus and Ligier, the latter now being run by Tom Walkinshaw, the subject of Benetton's 'management changes' following the fuel filter controversy. Herbert's appointment was ironic because he was sacked from Benetton by Briatore in mid-1989 when it became apparent his ankles had not healed enough to drive a F1 car following his horrific F3000 accident the previous year. Nevertheless, Herbert got within 0.4sec of Schumacher during his first test and then qualified within 0.6sec off him in Japan, whereas Verstappen and Lehto were on average 1.9 and 2.2sec slower than Schumacher respectively.

When asked about the B194, Herbert said: "It's got a lot more traction than the Lotus ever had. You go into a corner, you turn and you floor it. Spinning the wheels is actually quite difficult, whereas with the Lotus you could do it easily and you had to feed the power in and be careful."[162] Although the car was an improvement for him, it became apparent the Englishman didn't get along with Benetton's team boss. In his autobiography, Herbert detailed how Briatore did not fully support his efforts at Benetton, citing the example that Schumacher's telemetry data was withheld from him. Herbert also explained how rarely he tested the car while noting Briatore was never happy whenever he did well.

Had there been something on Schumacher's car which circumvented the rules during 1994, then one might have expected Johnny to have also mentioned this. Particularly as it would have been another way to 'have a dig' at Briatore. Instead, Herbert said the following within his autobiography. "The fact that the car had been designed to suit Michael's style of driving was understandable, and shouldn't really have been much of a problem, so long as I was able to acclimatise and get used to it. The only way I could do this was by testing, but, as with the data, it was a privilege that would be made available to Michael and not me."

Elsewhere, Wendlinger tested an F1 car for the first time since his near-fatal crash. It was held in rainy conditions at the Paul Ricard circuit and, afterwards, it was announced he would race in Japan. However during another test, held in dry conditions at Barcelona soon afterwards, the Austrian developed neck pains after only 15 laps and thus decided against racing for the remainder of 1994. Wendlinger later told *Motor Sport* magazine it took until February 1995 to drive with "almost no pain", underlining how easy it was for drivers to return too quickly following an accident. Ironically, Lehto substituted for Wendlinger in what would be his final two F1 races. The Finn qualified on average 1.3sec behind his Sauber teammate (Frentzen) during those two races, which puts his Benetton performances into context.

162. *Autosport*, 10 November 1994

Chapter 12

During a practice session for the following race, the Japanese Grand Prix, Schumacher's car virtually stopped out on circuit which aroused the suspicion of the FIA. At the time there was continued speculation that Benetton had an illicit electronic device which erased itself automatically once the engine died. Mosley later admitted that the FIA took action in Japan. "We took all the control units off the first three cars in the race (Williams, Benetton and Ferrari), and rushed them back to England. Our people went through the whole lot line by line. There was one small query on one, but it wouldn't have made any material difference."[163]

Many believed the FIA was unwilling to prove the launch control software previously found on Schumacher's car was illegal. Because the software was from Imola and doing so would prove Senna was killed racing against an illegal Benetton which, it was claimed, would open the door to various lawsuits against the FIA. Some believed this was the real reason the FIA didn't punish Benetton over the launch control findings. However, the Suzuka black boxes spot checks cast doubt over this theory because it confirmed the FIA was regularly undertaking random legality checks throughout 1994.

If the FIA didn't want Schumacher punished, because of lawsuits or having a German champion was important for F1, then why would they carry out these checks during races where Schumacher was a podium finisher? Instead, they could have conducted a spot

The FIA's suspicion was aroused by Schumacher's car. They therefore checked the electronics of the podium finishers, and all were declared legal. ***Photo: Morio***

Mansell's garage became a Coulthard-free zone and mechanics jokingly placed a photo of him with a red diagonal stripe across it. ***Photo: Alastair Ladd***

check at a race which Schumacher was banned from or had retired. This would have resulted in not needing to penalise Schumacher or Benetton, if that was their intention, yet the FIA would be seen to be policing the sport also.

It wasn't just the car's electronics that was being checked either. After races the FIA undertook random inspections on things like engine sizes, throttle linkages etc. Naturally enough, the

Schumacher apologised for suggesting Hill was a second-rate driver. It was an attempt to repair his battered reputation.
Photo: Motorsport Images/LAT

The race saw a sensational battle between the two rivals. Hill emerged the winner in what he described as his greatest F1 drive.
Photo: Motorsport Images/LAT

winner attracted the most attention from scrutineers, meaning Schumacher's Benetton was checked more than others because he won the most races during 1994. In addition, checks were carried out throughout qualifying because cars entering the pits were randomly called into a special area and given an inspection. Officials also scrutinised cars before an event and immediately after the race, during which team personnel were not allowed to touch the cars for a period of time. Rival teams also spied on one another and recorded their sounds, took video footage or photos of anything suspicious. *Autosport* magazine reported at Suzuka a Williams team man watched every move made in the Benetton pit. "It's nothing sinister," said their team manager, Ian Harrison, "they watch us and we watch them. It's being efficient really."

When asked about electronic devices on cars which deleted automatically, Mosley replied: "Ah, you're talking about 'volatile memory.' Yes, we're paying particular attention to that, and if we find any in the system, we'll know exactly what it's there for. Of course, the volatile memory itself needs some sort of operating system to activate it – to make it do what it's not supposed to do."[164] Despite the above, many remained cynical that certain teams had something beyond detection in 1994. If so they would have been extremely brave running those illegal devices at Suzuka, given how much pressure Mosley was under from the media to penalise any instance of cheating. It was felt Mosley had been overly lenient to Ferrari, Benetton and McLaren in previous cases, and given the rules had since been tightened, he could now justifiably show little sympathy to the next offender.

Mansell decided to do a bit of legislating himself in Japan. He barred Coulthard, the man he was competing against for the 1995 Williams drive, from entering his garage during the weekend. Come the race, the heavens opened and it was held during an appalling rain storm. Various drivers, including Hill, questioned the safety of racing in such conditions. Numerous cars crashed out due to aquaplaning, yet the safety car wasn't deployed until Martin Brundle narrowly missed hitting a tractor and instead collided with a marshal.

"I really thought my number was up," fumed the Englishman who had feared for his life and that of the marshal who fortunately suffered nothing worse than a broken leg. His crash had been eerily similar to Jules Bianchi's fatal accident at the same spot in 2014. Somewhat ironically, Brundle had warned of these dangers and was one of the drivers screaming for a safety car over his radio when his car aquaplaned off the track. Perhaps another case of race officials showing ineptitude in 1994?

A sensational battle between the two championship protagonists developed once the race restarted with Hill eventually emerging the winner in what he later described as his greatest ever drive in F1. Schumacher, despite being on the wrong strategy, finished a close second meaning he now led the championship by just a single point going into the final race. The stage was set, for what would become one of the most controversial championship deciders in F1 history.

163. *Autosport,* 24 November 1994
164. *Autosport,* 24 November 1994

AUSTRALIA AND THE AFTERMATH

November 1994

"We had not factored in the possibility that he might do whatever he needed to stop me passing him."

Damon Hill, Williams driver

"There were so many things that could have gone wrong and stopped me being champion. Then I realised I was champion and it was satisfying."

Michael Schumacher, Benetton driver

Moments before Schumacher and Hill came together…

Photo: Motorsport Images/LAT

Standings before the 1994 Australian Grand Prix

DRIVERS' CHAMPIONSHIP			CONSTRUCTORS' CHAMPIONSHIP		
Pos	Driver	Points	Pos	Constructor	Points
1	Michael Schumacher	92	1	Williams-Renault	108
2	Damon Hill	91	2	Benetton-Ford	103
3	Gerhard Berger	35	3	Ferrari	64

Steve Matchett (pictured in 2005): "Nearly all of the drivers we have had in the B194 during the year have commented on the car's unique handling characteristics, and how difficult it is to drive until they get used to it." **Photo: Dan Smith**

The Adelaide circuit played host to the controversial 1994 championship decider. **Photo: Calistemon**

For the first time in eight years, the final race would decide the F1 Drivers' Championship and the two contenders, Hill and Schumacher, had never been in this position before. Moreover, both had reason to feel they deserved this championship after what was a tragic and turbulent season for everyone. An unknown factor was their teammates and how that might spice things up, which added to the palpable tension that weekend. Perhaps fittingly, and in keeping with the rest of 1994, things ended in yet more acrimony.

Hill caused a sensation at Adelaide, the host of the Australian Grand Prix, from the moment he landed. In front of the world's media he announced: "I don't feel like driving my nuts off for the sort of money you pay someone with no experience." Hill had felt unappreciated within Williams and wanted to make that known. His timing was unfortunate, however, not only because of the championship but Hill had been out qualified by his teammate. At least he could count on having the best car in F1 as the FW16 had progressively improved throughout the season. According to its designer, Adrian Newey: "We had a pretty good car by the end of the year, as the results showed. If anything, we had a car that was slightly quicker than the Benetton. That was satisfying, the fact that we had managed to turn the car around, especially after Imola."

Pat Symonds, Schumacher's race engineer in 1994 concurred: "We produced an absolutely wonderful [Benetton] car. The changes that were made to the technical regulations after Imola, things like cutting the diffuser down, putting vents in the airboxes, putting the plank on, each one of them made our absolutely wonderful car average, or even below average, because I think by the end of the season the Williams was a better car."[166] Schumacher knew the fight would be tough given the strength of the Williams' driver line-up. It added to the pressure he was under, particularly as the German couldn't rely on any support from his own teammate.

This was because Herbert qualified 1.5sec off Schumacher and later admitted he "struggled against Michael in Australia" because Schumacher was determined to win the championship. However, at the time Herbert commented "I don't know why I was that far off him [Schumacher]... The car's a bit different style wise. I know

when I did the testing after a good day I could actually get the thing to work really well. So I need to get into that sort of rhythm."[167] The test referred to is where he lapped within 0.4sec of Schumacher – a gap slightly deceptive because Schumacher set his time the day before Herbert. Generally at testing sessions and race weekends, the track gets quicker with each passing day as more rubber is laid from cars lapping the circuit.

In his book *Life in the Fast Lane*, Steve Matchett (Herbert's Benetton mechanic) added: "I'm sure he [Johnny] would have gone a lot quicker on Saturday if the rain had held off. In testing he had been much closer to Michael's times than he was here, and I think he just needed more experience with the car. Not so he could play around with different set-ups, but more time getting used to how the car reacts, and how far it can be pushed before it lets go."

Indeed, Herbert had noted the Benetton's "unique handling" after his initial test: "I'd heard that it's twitchy, and it is. But you have to push beyond that. And when you do, it becomes quite stable."[168] This implies confidence was a big part of drivers unlocking the B194 speed, possibly via Benetton's exhaust blown diffuser discussed earlier. Schumacher famously exuded supreme confidence throughout his whole career, whereas his 1994 teammates progressively lost theirs through various crashes and poor results.

Herbert also admitted to indulging in a bit of trial and error to learn the car's characteristics during the previous race before crashing out. So he would hardly have been full of confidence in the car during Australia. Moreover, Adelaide was a street circuit where concrete barriers lined the track ensuring drivers paid a heavy price for even the small mistakes. For this reason, Herbert likely exercised more caution here than during testing at Barcelona or the previous race, particularly as Benetton needed both cars finishing in the points to secure the constructors championship. It is often overlooked that even Schumacher found the mid-1990s Benetton's difficult to drive as he later alluded to.

165. *Motor Sport*, December 2004
166. *Autosport*, 6 August 2014
167. *Autosport*, 17 November 1994
168. *Motoring News*, 26 October 1994

Damon Hill: "I mean, in your Benetton days, the on-board camera would show you doing 6000 revs per minute with your arms! You used to be very busy in the car, and you seem to have calmed down a bit now [in 1999]."

Michael Schumacher: "This is true, but I'll tell you the reason why. You remember when I left Benetton, and [Jean] Alesi and [Gerhard] Berger took their first steps in that Benetton? You remember how many crashes they had?"

Damon Hill: "Yes, I do remember."

Michael Schumacher: "Well, if you had ever driven those cars, Damon, you would know why I was driving it that way. I mean, that it was really unbelievable. Really difficult to drive. It was so edgy. But it was fast when you just drove it exactly on that edge. Now, though, there have been a lot of aerodynamic improvements to the cars and so the cars I have driven have been a lot more stable. And that applies to most of the cars today."[169]

Schumacher's superior talent and fitness kept those Benettons in line throughout the duration of a race. When he departed Benetton, Berger was his replacement and confident he could tame the car equally as well as Schumacher, however this illusion was soon shattered. "On the first day I comfortably got close to Michael's time and then thought 'Tomorrow, I'll just do those few extra tenths'. But when I tried it, I crashed three or four times and that made me think 'wow Michael'. The car was nervous but he managed to hold it there not just for one lap right on the edge, but for 50, 60 or 70 laps."[170] Clearly, Schumacher drove with a precision that others couldn't and this was especially evident in the mid-1990s Benettons.

In his recent book, Adrian Newey suggested Schumacher never showed a similar level of superiority over teammates than he had shown in 1994, possibly implying Benetton gave Schumacher illegal driver aids. That point is incorrect, however, because in 1995 Herbert qualified on average 1.6sec away from Schumacher throughout that season. Herbert was an experienced driver by then, unlike Verstappen. Despite the legacy of his Formula 3000 crash which caused him problems, by 1995 the Brit was as fit as he ever

was in F1, unlike Lehto during 1994. Worth noting, Verstappen and Lehto were on average 1.9 and 2.2sec off Schumacher in 1994, while Schumacher out-qualified Patrese and Irvine by over a second on many occasions in 1993 and 1996 respectively. Patrese, Herbert and Irvine were all race winners and generally regarded as better grand prix drivers than Lehto or Verstappen, so these gaps do make sense upon closer scrutiny.

Outside of Benetton, Senna out-qualified Andretti by an average of 1.4sec during 1993 when electronic driver aids (ie traction and launch control) were permitted. It is likely this gap would have been larger had Senna and Andretti driven for McLaren during 1994 instead when the cars were (supposedly) shed of these devices because superior drivers like Senna or Schumacher qualities were more evident in difficult cars. Conversely, as cars became more stable during the late 1990s Schumacher's advantage over teammates lessened, as confirmed by Irvine[171] who drove alongside the German from 1996 to 1999.

Furthermore, there are no serious suggestions of Benetton using illegal electronic aids in 1995. This is partly because they changed their engine supplier to Renault so installed the same Magenti Marelli electronics which Williams used. Therefore the average gap of 1.6sec between Herbert and Schumacher during 1995 can only be down to skill and how well the car suited them. Newey's implication above also begs the question why would Benetton hamper the second driver when they were in the fight for the 1994 Constructors' Championship?

Some suggested Benetton was solely interested in winning the 1994 Drivers' Championship with Schumacher, so having outlawed electronics in the second Benetton wasn't necessary for this. However, this argument does not hold water because a team's prize money is determined by its placing within the Constructor's Championship. It is well known that certain teams like Williams cared more about the Constructor's Championship rather than the drivers' title. Antony John Dennis also believed Benetton mechanics were paid a bonus depending on how many points they accrued within the Constructor's Championship. Therefore had

Senna out-qualified Andretti by an average of 1.4sec in the driver aids laden 1993 McLaren. Can comparisons be drawn between this and Benetton in 1994? ***Photo: Martin Lee***

Herbert (pictured in 1989): "I used to live on the edge when I was braking in the wet and I could feel everything through the tips of my toes, but I didn't have that after my feet had been smashed up in my (Formula 3000) crash."
Photo: Antony John Dennis

Schumacher walking back after his practice crash. By now, every Benetton action was scrutinised to the nth degree. **Photo: Adrian Musolino**

Mansell took pole and later claimed he was told not to make a good start and "watch the race, do not interfere." **Photo: Alastair Ladd**

Benetton personnel, as some have suggested, purposely hampered the second car, then they were also causing themselves financial pain in that process.

Benetton desperately trying to win the Constructors' Championship was the reason they replaced their second driver regularly throughout 1994, a policy which was extremely risky from a bean-spilling point of view had their second driver felt aggrieved at looking bad in comparison to the sister car. Also, had the second Benetton been taking points away from Hill, Schumacher's rival, then it would have made winning the Driver's Championship much easier. Yet another reason why it was in Benetton's interest to ensure their second car was as competitive as possible.

During Friday qualifying, Schumacher crashed his car after losing the rear end over a kerb. Had he been using illegal traction control in 1994, then it certainly wasn't in operation at that moment, as it would have prevented the back end from stepping out on him. Schumacher's car was destroyed as a result and what his mechanics did next sparked yet more rumours. Instead of giving the German the spare car, the team built a new B194 around the emergency spare chassis. Many observers concluded Benetton had illegal devices installed on that car whereas their spare car didn't.

It has been claimed the emergency spare chassis, along with the various components (ie gearbox etc), were all fresher than those within their spare car. Because there was a 50 percent chance Herbert would need that spare car, and naturally enough the team wanted to give Michael the best equipment for the Drivers' Championship. Moreover, Benetton would have still needed to build another spare car for the rest of the weekend, so their actions aren't unusual according to Paul West of Williams.

"Building a car using the emergency spare tub is normal practice. I know that we did it for Riccardo [Patrese] at Silverstone in 1992 and for Damon [Hill] in Suzuka 1995 and there may have been other times. The emergency spare tub would be built up with new components whereas the spare car may have higher mileage components. So that is another reason to give the driver the better equipment and, as Patrick [Head], used to say, "The mechanics are

here to work, not for a holiday," so another reason to build a new car. When Damon finished upside down in Portugal 1994 (during a practice session), there was a possibility that the spare tub would be used. But the damage to his race car was only cosmetic so it was raced but we would have done the same as Benetton if needed."

The happiest man in Adelaide after qualifying was Bertrand Gachot who, once again, failed make the race with his unloved Pacific. Afterwards he proudly exclaimed: "Today is a great day. I don't have to drive the PR01 anymore". Hill finished third on the grid, Schumacher second, and Mansell – not having read the script – claimed his final pole position. Most races in 1994 had been dull affairs, usually dominated by one driver, however the Australian Grand Prix was enthralling. Schumacher and Hill shot past Mansell to lead from the start and begin their private duel for the championship. Mansell later admitted: "I was told all sorts of things by the powers-that-be. 'You will not be part of this race, don't get a good start, watch the race, do not interfere...' So I deliberately didn't get a very good start and I just sat there and watched."[172]

Schumacher tried stretching his narrow lead while Hill maintained a constant pressure on the German. The pace at the front was furious, as evidenced by their brake wear, which was double that of their teammates'. Schumacher eventually cracked on lap 36: "I got caught out on a bump when the car stepped out and went sideways, but I caught it," he later explained. "Then I had to go on the white line and I had to use the run-off area. I went over the grass, and touched the wall."[173] Schumacher's car was damaged by that brush against the wall, however crucially Hill didn't see this impact having been too far behind the German. Damon closed up on to his rival's tail as Schumacher rejoined the track. Sensing this may be his only opportunity to overtake, Hill then dived inside Schumacher at the following corner and the German turned in on him.

169. *F1 Racing*, November 1999
170. *Autosport*
171. *Legends of F1: Eddie Irvine*, Sky F1 (2016)

172. *Autosport*, 7 August 2014
173. *F1 News*, 23 November 1994

Chapter 13

The two cars made contact, with the force of the impact pitching Schumacher's Benetton onto two wheels before it landed upright and hit the tyre wall head on. For a moment it looked like Hill had survived the collision but as he crawled back to the pits it was clear something was wrong. Once in the pits, TV cameras showed the issue, a front wishbone had been bent by the impact. Despite Patrick Head's best attempts to pull it straight using brute force, it was beyond repair. The TV coverage then switched to the trackside spot where Schumacher was standing, his helmet now removed and the German looking pensive expecting Hill's Williams to flash past at any moment. As time ticked by and it became clearer that Hill had retired, the German's expression gradually changed as the realisation that he was 1994 World Champion dawned upon him.

Most believed it was a cynical move by Schumacher who knew his car was damaged and that taking Hill out of the race was the only way he could win the championship. Schumacher and Benetton were already unpopular within the F1 paddock so this incident only underlined that negative feeling. However, other racing drivers including Hill himself have since indicated they might have done the same as Schumacher in that situation. Conversely, some believed Hill should have been more circumspect before diving down the inside as he did, but it's easy to be wise after the event. Nevertheless, the vast majority felt sympathy for Hill at Adelaide.

"We at Williams were already 100 percent certain that Michael was guilty of foul play," said a furious Patrick Head. "He was about to drive his stricken Benetton up the slip-road when he spotted Damon's Williams about to pass him and abruptly veered across the track to prevent that happening. We seriously considered lodging a formal protest there and then, on the grounds that it had been so blatant, but decided against it simply because of what had happened earlier in the year. Because 1994 was the terrible year it was – in other words, because Ayrton Senna had been killed in one of our cars at Imola – we didn't really think it would have been right for Damon to win the World Championship that year, especially if he'd done so in court, so we didn't protest.

"But had it been any other year – or had Ayrton not been killed in one of our cars – then most certainly we'd have lodged a formal protest..."[174] This incident is often used to devalue Schumacher's standing within the sport and not without justification. Consequently, Schumacher was a deeply unpopular driver because of this and other similar incidents. Whatever your view, it has to be seen within the context of everything that happened in 1994, for instance let's put ourselves in Schumacher's shoes on that starting grid at Adelaide 1994:

■ You are 25 years old and still relatively inexperienced.
■ You have driven superbly all year long yet people (rightly or wrongly) believe you are cheating via illegal driver aids.
■ You believe politics have cheated you out of four race victories.
■ You feel your name has been disgraced unfairly, and vilified in the press.
■ You have been dragged through the FIA courts several times.
■ Imola was an awakening to how short life can be as an F1 driver.
■ Hockenheim was a wake up to the potential of pit stop fires.
■ You've seen the Williams become a better car than yours, partly because of FIA rule changes.
■ You've all the pressure of fighting for your first championship.
■ You've seen the 1989 and 1990 championships won by drivers crashing into one another.
■ You've all the pressure of carrying your team to their first Constructors' Championship because your teammates have not delivered.

Williams was forced to retire Hill's car due to the damage sustained from the Schumacher incident. It cost him the 1994 title. **Photo: Alastair Ladd**

Senna won the 1990 Drivers' Championship after taking out his rival, a move which went unpunished. Did that influence Schumacher's actions at Adelaide? **Photo: Stuart Seeger**

Schumacher's 1994 Drivers' Championship would forever be perceived with suspicion. **Photo: Motorsport Images/LAT**

After the accident Schumacher claimed: "We just ran over each other. It is racing."[175] Pat Symonds, Schumacher's race engineer in 1994, gave more insight into Schumacher's frame of mind before the race. "He was pretty damn motivated to win the world championship, and now he had the chance to do it. I don't know how all that affected him, but it was probably the same as me. It was probably this mix of absolute determination to prove them wrong and the absolute horror of being accused of things that were not correct."

When asked about the collision, Symonds retorted: "There wasn't a moment of enjoyment in it, there really wasn't. I remember after the accident I just went ballistic, I'm the calmest person in the pitlane, and that was too much for me. I honestly didn't believe that we'd won the championship. I thought, 'Here we go again, another bloody enquiry'. I didn't believe that he did it on purpose. I know the steering was broken, I could see the data, and I didn't think that he had control of the car. I guess after 1997 with [Jacques] Villeneuve, and then Monaco 2006, I wondered about 1994. As I said earlier, there were times when Michael's judgement wasn't very good."[176]

Perhaps those later incidents Symonds referred to happened because Schumacher escaped with Adelaide 1994 unpunished which clearly was wrong. When recalling the collision in his autobiography, Max Mosley stated: "My private view was that

Michael had been very lucky not to be penalised and thus lose his World Championship win. But the stewards had looked into the incident and came to the opposite conclusion. It was a matter of opinion and it would have been wrong to interfere, particular after criticising Balestre for doing just that a few years before." Yet, on the face of things, there appeared to be no qualms about increasing Schumacher's original penalty following the black flag at Silverstone. Whatever the case, Mosley's implication from his comment above seems, had the matter been left to him, Schumacher would have been stripped of his 1994 title.

At Adelaide, race stewards came to their decision of not taking action against Schumacher after investigating video footage along with amateur footage of the collision. Most agreed Schumacher did ultimately deserved the 1994 Drivers' Championship, even despite Adelaide. So it would have been wrong to interfere after the race, particularly as Williams had not appealed and everyone wanted to just draw a line under 1994. However, the investigation was apparently a warning that the powers-that-be could have disqualified Schumacher had they deemed it necessary. Indeed, they did disqualify Schumacher from the 1997 championship after a similar occurrence at that year's final race.

174. Racefans, 22 August 2007
175. F1 News, 23 November 1994
176. Autosport, 6 August 2014

After Adelaide 1994, Schumacher was on a charm offensive. He paid tribute to Senna, saying "for me it was always clear that I wasn't going to win the championship, and Ayrton was going to win the championship. But he hasn't been there for the last races. And I'd like to take this championship and give it to him. Because he is the driver who should have earned it. He had the best car, he was the best driver, and that's my feelings about him." Schumacher also publicly apologised for his earlier outburst towards Hill in an attempt to repair his battered reputation, however the damage had been done. In hindsight, 1994 was the year where the public's perception of Schumacher flipped from the charming upstart taking the fight to the dominate Williams to being viewed with suspicion. It was a perception Schumacher never shook off.

Of course, it was easy to be magnanimous in victory, but at least Schumacher made the effort. Despite his attempts at reconciliation, the British tabloids continued to vilify Schumacher for the collision in the days following the race, their headlines included "SCHU DIRTY RAT". *The Sun* and *The Mirror* newspapers even started petitions to strip Schumacher of his title. *The Mirror* reported 99 percent support came in favour of this, prompting them to take their petition to Max Mosley's office. "It's quite fantastic, just amazing – all this support for Damon. It's marvellous – but unfortunately, it's misplaced," was the reply back. Certain newspapers even criticised Schumacher for smiling upon learning he had won his first Drivers' Championship, given the circumstances.

According to his autobiography, Hill was advised by Barry Sheene not to say anything controversial in the immediate aftermath of the incident and Damon revealed this was the best advice he was ever given. Instead, Hill remarked: "I've nothing against him. When a championship is decided at the last race, these things can happen." As a result, many media outlets praised Hill for showing such dignity. It was unusual in F1: a world used to drivers bitching about one another in the aftermath of any collision. British newspaper's opinion of Hill changed spectacularly 12 months later, but for now he was praised as a hero, even winning the 1994 BBC Sports Personality of the Year.

After that final race, Martin Brundle put his case forward to become Schumacher's teammate for 1995, and in doing so had a dig at Benetton's recent second drivers. "Probably the best seat for me, other than McLaren, is the second Benetton ride. I think I'm the only guy who could mentally cope with Schumacher – and I think I proved I did before [in 1992]. He destroyed me over four races but I came through the other end and did a solid job against him. I think I averaged one second off him the whole year – if only people realised then what a megastar he was. Perhaps I'd still be driving a Benetton! Nobody's done a remotely similar job since."[177]

Brundle was Schumacher's teammate during 1992, and has never suggested the German had any illegal advantages during their time together, in fact his above comments imply the opposite. Patrese, Schumacher's 1993 teammate, and on average 1.14 seconds slower than him, noted "...and Michael Schumacher was very good in a bad car that is where he can destroy his team-mate. I was talking inside the team about the faults the car had, but they said I was just making excuses, because Schumacher was quicker than me...With Michael I always got on well. As we know now (in 2010), he was special. After me Verstappen, Lehto, Herbert, none of them found it easy racing with Schumacher."[178]

Perhaps the above comments should be considered when assessing whether Schumacher used illegal driver aids in 1994. Patrese was originally employed on an equal footing to Schumacher, however after a few races he fell out with Benetton's senior management. According to Paul West, Patrese's Williams mechanic in 1992, "I only spoke to Riccardo a few times in 1993, and he was unimpressed that Walkinshaw and Briatore didn't stay to see him finish second in Hungary".

Paul West: "Patrese felt Schumacher was getting better treatment and equipment within Benetton in 1993." ***Photo: Martin Lee***

Brundle: "I think very few people could mentally cope with Michael's speed and confidence like I did." *Photo: Alastair Ladd*

If by mid-1993 onwards Schumacher was Benetton's number one driver and was therefore receiving better equipment (such as engines updates first), it's a position he earned by beating his teammates to that point, just as Senna did it at Lotus. Every F1 team has this same philosophy that their fastest driver will receive any upgrades first. However, any superior equipment Schumacher possibly received in 1993 couldn't have been illicit gimzos because they were not banned by this point. Schumacher's detractors have suggested he had an easy ride

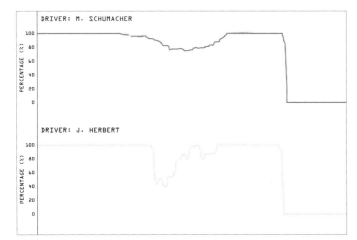

Fig 10. Comparing Schumacher's use of the throttle with that of his teammate Herbert. *Image: www.neilwhitedesign.co.uk*

to this position at Benetton and, once he was there, illegal advantages in 1994 cemented it. Proof this wasn't the case can be seen when Schumacher drove the Ligier F1 car in 1994.

Schumacher tested the Ligier for one day in December 1994, because Renault wanted him to try engine maps in preparation for the following year. *Autosport* magazine reported Schumacher was one second quicker than regular Ligier driver Olivier Panis who also drove that day. Moreover, Ligier was amazed with Schumacher's skill and technical ability, thus demonstrating Schumacher could destroy other drivers in equal cars even when not driving a Benetton, so there wasn't any possibility for illegal driver aids.

Panis later insisted this was a "driving lesson" for him and after studying Schumacher's telemetry data he managed to lap within 0.13sec on subsequent days when Schumacher wasn't driving. Vincent Gaillardot of Renault noted: "Michael was excellent at keeping an identical throttle position throughout a turn. I used his skills to show Olivier Panis what to do."[179] Frank Dernie, by this point Ligier's Technical Director, confirmed: "Panis saw several things Schumacher did which helped including use of left foot braking." A BBC documentary which aired in 1995 compared the German's telemetry with his then teammate Herbert's. Fig 10 is an illustration of how it looked.

177. *Autosport*, 1 December 1994   179 *Sport Auto*
178. *Motor Sport*, May 2010

This illustrated what Gaillardot said above, because you can see how precise and constant Schumacher's throttle movements were in comparison with Herbert's. Being that progressive on the throttle stabilised the pitch of the car through a turn whilst generating additional grip via the exhaust blown diffusers. Schumacher's braking technique wasn't shown on this telemetry trace, however he would have been brushing the brake pedal simultaneously with his left foot to keep as much throttle open as possible through the corner, whereas Herbert was unable to left-foot brake based on his earlier comments and his admission of a lack of sensitivity in his feet.

Christian Silk, Herbert's race engineer in 1994, feels the above telemetry trace was typical of the differences between the two drivers. "Schumacher was really good at listening to the team and adjusting his driving depending on what engineers wanted him to do," Silk explained. "Like keeping the throttle on throughout a corner in order to maximise the exhaust blown diffuser, irrespective of any fear factor." Gaillardot added: "That year [1995], the key was the blowing of the exhausts into the diffuser. At Benetton, we had found a trick, and of course we didn't tell our classmates who worked at Williams...

"Benetton wanted to go even further than Williams in integrating the engine with the chassis. Michael too. He didn't want to hear about max power. Only the final chrono counted. The blowing

required some adaptation work on the part of the pilot." Michael Schumacher, still in the interview in 2010, noted: "The difference in aero support between the phases where I accelerated and where I released the pedal was very significant. We worked to reduce this effect. Renault brought several solutions: butterflies always open, ignition delayed... We focused mainly on partial loads."[180]

Could the above explain why Schumacher held back his telemetry from Herbert during 1995? Indeed, the newly crowned World Champion admitted "during the [1994/95] winter tests, the difference between Herbert's performance and mine was small in some tests. I have asked the team – which has accepted – that the data concerning my driving wasn't showed to him. I don't see why I would have offered him the means of, maybe, beating me."[181] Both Herbert and Panis would have needed to consistently see Schumacher's telemetry over a variety of tracks in order to fully benefit from it.

This selfish act from Schumacher is often derided as him not being sportsmanlike in his quest for victory. However, many former champions played similar tricks, as Paul West confirmed: "The one thing Mansell did do which we only found out later was to adjust the ride height switches in his car as he was coming in the pits. Our engineer John Russell would make a note of these settings to assist Riccardo [Patrese]. Mansell would tell his engineer Dave Brown the correct settings when they were alone, not exactly being a team

Benetton's 1996 drivers Alesi (pictured) and Berger both found the car difficult to drive and crashed it numerous times during pre-season. Former Benetton mechanic Paul Seaby states that this was because neither could get used to the B195's exhaust-blown diffuser. ***Photo: Alastair Ladd***

Interesting parallels can be drawn between Mansell in 1992 and Schumacher in 1994 and their respective teammates.
Photo: wileynorwichphoto

Schumacher reportedly held back telemetry from Herbert in 1995 perhaps because he did not want Johnny gaining from his driving secrets, as Panis had done. **Photo: Alastair Ladd**

player but you always want to beat your teammate." Similar stories exist of Piquet and Mansell not sharing data during 1986 when they were teammates, and others examples. Conversely, Verstappen admitted Schumacher always shared data with him during 1994 because it was his first year and Jos needed to learn quickly.[182]

Some drivers are technical in their approach, ie they want to understand how the car works and how they can adjust their driving to enhance its grip. Schumacher keeping a constant throttle (via left-foot braking) to benefit the car's pitch and exhaust blown diffuser is an example. Whereas other drivers just react to the car's grip instead of trying to manipulate it, like Schumacher's successor at Benetton, Jean Alesi. "When I went to Benetton in 1996 it was too late in my career to try and teach me a whole new way of driving," said the Frenchman. "I just drive, I don't like engineers telling me how to do it. Michael has improved a lot since he was at Benetton, because there he was just a robot. The team tell you about the aero balance of the car and how best to drive it, and Michael is like a tape: you tell him what to do, he takes it in, and he does it. Then when the car did something he wasn't expecting he usually spun. At Ferrari he learnt to think for himself."[183]

History suggests reactive drivers like Alesi are not as successful as their technically minded counterparts, because you unlock more performance by manipulating a car's grip through clever driving than you would merely reacting to it. Growing up as an Alesi fan during the mid-1990s, I learnt this lesson watching Jean constantly losing races to technically minded drivers like Schumacher and Hill. According to John Watson's Eurosport commentary during 1994, Verstappen and Lehto failed to adapt their driving to utilise Benetton's exhaust blown diffuser, so must therefore be considered reactive drivers as a result. History demonstrates in these situations, reactive drivers can become paranoid their technically minded teammates are receiving better equipment than them, when in fact it is their approach which is proving to be quicker.

Frank Dernie added: "I think Lehto had not expected Schumacher to be as quick as he was. The massive crash he had where he broke his neck was a combination of factors, one was certainly deterioration of the track as the dew dropped but I am fairly sure Lehto was convinced the damper testing we were doing on his car

was the reason for Schumacher being quicker than him earlier, so when we put standard dampers on he was expecting more extra grip than he got." Another example was in early 1992 when Patrese was being convincingly paced by his Williams teammate Mansell.

Patrese then became convinced Mansell had received additional electronic assistance. The Englishman thought to himself: "I'm not having this all year," so let Patrese test his car during a practice session in Brazil. After which the Italian realised both cars were equal and the performance gaps between them was down to Mansell's ability to utilise active suspension better. Patrese had been wary of it due to a testing crash he suffered at Tamburello, the same corner which claimed Senna, whereas Mansell learnt to ignore any fears over active suspension. This example also illustrated what an important factor confidence was among drivers, because essentially that was the reason Mansell averaged 0.9sec quicker than Patrese during 1992. The two drivers had been much closer when active suspension wasn't used in 1991.

It's worth noting that Verstappen has never repeated the claims he made in 2011 that Benetton installed illegal electronic aids solely in Schumacher's car and even contradicted them in subsequent interviews as highlighted earlier. Therefore one has to question whether he still holds those views? Interestingly, Verstappen continued employment with Benetton during 1995 as its reserve driver, then he raced for Walkinshaw (Benetton's 1994 Engineering Director) in 1996 and 2000/01. So if Verstappen truly believed Benetton and its Engineering Director had cheated him during 1994, one has to ask why did he continue working for them and their Engineering Director in subsequent years? Furthermore, why did he not seek further proof from both to support his thus far inconclusive claims? Walkinshaw sadly passed away in 2010 while Verstappen's comments were made a year later, so there wouldn't have been any comeback from Walkinshaw.

This apparent contradiction gives us plenty to think about as we turn our attention towards the key players at Benetton and what their history might suggest regarding the 1994 controversies.

180. *Sport Auto*
181. *L'Automobile*, December 1995

182. *Autosport*, 11 May 1995
183. *F1 Racing*, August 1999

FURTHER BENETTON ALLEGATIONS

After 1994

"I never had any trouble with Tom [Walkinshaw]. He was totally straight and honest with me, and he never asked me to cheat."

Frank Dernie, Benetton's Chief Engineer

"Hey guys, you know me. I no know the difference – fuel filter, coffee filter, whatever! Speak to the tech guys..."

Flavio Briatore, Benetton's Commercial Director

In 2009 Briatore was given a lifetime F1 ban for race fixing. He had been Benetton's commercial director in 1994. ***Photo: Bert van Dijk***

Standings after the 1994 season

DRIVERS' CHAMPIONSHIP		
Pos	Driver	Points
1	Michael Schumacher	92
2	Damon Hill	91
3	Gerhard Berger	41

CONSTRUCTORS' CHAMPIONSHIP		
Pos	Constructor	Points
1	Williams-Renault	118
2	Benetton-Ford	103
3	Ferrari	71

Spot the difference. Above is the Walkinshaw run 1995 Ligier…
Photo: Károly Méhes

…which looked identical to the 1995 Benetton. Mosley visited the Ligier factory, presumably to investigate this? *Photo: Alf van Beem*

This chapter seeks to separate fact from fiction regarding common myths surrounding the Benetton allegations, thus the extent of their culpability will become clear.

One reason several observers believed Benetton strayed beyond the rules in 1994 is because of its Engineering Director, Tom Walkinshaw. The Scot was no stranger to controversy or arguments over rule interpretations before 1994, leading many to conclude that he and Benetton were guilty by association. Let us explore Walkinshaw's past to establish whether this view is valid.

After a brief spell as a racing driver, Walkinshaw founded his own team, Tom Walkinshaw Racing (TWR), in 1976. His first brush with the authorities came in 1983 when TWR's Rover saloons were disqualified from the British Touring Car Championship (BTCC) series after a lengthy legal battle. His driver that year, Steve Soper, explained what occurred: "Then, well into the 1984 season, I lost my 1983 British title over a protest about the Rover's legality. Tom was very clever at building his cars to exploit the rules to their utmost, but he upset quite a few people along the way. Whenever Frank Sytner and BMW protested our cars we always survived but, finally, we were thrown out because Tom had modified the hydraulic tappets – no performance advantage, but for maintenance, so they

The Walkinshaw-run Jaguar was excluded from Le Mans in 1993. Brabham felt "robbed" because "there was a lot of politics going on at the time."
Photo: Christian Madden

could be more quickly adjusted. But it wasn't in the rules, so we were out. At that point, Austin-Rover withdrew in a huff, so I had nothing to drive in the championship I'd won the year before."[184]

Walkinshaw then persuaded the British Racing Drivers' Club (BRDC), owner of Silverstone, to purchase some car dealerships from him. However, the deal collapsed amid legal acrimony in 1993. Meanwhile at the Le Mans 24-hour that year, TWR ran a Jaguar XJ220C which won its class but was subsequently excluded. The car was originally entered under North American (IMSA) rules which permitted racing without catalytic converters. It passed scrutiny but, shortly before the race, organiser l'Automobile Club de l'Ouest (ACO) disqualified the TWR Jaguars for not having catalytic converters. The team competed in the race under appeal but a month later the appeal was overturned because it was lodged too late. At the time, ACO steward, Alain Bertaut, was an old adversary of Walkinshaw's.

One of the drivers, David Brabham, recently admitted: "Tom and the ACO hated each other, so we were wrapped up in all of that mess. And, of course, there were other politics going on with Jaguar. And Tom was a master at playing that kind of game."[185] In recent years, rumours have surfaced that Walkinshaw was deliberately late in his appeal against the 1993 Le Mans disqualification because he was unhappy with Ford's recent acquisition of Jaguar. The Jaguar/TWR relationship had been successful throughout the 1980s and early 1990s, but it was in decline at the time. By 1994, the Walkinshaw run JaguarSport team was liquidated.

When Walkinshaw ran Ligier F1, its 1995 cars looked suspiciously like Benetton's. Max Mosley paid a visit to the Ligier factory pre-season, presumably to investigate, but no further action was taken. Autosport quoted Walkinshaw (January 1995): "Mechanically, it [the Ligier] is totally different [from the Benetton] and structurally it is quite different as well. Aerodynamically, it's as close as we can make it to being the same. I don't know how you would end up with anything else if you take a core of engineers who have been working on the Benetton. Of course the damn thing looks the same. But if you go into the detail of the car, there is nothing interchangeable"

184. *Motor Sport*, February 2014
185. *Motor Sport* podcast, December 2017

These examples prove that Walkinshaw did pushed grey areas, exploit rules and, in the 1983 BTCC case above, he strayed beyond what was acceptable. The Scot also made enemies, particularly with those within positions of authority, such as Mosley and Bertaut of the ACO, so anything could have been possible in 1994. However, in reality, Walkinshaw had limited input on the 1994 Benetton as Frank Dernie, who worked with him from 1991 to 1997, alluded to. "Tom [Walkinshaw] had no day-to-day role at Benetton. He was at meetings from time to time and all the races but not often at the factory. Ross [Brawn] was the only one of us who reported directly to Tom, it would be impossible to guess what work came directly from Tom and what was from Ross. I fell out with Tom and resigned eventually, but he never involved me in any discussion of or involvement in doing anything outside the rules."

Another Benetton insider added "[In 1993] Walkinshaw was at odd tests and all races, Pat Symonds was another man in charge of testing with Ross [Brawn]." The reason for Walkinshaw's limited involvement in the 1994 Benetton was that, during the winter of 1993, TWR was heavily involved in other projects. For instance, it were taking the revolutionary Volvo 850 estate car into the BTCC in 1994. Therefore during the latter half of 1993, Walkinshaw was sourcing the drivers, staff, and facilities for that. His other projects at the time included partly running an F3000 team, bidding to take over the Silverstone lease, and fighting the aforementioned legal case against the BRDC and its investment in car dealerships.

In addition, TWR was also looking to enter Indycars for 1994, while managing the production of the new Aston Martin DB7 and Jaguar XJ220. By 1994, TWR was a global business empire with sites in the UK, Sweden, Australia and the USA, employing circa 1300 people. Given all this, it seems doubtful Walkinshaw spent any significant time at Benetton forcing them to install illegal driver aids. Likewise, would Walkinshaw have taken time out of his busy diary to ensure any cheating instructions were being carried out by his Benetton sub-ordinates? In any case, his instructions would have been passed down to Ross Brawn, who most regard as an ethical competitor.

Hill drove for Walkinshaw's Arrows team in 1997. In his autobiography, Hill recalled a pre-season dinner where Walkinshaw told a sponsor "if you want to win in F1 you've got to cheat." Hill wasn't sure if Walkinshaw was joking but soon realised he would be implicated should any cheating occur. Damon was reigning F1 World Champion at the time, so being involved in cheating would have significant ramifications for him and the sport. However, this incident didn't deter the reigning F1 world champion from driving for Walkinshaw during 1997 because he regarded John Barnard and Frank Dernie as ethical competitors. Hill realised they were the ones who built the car in reality, not Walkinshaw, and its equivalent at Benetton during 1994 would have been Brawn and Byrne.

Since his arrival at Benetton in July 1991, Walkinshaw was primarily involved in reorganising the technical functions and laying the foundation for future success. This involved bringing Schumacher, Brawn, Byrne and Symonds into the team. Walkinshaw also ensured they were given the resources to fulfil their talents, which included acquiring new premises at Enstone and arranging the team to move there in 1992. The Scot was also instrumental in keeping Ford working closely with Benetton until the end of 1994 and managing the engineering office budget.

By early 1994, Walkinshaw was involved in the Ligier purchase, along with fellow Benetton director Briatore. Walkinshaw then carried out a similar role here by placing several key engineers like Frank Dernie in Ligier to restructure them. After the Hockenheim fire and the subsequent Benetton 'management changes', Walkinshaw was moved over to Ligier full-time. The bottom line being that any cheating requests from Walkinshaw to Benetton in 1994 would need to have been delegated to others given his various roles. Twenty-five years later, nobody has come forward

The TWR-run 1994 Volvo BTCC car. When the B194 undertook its first major pre-season test at Barcelona, Walkinshaw was not present because he was at the Volvo 850 launch in Sweden instead. *Photo: Martin Lee*

In reality, Walkinshaw had little day-to-day influence on his cars.
Photo: Race27

Briatore's alleged involvement in fixing the 2008 Singapore Grand Prix raised new doubts over Benetton in 1994.
Photo: chensiyuan; ptttf

admitting that was the case. The likes of Brawn, Brundle, Win Percy, Kenny Brack and Jan Lammers have worked with Walkinshaw for many years. They all list his faults as pushing grey areas and promising things that never happen, but they do not label Walkinshaw as a cheat.

Walkinshaw was possibly responsible for attempting to take advantage of the Silverstone stop-go penalty being communicated late to Benetton, perhaps another example of him pushing grey areas. Others in F1 would probably have done the same in that position, hence why certain rules surrounding stop-go penalties were changed soon afterwards. Similarly, this book contains many examples where others have pushed 'grey areas' but have largely gone unpunished during 1994.

However, Walkinshaw failed to appreciate Silverstone 1994 was politically a very dangerous time for Benetton to be doing that. It is often overlooked that Walkinshaw has not been found guilty of cheating in F1 outside of 1994 despite being involved for over 10 years. Bad business deals yes, aggrieved off investors yes, Ligiers looking suspiciously like Benetton's yes, but no proven cheating.

Another reason used to condemn Benetton for 1994 was who its commercial director was – Flavio Briatore, a man initially given a lifetime ban from F1 after his alleged involvement in fixing the 2008 Singapore Grand Prix. Does this therefore suggest he was willing to instigate any old scam in 1994? Again, let us look at the facts behind this common assumption. Briatore had an unconventional route to becoming an F1 team principal. He worked in several jobs, from ski instructor to insurance salesman, before being convicted on fraud charges during the 1980s. Briatore then received prison sentences totalling four years. However, he fled his native Italy to avoid imprisonment and his convictions were later extinguished by amnesty. Meanwhile, Briatore made his fortune opening Benetton stores across America, which led to him running the Benetton F1 team at the start of 1989.

Briatore had no knowledge of F1 before 1989, nor was he passionate about racing or technology within the sport. Instead his approach was to manage the team like he managed any other company: Improving its people, marketing and return on investment by giving the team a new exciting and glamorous image, thereby ensuring the Benetton brand received good exposure within F1. Briatore acknowledged his skills didn't lie in the engineering aspects of the team, so he left that others. The

allegations against Benetton in 1994 all related to technical issues such as illegal electronic devices, removal of a fuel filter, the plank, and the Silverstone black flag. Given his ignorance over technical matters, it is therefore doubtful he would have been the 'brains' behind them.

Various people who worked with Briatore, including Matchett, Brawn and Herbert, all confirmed he wasn't interested in the technical side of F1 – instead, he viewed it as a business. This explained why Briatore was always looking for the most cost-effective way to run his team, unlike some rivals. For instance, McLaren would usually hire the two best drivers available, irrespective of the cost, whereas Briatore was a believer in having a clear number one and number two driver policy. The Italian's reasoning being Benetton's second driver didn't need a superstar's salary because all they needed was a solid points finisher who helped them win the Constructors' Championship.

That was originally the plan for Lehto, who wasn't being paid remuneration for 1994. Instead, he had a sponsor help (Fazer). Briatore's policy also meant he could be ruthless and replace the second drivers whenever they underperformed, as demonstrated throughout 1994, their feelings not seemingly mattering as Frank Dernie alluded to: "The [pre-season testing] accident and subsequent poor treatment by Benetton management was a big part of demoralising him [Lehto] in my opinion." Briatore personally managed many other drivers who were capable of filling the void as a solid number two, hence his lack of empathy. However, it was his sacking of Piquet Jr, the team's second driver during 2009, which led to the Italian's downfall.

During the 2008 Singapore Grand Prix, Piquet Jr crashed at precisely the right moment to hand a sporting advantage to his teammate Alonso, who subsequently won the race having started a distant 15th. At the time, Piquet described his crash as a simple mistake, despite paddock rumours suggesting the circumstances surrounding it was suspicious, as was Alonso's peculiar race strategy. After Piquet Jr was dismissed in 2009, the disgruntle driver then claimed he was ordered to crash on purpose during this race by Briatore and Symonds who knew the ensuing safety car would benefit Alonso's race. That sparked an investigation by the FIA into race-fixing charges. By 2009, Benetton had morphed into Renault and they announced they wouldn't contest these charges and Briatore and Symonds had left the team.

During the subsequent FIA hearing, the Renault F1 team was given a warning. Briatore was banned from all F1 events indefinitely, and Symonds received a five-year ban. These bans were subsequently overturned by a French court, although both agreed not to work in F1 for three years as part of a later settlement. Benetton's former boss has always maintained he wasn't involved in the crash conspiracy, and this was the reason his lifetime ban was overturned and that every report from the race stewards also concluded this.[186] Meanwhile, Piquet Jr escaped punishment for his involvement because of the evidence he gave. He has always maintained Briatore and Symonds asked him to stage the crash while Symonds has insisted the idea came from Piquet Jr himself as a way assist his 2009 contract negotiations. Piquet Jr did struggle during 2008 so it was surprising when he was retained by Renault for 2009, where he was sacked mid-season for his lack of performances.

Only those involved know what Briatore's true part of this scandal was. Perhaps he pressured the team to win 'by any means necessary', however it seems unlikely he would have initially proposed the idea of crashing on purpose. For the same reason, he was never credited for Renault's/Benetton's race-winning strategies during previous events. Briatore wasn't interested in the strategic details of F1 races so left that to others – he was only interested in the end result. However, if Briatore did instigate the 2008 Singapore conspiracy then it is understandable and natural to view his F1 past, like 1994, with greater suspicions.

Likewise the same applies to Pat Symonds, Schumacher's race engineer in 1994, who also implicated by Piquet Jr in the 2008 conspiracy. Symonds was Renault's Executive Director of Engineering in 2008, so it seems more likely the idea came from him or Piquet Jr rather than Briatore. However, Mosley described Symonds as a "completely honest person"[187] because he immediately confessed his involvement within the 2008 scandal to Mosley once the FIA investigation started. Similarly respected F1 journalist Simon Taylor described Symonds as "honest and honourable"[188] after interviewing him in 2012 over that controversy. Piquet Jr has always maintained the idea came from Briatore and Symonds and the reason he undertook it was: "It actually felt good to agree to do something for the team after all the criticism I had taken. I didn't even consider the morality of it."

What is clear, however, is that Briatore upset key personnel at Benetton during the mid-1990s, which is partly why Schumacher, Brawn, Toet and others left the team. In addition to their own personal grievances, all were upset over how Briatore handled the politics of 1994, which tarnished their own names. Despite this, they, along with hundreds of other former employees, have never since stated Briatore ordered them to cheat in 1994. The Piquet Jr and Verstappen examples showed how easy it was for a disgruntled

Briatore has maintained he wasn't involved in the crash conspiracy, hence his lifetime ban later being overturned. *Photo: Ultra7*

Piquet Jr escaped punishment after blowing the whistle and giving evidence. He has always maintained Briatore and Symonds asked him to stage the crash. *Photo: Ann64*

Many ex-Benetton employees, including all its 1994 drivers, have stated a grievance against Briatore. However, to date only Verstappen has claimed he cheated in 1994. *Photo: Ford*

Ferrari was accused of having illegal driver aids in 1998, after Schumacher and key ex-Benetton staff joined. What does this tell us about the 1994 Benetton allegations? ***Photo: www.williamsdb.com***

ex-employee of Briatore's to make such claims, even when their evidence is not conclusive. However, no other Benetton, Ford, Cosworth, LDRA, or FIA employee has supported Verstappen's claims since, they cannot all still be working in motorsport.

In 1996 Schumacher moved to Ferrari, and by 1997 key Benetton figures like Brawn or Byrne joined him. Ferrari then went from being an occasional race winner to serial championship contenders over a sustained period. Questions have since been asked, why did Schumacher and his former Benetton colleagues stick together? Was it because they all circumvented the rules in 1994 and subsequently at Ferrari? The truth is that, once Schumacher arrived at Ferrari, he did work with their existing technical team in 1996, thereby proving his superior skill didn't rely on his former Benetton colleagues, as confirmed by his 1996 teammate Eddie Irvine. "We were really in the shit in 1996. I remember when the car came out I said, 'That looks worryingly different from everyone else's car.' It turned out everyone else was right and we were wrong... He won three races, which is one of the greatest achievements in motor racing history. He had four pole positions with it and I stood there in awe of his performances that year. That was the year that Michael really earned his money."[189]

Because the 1996 car was so poor and unreliable, it soon became apparent that Ferrari's technical team needed restructuring and strengthening in order to be championship winners. Hence the

reason Schumacher called his former Benetton colleagues, because he knew they could sort out Ferrari's technical woes. If Schumacher *et al* did use illicit methods to turn Ferrari around, then one would expect an immediate jump in performance after their cheating took effect. However, this didn't occur and instead the Ferrari didn't become the best car in F1 until 2000, thereby underlining their rise was gradual and over a number of years. Moreover, at Benetton, it is alleged that they cheated on Schumacher's car but not the number two car, yet there was never this same suggestion at Ferrari even though the same senior figures were involved.

Despite this, speculation continued that Schumacher and his ex-Benetton colleagues were somehow using outlawed devices at Ferrari. For instance, during the summer of 1998, rumours circulated that Ferrari was running illegal driver aids to help them under braking and acceleration. McLaren's Ron Dennis, Ferrari's bitter rivals for the championship, suspected an intelligent brake-balance system, so he visited Ferrari during the Austrian Grand Prix and threatened to protest if his suspicions continued. At the following race in Germany, Ferrari then performed poorly, leading to suggestions they had removed this system after McLaren's actions.

186. *Architects of F1: Flavio Briatore*, Sky F1 (2016)
187. *Architects of F1: Max Mosley*, Sky F1 (2016)
188. *The Times*, 8 December 2010
189. *Michael Schumacher: The Edge of Greatness* by James Allen (2008)

Mosley felt inclined to dismiss these suggestions: "I know McLaren talks about that. There are interesting things at Ferrari, yet nothing illegal. I believe McLaren has understood that and is well on the way to finding an equivalent system."[190] Brawn added "It's just bullshit. You cannot defend yourself against an accusation like that, so it's a very nasty, malicious thing to say. If someone says you have a fantastic system that no-one can detect, how can you prove them wrong? We [Ferrari] are one of the few teams that have our software scrutineered before we actually use it. So we are very sure, and the FIA is very sure, that our software is completely legal."[191]

For whatever reason, Germany proved an exception as Ferrari was competitive for the rest of 1998. At the next race, Hungary, Dennis tried defusing the situation: "Anyone can rerun the tapes from Austria and you can see the wrong wheels are locking up into the corners – it's not the unloaded wheel that's locking up, but the loaded one. We believe that now there has been either an optimisation of the system – or something has changed – because now there's every reason to believe that the system is in accordance with the regulations. And to substantiate that view we have, over the past four weeks, asked many questions of the FIA and sought clarification."[192]

All this came months after Ferrari had successfully protested against McLaren's braking system which allowed its drivers to apply the brakes on the rear wheels independently, assisting both turn-in and traction. Dennis was livid how his system had been banned

Schumacher felt upset that his victories and hard work during 1994 were overshadowed by accusations of illegal electronics. **Photo: Ford**

following Ferrari's protest in early 1998, when McLaren had been dominating races, particularly as the system had previously been permitted in late 1997 when McLaren wasn't as competitive. It would be understandable if Dennis's main motivation for threatening Ferrari later that summer was payback. In the end, he didn't protest against Ferrari, nor did anyone else, so whatever devices the Italian team were running in 1998 was deemed legal.

Dennis might feel had Ferrari's devices been on the McLaren the outcome may have been different. In any case, it boils down to how rules were interpreted so one couldn't call any Ferrari devices cheating, for the same reason one cannot call McLaren's braking system in 1998 cheating either. Essentially, both teams invented clever new technologies which were not previously legislated for. F1 rules needed to be clarified as these new devices appeared, similar to how English law is constantly updated following judgements. During 1998, teams were experimenting with throttle maps, and other devices to emulate traction control within the interpretation of the rules. Dennis admitted "Ferrari seems to be doing quite a good job of it,"[193] but didn't actually suggest their system was illegal.

Nevertheless, dark rumours continued to spread that Schumacher and his ex-Benetton colleagues knew how to cheat in some way with undetectable traction control, thus underlining the possibility they also did so in 1994. These rumours were so rife that Schumacher felt compelled to respond prior to the 1998 Hungarian Grand Prix: "I would never use an illegal system because there are too many big players involved in F1. I know in 1994 that we didn't have anything illegal, but there was so much talk about it that it became like the truth. I was really upset, after victories that we fought and worked for really hard. You will always have engineers trying to get the best out of what you are legally allowed to do. You try to develop something that gives you a little support, and it may come out to something similar to traction control, but it's not traction control."[194] Patrick Head stated he was assured by the FIA that Ferrari's 1998 software was within the rules. Consequently, Williams, McLaren and other teams worked on developing their own systems.

During 1998, many decisions went in Ferrari's favour which was convenient for the championship fight. **Photo: Alastair Ladd**

The 1996 Ferrari did not suddenly become a rocket during starts as a result of Tad Czapski joining. ***Photo: Matthias v.d. Elbe***

However, two years later it emerged at least one team had done something they shouldn't have with their software. Mosley wouldn't name the team/s, but insisted the infringement occurred in 1999 and those involved were not in contention for the world championship,[195] which therefore ruled out McLaren and Ferrari. As a result, new regulations were hurriedly introduced for the 2000 British Grand Prix (explained shortly) to eliminate the problem. Because nobody knew who the culprits were, this heightened suspicions during that race, especially against Schumacher and his former Benetton colleagues who were usually the target for such allegations. Schumacher only added to this innuendo after spinning off during a practice session that weekend. He found himself stuck on the wet grass spinning the rear wheels he was then observed holding and pressing buttons on the steering wheel before attempting to move again.

After a few seconds, his fuel flap opened and he pulled away from the wet grass with no wheelspin whatsoever[196] which only fuelled speculation, because a new regulation introduced for that race stipulated whenever the pit-lane speed limiter button was activated the fuel flap must automatically open as well. The FIA wanted to tell when teams operated their pit-lane speed limiters in case any had used it as traction control covertly. Brawn admitted Schumacher must have therefore turned on his pitlane limiter button to drive off the wet grass, adding "I don't know why he did that". However, Brawn denied the suggestion Ferrari had used it as illegal traction control. "There's not a problem. How would we use it at the start, the fuel flap would open and the rear light would come on (another visual aid the FIA insisted on), so what is there to say?"

Willem Toet, who worked at Ferrari until 1999, but was with rivals BAR-Honda at the time, gave his thoughts on this incident. "No traction control system helps when you have zero grip. For sure, Michael will have been on the radio a number of times to inform the pits what was going on. Reverse was [on purpose] hard to get and then not instant to get out of. It was hydraulically activated like all the gears and the team didn't want it to be selected accidentally. The most likely scenario is that he was selecting reverse, then first

and also talking on the radio. He was more than smart enough to know that minimising wheelspin via clutch control was the best way out of a muddy situation. A traction control system, legal or not, wouldn't have been active in these circumstances – you just couldn't use obvious sensors like wheel speed sensors, which were banned on rear wheels for Silverstone 2000). I am confident that traction control had nothing to do with what Michael tried to do – and clearly, the FIA didn't find anything. However, what he did I have no idea."

Another F1 designer at the time believed Schumacher was changing the differential, which was allowed when the car was stationary and would help prevent wheelspin. "Everyone said Ferrari cheated. I was at Ferrari so I know they don't," claimed Irvine, who was driving for Jaguar at the time. In 2001, traction control was legalised following complaints from F1 engineers that it was impossible to police because of all the suspicion and innuendo as highlighted above. This had not affected F1's pecking order significantly, thereby suggesting that Schumacher and his ex-Benetton colleagues at Ferrari were not finding ways around the traction control ban prior to 2001.

Tad Czapski was Benetton's electronics whiz during 1994 and one of the few to immediately follow Schumacher to Ferrari in 1996. Czapski's clever electronics undoubtedly pushed boundaries, but success in F1 is usually a team effort. So it seems unlikely that was the only reason behind Benetton's good starts/good traction, which is the view held by those who believed the B194 had illegal electronics. The 1996 season is a prime example of this because, after Czapski's move, the Ferrari remained average during starts throughout 1996. This was despite Eddie Irvine claiming he was really good at getting off the line[197] and Schumacher having practised them intensively at Benetton. Meanwhile, the Benetton continued to make good starts even after Czapski's departure.

190. *Autosport*, 6 August 1998
191. *Autosport*, 20 August 1998
192. *Autosport*, 20 August 1998
193. *Autosport*, 16 July 1998
194. *Autosport*, 20 August 2000
195. *Autosport*, 20 August 2000
196. *Autosport*, 27 April 2000
197. *Legends of F1: Eddie Irvine*, Sky F1 (2016)

According to Toet, Schumacher was especially good in cars without traction control. **Photo: Iwao**

Benetton/Renault has always been good at starts and traction. Was this due to a combination of factors or just clever electronics? **Photo: Ford**

It seems more likely, the reason behind the 1994 Benetton good starts/traction was a combination of factors. In addition to the heavy duty clutch, which allowed its drivers to practice their starts, and the legal traction control system, Willem Toet described other contributing factors: "The Cosworth was definitely torquey and – even more importantly – controllable, which played a big part in the traction of the car – just as with my hillclimb car, which was miles better off the line and out of corners than other cars. I didn't use traction control most of the time and it didn't help when I tried it. On the Benetton, we also had a fairly low weight distribution (a bit less weight on the front, a bit more on the rear) than some other cars – there were no weight distribution rules in those days." More weight on the rear wheels benefitted traction, as did keeping the centre of gravity as low as possible, both of which could be achieved because Benetton integrated a smaller V8 engine into its chassis, compared to its rivals. Because Benetton's car was lighter than rivals, ballast could be added around the rear wheels to assist traction.

Toet added: "Then we had a tiny bit less downforce (peak) than the Williams – but with a more controllable aero package. Not easy to drive at all, but easier than the Williams and more modern knowledge tells me that also played a big part in traction." Frank Dernie concurs: "In my opinion, the Benetton traction was an aerodynamic effect which Rory [Byrne] worked very hard on. Nobody sane would have mentioned this at the time because

For 2004, launch control was again banned in F1. Nevertheless, the two Renaults leapt-off the line at most races. **Photo: Rick Dikeman**

it was probably Benetton's biggest secret." Because Benetton's aerodynamics worked over a wider range of height and pitch changes than its rivals, it therefore maintained more consistent traction level coming out of corners than others. Remember, it only takes a momentary loss of grip to cause wheelspin which then requires remedial action from the driver. The final piece of the jigsaw was Schumacher's throttle control, which was incredibly precise and consistent as evidenced by the earlier telemetry traces. Nevertheless, Toet provided more insight.

"One of the early surprises was Michael trying to cope with a car that didn't have traction control and trying to get the best out of it. One of the ways he described it was: he would push the accelerator to come out of the corner, the car would start to slide so he'd come off the 'gas' again, but this was happening faster than we could believe and, at the time, I think we were only logging the throttle position at 10 or 20 times per second. When we started logging the throttle position at higher frequencies, we could see what he was doing. We realised that he was pushing the car into a slide, the yaw rate would begin to increase, then he would back off the throttle and the yaw rate would begin to decrease until he would get back on the throttle again. Something we had not seen at that speed before from other drivers."[198] This explained why Irvine believed Schumacher was excellent at mapping the engine, and at throttle response work.[199]

Conversely, Dickie Stanford, Williams' Chief Mechanic in 1994, admitted it took them a few races into that season before finding "the sweet spot to run the car ride height wise and (rear) suspension settings"[200] This suggests Williams' traction wouldn't have been ideal until then. Given all the above, was it any wonder why Senna was lamenting the gulf in traction between his Williams and Schumacher's car? Benetton/Renault's race starts and traction didn't noticeably improved after Czapski re-joined them in 2001, thus illustrating his electronics were certainly part of the equation but, as in 1994, it wasn't the only reason. For instance, between 2001 and 2004 Benetton/Renault used a revolutionary engine with an extremely wide V-angle (111deg whereas other engines were between 72 and 90deg). This allowed Benetton/Renault to install its engine lower into their car than others, giving them acceleration benefits at the cost of reliability.

Was it any wonder why Senna was lamenting the gulf in traction between his Williams and Schumacher's car? ***Photo: Martin Lee***

For 2004, launch control was banned from F1 once again after a brief hiatus since 2001. After the Australian Grand Prix, Alonso said his start had been "just as good" as a 2003 electronically assisted one – it left Renault rivals wondering. The 2004 rules stated that traction-control could only kick-in after the car has reached 62mph (100km/h), meaning the starts should have been up to the driver. "The start is one of the best times to overtake in F1," Renault's Pat Symonds told *Autosport* at the time, "so obviously we work very hard at that."

According to an *Autosprint* article, the reason behind Renault's great starts at the time was that its car was built with greater weight around the rear wheels than competitors. This was due to a more robust clutch and sturdier driveshaft, transmission etc, which all allowed the Renault drivers to perform a starting technique that would be damaging for other (more fragile) cars. Essentially, there were two design philosophies very different in their objectives. The one preferred by most teams gave priority to lightness, while Renault's heavier but sturdier components could withstand maximum engine revs, and holding the car on the clutch biting point for several seconds (with the brake on) for super-quick starts.[201] The above example showed good starts and traction has always been Benetton/Renault's priority and it has always been a team effort, so not just reliant on the electronics of one man.

However, let's assume for a moment that Benetton did have illegal software in 1994. How easy would it have been to hide this from the hundreds of employees of Benetton, Ford, Elf, FIA, LDRA etc? Paul West of Williams gives his thoughts: "All I would say is that if we, Williams, had any 'tricky' software, it would be hard to not be aware of it because we, the mechanics, would be party to what the driver needed to do to use it, either by direct instruction

or over the radio at the start, say, for launch control or for traction control during the race.

"I am not a great diplomat and am prone to 'go off on one', so even if Benetton were doing something illegal I wouldn't have been in the loop, even though I was Chief Engineer. Having written that, since there were only two people present every time the car ran, whether testing, racing or shakedown, Tad Czapski and myself, it would have been very difficult but not impossible for a launch control to have been tested without my knowing about it." Czapski was hired by Walkinshaw in the autumn of 1992 to work on Benetton's advanced electronics which included active suspension, semi-automatic gearboxes and traction control. He then followed Schumacher to Ferrari but, in 2001, returned to Benetton. Czapski was contacted but declined to contribute towards this book.

Pat Symonds, Schumacher's race engineer in 1994, believed: "If someone wanted to be really devious, they could have hidden it from me, but they couldn't have hidden it from him – Michael would have had to be involved, and I don't think he would have been. He did some things that were unsporting, let's say, but he always did them on the spur of the moment. His instantaneous decision-making was sometimes not very good. But I don't think he ever had any preconceived ideas of doing anything wrong. That's why I don't think he would have gone along with anything like launch control, and absolutely he would have had to have known about it."[202]

In the next chapter, we will explore the remaining arguments behind this topic, and give a final summary.

198. Willem Toet, LinkedIn blog, 9 December 2015
199. *Legends of F1: Eddie Irvine*, Sky F1 (2016)
200. *Motor Sport* podcast, February 2018
201. *Autosprint*, 13 October 2004
202. *Autosport*, 6 August 2014

PEMBREY TEST AND CONCLUSIONS

April 1994 and beyond

"I do remember that day at Pembrey... just [Benetton] doing start practice in front of us, not realising that there was somebody from Williams present."

Jonathan Williams, son of Williams team owner

"The Pembrey test Williams suspicions I know about, neither Dickie Stanford nor Jonathan Williams could possibly know [what Benetton was testing there]"

Frank Dernie, Benetton's Chief Mechanic

Did Benetton use traction control during a Pembrey test in April 1994? ***Photo: Antony John Dennis***

Pembrey, situated near Swansea, was an unusual testing venue for Benetton (pictured in 1993) which was located in Oxfordshire.
Photo: Richard Francis

As in the previous chapter, we seek to analyse any outstanding allegations surrounding Benetton in 1994 thus allowing you to reach a definitive conclusion on the matter. In February 2018, it emerged Benetton aroused suspicion of using illegal traction control during a Pembrey testing session. Jonathan Williams, the son of legendary team owner Frank Williams explained: "It must have been in between the [Pacific] Grand Prix at Aida, the race at which Ayrton observed what he considered was traction control [on Schumacher's Benetton], and Imola, because it was JJ Lehto coming back [after his pre-season neck injury] to replace Jos Verstappen for the third race.

"We were at Pembrey in our trucks, camped out on the pit apron, and Benetton did turn up that night and went into the scrutineering hut in the centre of the track. So, apart from knowing there were two teams on site, you were not seeing each other. On Friday, somebody from Benetton who I didn't know came down to us and said, 'What's your program for the afternoon? We'd like to do some start practice and you're on the pit straight, so we'd like to do some start practice right in front of you.' We said, 'Actually, we've got a bit of a [free] slot then,' and so we all went on the pit wall and watched it. I'm not going to name names, but a Madgwick [Formula 3000] mechanic, who then went on to be a hugely successful systems engineer for two Formula 1 teams, both during their championship-winning periods, said to me: 'Just look at the tire marks and listen.' He was educating me on traction control."

"What really, in hindsight, rammed it home to me was when an ex-Williams employee, again nameless, who was at Benetton came down and watched, and then saw me, and very quickly scuttled back. They stopped start testing, knowing that they were in front of somebody from Williams. I've never told that story in public before, but it was 20-plus years ago, and there are enough people actually saying that the car was equipped with traction control for me to not feel concerned about that story being out there."[203] So did Benetton give the game away, or was Williams being paranoid?

Jonathan Williams certainly deserved credit for these comments, since most were unwilling to talk openly about allegations they cannot prove. Similarly, if one was going to test illegal traction control then a discreet venue where no other F1 team was present would have been ideal. Williams' comments suggest only Benetton and Madgwick, a Formula 3000 team was present that day. While F1 teams did test at Pembrey at the time, it certainly wasn't a go to venue like Silverstone.

Benetton (pictured in 1993) was the only F1 team present that day at Pembrey, adding to the suspicions. ***Photo: Richard Francis***

Antony John Dennis attended the majority of Benetton tests during 1993/94 in his role as a Race/Test Field Technician to Benetton but wasn't present at this one. Nevertheless, he believes Benetton was at Pembrey then for suitability, availability and cost saving reasons. F1 teams usually tested at Silverstone all together under pre-planned FOCA tests[204]. This was so they could share the costs of the required medical facilities and marshalling, because 'Silverstone Syd' (the circuit's chief fire marshal) usually brought a huge entourage. Pembrey, being a much smaller track, therefore wouldn't have needed as many facilities. Antony John Dennis also added: "Down time is very expensive when you are renting a race track, a helicopter, a doctor and several marshals."

The official reason for the test was to assess JJ Lehto's race fitness following his horrific pre-season testing accident, as Jonathan Williams alluded to, and this may have been another reason Pembrey was chosen as the venue because the Welsh circuit was bumpier than other tracks, providing a greater challenge to Lehto's neck. In addition, Pembrey offered a greater variety of high speed corners together with heavy braking zones than Silverstone, which was mostly high-speed corners and little else. After this test Lehto remarked: "It [Pembrey] is one of the bumpiest tracks I've ever driven on, but I felt no pain and there were no after effects. If I can do 90 laps there I can race at Imola."[205]

At the time, Williams was testing at the similarly remote Nogaro circuit in France, precisely because it was bumpy and they needed to assess its aerodynamic problems on this kind of track. The relative secrecy at Pembrey would have also allowed Lehto to perform at his own pace, without any unnecessary pressure or distractions one would find at a higher profile FOCA test. For instance, the Lehto/Pembrey test wasn't reported in *Motor Sport* or *F1 News* magazines. This was important, because Lehto wasn't yet confirmed as driving in the next grand prix so this Pembrey test was effectively an audition for him. While there were no major race events taking place at Silverstone that day, it is possible that it was busy with other activities such as work being carried out to the track or corporate activities etc.

203. *Motor Sport*, 7 February 2018
204. F1 Constructors' Association (FOCA) tests involved all the teams testing at one circuit at the same time. An example was the pre-season Imola test discussed at the end of chapter two
205. *Autosport*, 28 April 1994

At Pembrey the first corner was a tight hairpin, a short distance away from the pit buildings, so one might have expected Jonathan Williams and others present to have heard traction control in operation during Lehto's 90-lap race run because during a test session the silence is only shattered by the cars running on the track, which in this case was two. Yet Williams' comments implied Benetton used traction control during starting practice only, which would suggest it was launch control and thus consistent with the LDRA findings but not with Verstappen's 2011 claims. Nor does Williams describe what kind of sound he heard when standing on the pit wall watching Benetton's starts, nor whether Lehto was executing a special paddle/button pressing sequence (as stated in the LDRA report) in order to engage launch control, and nor whether the Finn was flooring the throttle before his starts. All of which should have been noticeable to Williams so his accusations are somewhat weakened by his failure to provide these crucial details.

When asked about the Pembrey test, Frank Dernie, a former Williams engineer himself, replied: "Lots of people in other teams make gross and often incorrect guesses of what the competition are doing, particularly when they are getting beaten." Previously, it was explained how Dernie introduced lots of start practice within test plans over the winter of 1993/94 because Benetton had developed a unique heavy duty clutch which could cope with this along with Schumacher's 'distressing' starting technique. So could Benetton have been getting Lehto up to speed with this new clutch which would have been unfamiliar to him at Pembrey? Remember Hill commenting his great start at the Hungarian Grand Prix was due to him practising starts.[206] Those comments implied Williams had not been practising starts before Hungary to the extent Benetton was.

This might explain why the "ex-Williams" engineer who was at Benetton in 1994 stopped start practice at Pembrey upon seeing Jonathan Williams – because they didn't want Williams knowing about their heavy duty clutch which allowed Benetton drivers to practice starts and hone their technique more than others. Paul West of Williams stated: "As far as I remember, the clutches we [Williams] used were just straight out of the box with no modifications." So could Williams have been using a lighter, more fragile clutch than Benetton's which couldn't take as many starts

Antony John Dennis's comments regarding Pembrey are based on scientific experiments carried out during Benetton tests during 1992/93. The above photo was taken at Santa Pod. **Photo: Pete Henessy**

Pembrey is situated on flat land so the sound of Benetton's alleged traction control should have been noticeable. **Photo: Richard Francis**

before burning out. Similar to the 2004 Renault example explained earlier, sometimes the weight penalty is more than compensated by an improvement in driver starting technique which the sturdier equipment allows for.

When asked how many starts a typical F1 clutch could do in 1994, Paul West said: "I think four to five, possibly six, depending on how good the driver was at starts and clutch control." West also confirms that it took Williams 45 minutes to replace a clutch on the car and adds: "If we only had one driver testing, then one car is all we would take [to a test] but doing the race distance first and then practice starts makes sense. The team would be more interested in data from a race run and the starting practice is more for the benefit of the driver."

Therefore if Benetton was testing an illegal traction/launch control at Pembrey, one has to wonder why they would left such an important item of the test until the end of the day? Several problems could have arisen which would have resulted in no data being gathered on their allegedly illegal devices. Indeed, through pre-season testing, only weeks earlier, Benetton failed to make a race distance due engine reliability problems. The Brazilian race was the first time its new-for-1994 engine lasted the distance, and that was only after measures like limiting mileage in the morning warm-up and Schumacher backing off once Senna retired.

Also how comfortable would Benetton have been testing an illicit device in front of an F3000 team that would have been participating in support races during the European Grand Prix weekends? Madgwick was a professional team with knowledgeable technicians and very much a part of the F1 world for the majority of the season. Equally odd is that Benetton only brought Lehto to Pembrey – a driver who had yet to be confirmed as racing for them following his injuries. So it would have been a reckless decision for Benetton to impart such sensitive information to Lehto under these circumstances.

Nevertheless, let's assume Benetton was testing launch control that day – this still does not mean they cheated in 1994, since teams didn't have to adhere to race regulations during testing. Cheating can only occur during a race weekend, but would Benetton test something they had not intended to race? Willem Toet replied: "Now, but even more in the past, tests are used to develop systems. It was common practice then as it is now to test illegal devices in tests in order to assess the value of an idea. I have no idea if the Pembrey test electronics were legal for use in F1 or not but I'm sure

Antony John Dennis has no knowledge of launch control testing taking place after 1993. **Photo: Alastair Ladd**

they were development tests to evolve systems." In 1994, Williams had an anti-roll bar adjuster inside the FW16 cockpit for 'testing purposes only' which, if used during race weekends, would have been illegal. Similarly, Williams continued testing its continuously variable transmission (CVT) in 1993 even after it was declared illegal, for the reasons Toet alluded to.

Antony John Dennis (who wasn't present that day at Pembrey) believed Benetton was giving Lehto vital test miles, post-injury and pre-race. This normally included start testing, which ironically was usually undertaken at the end of the day, due to the high risk of clutch damage. "If you break a clutch at the beginning of the day, you could lose hours of testing replacing it," Dennis added. He also believed information would have been imparted to a driver on the fastest way to start, based on scientific experiments carried out during the development of launch control during 1992/93. Dennis cited the example of speed traps being set up along the start section of a track, with on-board logging of front and rear wheel speeds, throttle angle, revs, clutch accelerometers etc, so Benetton could accurately measure the performance of different kinds of starts (during 1992/93).

Dennis also responded to the idea that Benetton may have switched on its illegal during race weekends launch control at Pembrey. "Using launch control during testing could give a driver the feeling of what a fantastic start felt like through the seat of his pants, so next time around when that option wasn't available, or at races, the driver could try and replicate that great start feeling. The team could remind him; 'you need to hold X-rpm, and aim for Y percent wheel slip' in order to achieve the best getaway."

Alternatively, perhaps it was Benetton's legal traction control that Jonathan Williams heard at Pembrey, because this system worked intermittently, depending on how well tuned it was to current track conditions. That would explain why it was only heard during practice starts but not during Lehto's race runs, since the device could only be tuned to one set of parameters at a time, and track conditions are ever evolving. Track parameters varied every few laps because of tyre wear, improving track grip, ambient temperatures etc. Remember, Lehto did 90 laps that day.

Toet continued: "It's easy for people to look back and say that due to the sound or due to the marks on the road the car must have been illegal. However, they have completely missed the point that Benetton found a loophole in the rules that took advantage of a freedom installed to protect the engines from blowing up to manage acceleration. That advantage/understanding didn't spread to other teams for, in some cases, many years. Pushing the grey areas? Well of course! F1 rules have been written specifically to allow that.

"Are the people commenting wrong with their conclusions? Absolutely they're wrong – they don't understand the rules. Letter of the law counts – spirit doesn't exist. Did the FIA know that the rules could be 'abused' in this way? How exactly, no, but they wanted rules that could be interpreted in different ways to spice things up – and spice things up Benetton did! Will the argument continue into infinity? Probably, but it won't change the result and it won't change the fact that the doubters don't get it. The trick is often about finding loopholes. Ground effect, twin chassis, fan car, twin rear wings, twin towers, mass dampers, double diffusers, coanda exhausts. The rule makers love it when a team upsets the apple cart and steps up above the pack. Then they 'clarify' the rules and flatten the playing ground again until the next successful idea That's exactly what F1 had been about for the last 50 years."

The now infamous Pembrey test took place in late April, just after the Pacific Grand Prix where Ferrari had its variable rev limiter banned and teams like Sauber and Arrows had been viewed with suspicion. McLaren had previously stated the FIA was unable to police the traction control ban, essentially claiming it all boiled down to how honest teams were willing to be. All this had followed cheating accusations between Williams, Ferrari and McLaren throughout pre-season. Under that toxic backdrop, Jonathan Williams conclusions is understandable, but according to his colleague Richard Wise another early season test also gave rise to Williams' suspicions.

206. F1 News, 24 August 1994

"I remember standing at the front of the [Williams] garage with Ayrton – the first time I had ever really been 'alone' with him. Michael Schumacher drove out of his garage and stopped right in front of us. He then did a perfect traction control start leaving the tell-tale tyre marks within 10ft of us. I looked at Ayrton and he looked at me, shook his head and said 'that's what we are up against, how can we compete against that?'" When probed about the kind of tyre marks, Wise responded: "The black tyre grip marks were very short on/off/on/off, without any sideways sliding. Practice starts were very common in those days – not as common as in 1993 when traction control was permitted – but if you didn't want the opposition to see them, they would be done at the back of the circuit – on this occasion, Michael knew we were standing there so who knows why he did it right in from of us?

I would imagine that we and all the other cars did them [practice starts] at this test but this one stood out as it was obviously 'controlled' by something [which was obviously permitted while testing but not in a race situation]. It's very difficult to say what the reason for the Benetton starts was – they could have been anything to do with launch control. Normally any car doing any form of start procedure would do it after they had passed the last 'inhabited' garage, for both safety and secrecy reasons. On this occasion, it was strange that Michael decided to do it in front of us. It could have been the 'legal' system that Willem Toet describes."

Interestingly, Benetton's Joan Villadelprat admitted: "Benetton's plan was to defeat Williams and Ayrton Senna, even in the psychological war that was very big." Villadelprat's claim is backed up by Schumacher overtaking Senna during the formation lap in Brazil, and doing the same to Hill at Silverstone. Furthermore, Benetton appeared to try fooling Senna and Williams during morning warm-up at Imola 1994 by running at a pace which suggested a one-stop strategy, not the three-stop strategy Schumacher used during the race.

Perhaps Benetton, knowing that paranoia had descended upon F1 at the time, was engaging in mind games with Williams and Senna during that incident Richard Wise alludes to. Why else would Schumacher and Benetton blatantly do a start "obviously 'controlled' by something" in front of Williams? One Benetton mechanic, who had previously worked at Williams, was "always was a bit of a joker" according to Frank Dernie who adds "so it wouldn't surprise me at all if he was the source when winding up one of his old colleagues."

Whatever, the net result of this and what he heard during the Aida race caused Senna to tell key Williams personnel of his conviction that Schumacher's Benetton was different from the second Benetton, which differs from Jonathan Williams' account from the Pembrey test because both Benetton cars running an illegal device is not a commonly held view. If that were the case, it would make the significant time gaps between Schumacher and his teammates harder to fathom because, as detailed earlier, Schumacher's throttle technique was vastly superior to his teammates'.[207] Had both cars been using an illegal system it should have brought Schumacher's teammates closer to his times.

Senna's suspicions were aroused in Aida and, afterwards, he reportedly visited the Renault HQ where he demanded they recreate traction control, of which all records disappeared after the start.[208] In the book *The Death of Ayrton Senna*, it also was reported Senna was in Paris (12 miles north of the Renault HQ) ten days prior to Imola to watch a friendly football match between France and Brazil. Williams chief mechanic, Dickie Stanford, added "Ayrton was convinced that [Benetton] was doing something, and we [at Williams] were as well. I know the engine note was recorded and everything, I don't know whether [Williams or Renault] took it to the FIA, I don't know. I know they recorded it because we still record engine notes now. You can tell a lot [from engine notes]."[209]

In 1993 some F1 cars had traction control. Their tyre marks are light and on/off (circled in red), while non-traction control F1 cars left thick black lines. *Photo: Landmensch*

Richard Wise was Williams' timekeeper and, given his vantage point, nobody would have heard the cars better than him during tests.
Photo: Richard Wise

In addition to the mind games Benetton played on him, Senna found the Williams culture of "the driver is just an employee" very different to McLaren's, where his every wish was attended to. Both perhaps added to his woes during early 1994. **Photo: Instituto Ayrton Senna**

Nothing came of Renault's recordings of the B194. Renault then supplied engines to Benetton for 1995 and beyond. Today it owns the team. **Photo: Supermac1961**

Acoustic analysis is regularly used by F1 teams to determine the traction qualities of rival cars, based on revs and gearchanges so, it has developed considerably over the years. When quizzed about this, Paul West of Williams answered: "I know Renault recorded the Benetton during testing [in 1994] using equipment around various circuits and from their recordings they were convinced that traction control was being used. Bernard Dudot [Renault boss] tried to persuade Patrick Head [Williams Technical Director] to present their evidence to the FIA, but Patrick wanted 110 percent assurance that it was infallible and Dudot couldn't give him that assurance so it was never pursued." Williams also videoed Schumacher's starts at Imola during race day, and spied into Benetton's garage at the Suzuka race weekend.

So, with all this espionage and the fact a F1 Championship was at stake, one could only imagine the analysis undertaken by Renault and Williams on these recordings. Frank Williams has since added: "It didn't stack up that he [Senna] had been blown away by the Benetton, he wanted us to protest [against Benetton for illegal traction control] which we didn't do."[210] But what difference – if any might it have made had Williams protested against Benetton?

Schumacher's black box, which would have contained any traces of illegal driver devices, was scrutinised by the FIA after the San Marino, British, Hungarian and Japanese Grand Prix – significantly more than any other driver during the 1994 season.[211] As detailed earlier, the findings were queried after the San Marino Grand Prix, but the FIA decided there was insufficient evidence for action to be taken. The FIA also checked Schumacher's differential after Spain, his throttle actuator after Canada, and his engine after the European Grand Prix[212] which was in addition to the usual scrutineering and random checks carried out before and during an F1 race weekend.

Schumacher's only scrutineering failure was following Belgium after the plank infringement. Rob Seymour worked as a contractor for Ford Electronics within Benetton and was responsible for

the real-time telemetry, engine ECU and drivers display for the Cosworth engine. He attended all of the races during 1994 and, along with his colleagues, liaised with Charlie Whiting, the FIA's technical delegate, regarding data downloads post-race. Seymour stated: "There were three black boxes on the car – Tad's [Czapski] gearbox chassis controller, our [Ford Electronics] ECU and a Cosworth data recorder. The ECU held no data recording, so we used to hand the program e-prom to the FIA for comparison with a sample program lodged with them this happened at most events post-race in *parc fermé*.

"The one race I remember was Belgium where Charlie measured our plank and didn't want to see any data at all. When asked by Benetton's chief mechanic if he was to measure Hill's plank he said he didn't need to... we were the only team disqualified. I am unaware of other teams features as then there were rumours all over the place, also l do not know how many times Benetton had their software checked. I had data on any ignition cuts demanded from the chassis controller used for pitlane speed control. The traction control module used during 1993 was also a Ford device but not fitted in 1994."

Other drivers/teams were also checked post-race, but none more so than Schumacher. So any suggestion the FIA allowed Schumacher to cheat during 1994 because they wanted a German champion or to avoid a lawsuit after Senna's death is not supported by the above. Willem Toet summed up his feelings: "I think it is really funny how 'sure' people are that the Benetton was illegal when it was the most scrutinised car on the grid." Hill's ECU was checked after the 1994 Hungarian and Japanese Grand Prix without complaint.[213] Paul West provided more insight on this scrutineering process:

207. Discussed in chapter 13
208. *Sport Auto*
209. *Motor Sport*, 7 February 2018
210. *Senna* movie (2011)

211. *F1 News*, 8 March 1995
212. *F1 News*, 8 March 1995
213. *F1 News*, 8 March 1995

Chapter 15

Schumacher's 1994 helmet. The FIA carried out random checks on everything, including this. **Photo: Mike Fairholme Designs**

Renault was the best engine in 1994, but the Schumacher/Ford/Benetton combination was better than the Hill/Williams/Renault combination until late 1994. **Photo: Thesupermat**

"From memory, they also checked the black box after qualifying and, as it took about half an hour to check, it was a pain for us as we couldn't do any work on the car until they finished. We would go and have some lunch if it was going to take a long time. I didn't hear of any issues after they checked the black box [on Hill's Williams]. The cars were kept for an hour after the race [for scrutineering]. It was allowed for two guys per car to clean them but nothing else."

Many read Benetton's various penalties during 1994 as the FIA punishing them in other ways, because they couldn't nail them over the launch control affair. But how could Benetton concealed illegal devices given the constant microscope it has been under both then and since? What more could Benetton have done to defend itself or

At various times during a grand prix weekend, the cars would be checked for their legality. From 1994 onwards, this included checks to the cars' ECUs. **Photo: Károly Méhes**

the FIA to prove guilt? If cheating was able to slip through the FIA's net then should the driver aid ban have been imposed in 1994 if it couldn't be policed?

Interestingly, Schumacher's V8 engine car often eclipsed the V10 powered Williams. The 1994 season was the only one during the era where these two powerplants co-existed as competitors, and the V8 triumphed. However, in F1 it is not all about horsepower, it's how a car works as a package. Weight distribution, torque, fuel consumption, aero packaging etc all determine performance. Benetton's Ross Brawn added: "One of the development goals was to keep the car's centre of gravity as low as possible. The aerodynamics program was designed to deliver stable downforce. That had been forgotten at the time of the active chassis because the car was always kept in one position. The engine was developed in collaboration with the chassis engineers to ensure a perfect integration. The Benetton B194 rewarded us for this effort."[214]

Mark Blundell also pointed out that good cars developed a driver's confidence, thus allowing them to unlock more performance. The B194 was possibly the first car designed mainly for Schumacher's driving style, which may explain why the German performed at another level that year. Conversely, the Williams FW16, in its early season guise, wasn't a car that inspired confidence in its drivers. Once Williams' early season problems were resolved, Hill and Schumacher fought against each other just as in the latter half of 1993.

But how could Benetton win one grand prix in 1993, but eight races in 1994? That level of improvement had rarely been seen in F1 but comparisons did exist. For example, the Honda F1 team achieved one podium in 2008, because it had decided – as did Benetton in 1993 – to focus its resources on the following season's car earlier than others. This philosophy of short-term sacrifice led to long-term reward as they won the championship the following season as Brawn Grand Prix. The links between the two are Ross Brawn and a major rule change between those seasons.

Dave Shelton (pictured above in the B194): "When you're winning everyone thinks you're cheating. I was accused of cheating in the BOSS series, even though there were no fucking rules!" ***Photo: Dave Shelton***

During 1993, all the top cars had traction control so Benetton couldn't have cheated, and after every race, Schumacher either didn't finish or stood on the podium. So throughout the entire 1993 season only Senna, Prost and Hill ever finished ahead of him. Now consider Prost's retirement, Senna's death and that Williams was the team affected worst by the driver aids ban. Was Schumacher's domination in early 1994 really that surprising?

Benetton always maintained it were treated unfairly throughout 1994. Indeed, Pat Symonds, Schumacher's Race Engineer, said: "We'll never know what was behind it all. But there is no doubt that proper practices were ignored because people felt that the ends justified the means. I'm absolutely certain of that. What the end was, to this day I'm not quite sure." Whereas Joan Villadelprat, Benetton's Operation Director in 1994, added: "It was really hard year because there was a lot of things that happened to us. But I can guarantee you that as far as I know, the car was absolutely perfectly legal. I think we caught everybody by surprise. We broke the establishment a little bit. And when you do that, you always have a price to pay, and I think we paid that price through the year."[215] If Benetton had knowingly ran driver aids and managed to escape punishment over it, why would it antagonise the FIA by implying its other penalties were unfair?

Some felt Benetton's punishments were politically motivated and influenced by a need to make the championship exciting by allowing Hill and Williams to close up. Mosley dismissed this: "When you actually sit in on a hearing you do not think like that. Take the incident at Silverstone where Schumacher ignored the black flag. This was the equivalent of a football player ignoring the red card and the trainer on the touchline telling the player, don't take any notice, keep on playing... Schumacher might have made a mistake and broken his arm: nobody could foresee that Hill would actually win the two races when Schumacher was banned, nor predict that Benetton would mess up their settings on Schumacher's car leading to his disqualification [at Spa]."

"Who could have predicted that Hill would have blown Schumacher fair and square in the penultimate race at Suzuka? None of these things was predictable. But when you are considering a case as a member of the World Council you tend to only look at the actual incident in question. I think the atmosphere in the Council is very fair and very honest."[216] Nevertheless, it seems F1 did enjoy a revival of interest during late 1994 stemming from the Schumacher/Hill rivalry.

214. *Auto Motor und Sport*, 21 December 2014   216. *F1 News*, 22 February 1995
215. *Autosport*, 7 August 2014

Chapter 15

The level of controversy exhibited throughout 1994 has never been repeated within the sport since because the FIA learned from its mistakes that year as Mosley later noted. "The difficult area is when teams think that something is OK and we don't, which is why we go through this elaborate procedure of checking everything beforehand [for 1995 onwards]. It is in everybody's interest to discover these things before a race and not after a driver had been on the podium and drunk the champagne. The checking procedure will be carried out by LDRA and FIA Technical Delegate Charlie Whiting. At every race this year [1995] we will have at least one electronics specialist and a fuel specialist, operating out of a new purpose-built transporter."[217] As a result, the public rarely saw future accusations of teams cheating via electronics aids, because the FIA usually dealt with these matters internally, and before races.

As a consequence, the Benetton allegations stand out like a sore thumb among fans because all the sordid details of their investigation are within the public domain, hence why it has been furiously debated ever since. That it involved the driver leading the championship and Senna died believing Schumacher's Benetton was illegal all added to the public interest. Whereas the aforementioned teams with illegal devices during 1999 didn't create anything like the same amount of public interest or discussion amongst F1 fans because, unlike the Benetton case, the details were kept from the public. Thus the matter was quickly forgotten about, yet the alleged crime was still the same.

Benetton learnt in 1994 that, once you started beating the establishment, you better ensure all aspects of your operation are in good order, as any failing could be used against you. Benetton was

naïve to this so perhaps it contributed to the negative perceptions bestowed upon them. The politics that year were especially sensitive given the tragedies and the worldwide media spotlight shining on F1 afterwards. Equally, the rules were much less professional and defined in comparison to today.

For instance, it was detailed earlier how, before the Verstappen fuel fire, the FIA was unaware what instructions Intertechnique was giving teams as to what they could do with the refuelling equipment, because the FIA didn't know about the Larrousse letter initially. Thus the 1994 controversies have to be seen under the context that there were greater opportunities for misunderstandings between the FIA and teams until the rules were more clearly defined.

In my experience, most F1 fans believe Benetton cheated in 1994. However, the reasoning for that belief is not always sound. Essentially conspiracy theories are intriguing, exciting and believable when presented in an oversimplified way by those who reject the factual reality to those displeased about the results. When misinformation surrounding a subject is embellished, the truth becomes lost. This book hopes to reverse that trend by questioning commonly held opinions.

After 25 years of rumours and speculation on this subject, hopefully this retrospective helps clarify what actually occurred. Like him or not – and, despite all the problems with his heat-of-the-moment decision making – Schumacher was one of motorsport's greatest ever drivers. Likewise Benetton regularly outperformed its larger competitors during the mid-1990s. So if their 1994 successes were achieved legitimately, then F1 fans

The various Benetton controversies along with the Schumacher v Hill rivalry kept F1 newsworthy throughout 1994. *Photo: Alastair Ladd*

Perhaps Ratzenberger's and Senna's greatest legacy was F1 safety developments stemming from their deaths, like the higher cockpit sides.
Photo: tonylanciabeta

must credit them rather than diminish their achievements with accusations of cheating. If, on the other hand there was any truth behind the accusations, then – out of respect to Senna – that truth must be known.

Away from the acrimony lay a more profound sadness: the accidents throughout 1994. The deaths of Senna and Ratzenberger shocked F1 and, after some internal power struggles (detailed earlier), they eventually forced the sport to unite over improving safety. The resulting scientific approach towards safety saved countless lives within the world of motorsport.

But perhaps an even greater legacy was how this improvement over F1 safety filtered down to the average road car, thus saving tens of thousands of people across the world. Mosley explained "When Sid's [safety] committee started (after Monaco 1994) I said to him, maybe what we should do is have a look at what the governments are doing, because 50,000 a year are being killed on roads – and a high proportion of them were car passengers.

"It was logical to think that there must be quite a lot of research going on about how better to protect people in the cars, but when we got somebody to have a look we found nothing had changed since 1974 – and that was 20 years before. There were proposals from one part of the commission in Brussels to bring some things in. But these were being blocked by the industry part of the commission that was under the influence of the car industry. So we started a big thing in Brussels and got all that changed. It's reckoned that since 2000, there have been 100,000 fewer killed than would have been if there had been none of the measures... Of course, none of that would have happened without Senna's accident."[218] Or indeed Ratzenberger's accident, whose memory this book is proudly dedicated to.

217. *F1 News*, 22 February 1995
218. *Autosport*, 7 August 2014

Benetton had not been regularly winning prior to 1994, so perhaps they were naïve to the Machiavellian politics that can be associated with that.
Photo: Pete Henessy

BENETTON'S RACING RECORD IN F1

Year	Engine	Drivers	Points	WCC
1986	BMW M12/13 L4t	Teo Fabi		
		Gerhard Berger	19	6th
1987	Ford-Cosworth GBA 1.5 V6	Teo Fabi		
		Thierry Boutsen	28	5th
1988	Ford-Cosworth DFR 3.5 V8	Alessandro Nannini		
		Thierry Boutsen	39	3rd
1989	Ford-Cosworth DFR 3.5 V8	Alessandro Nannini		
	Ford HBA1 3.5 V8	Johnny Herbert		
	Ford HBA4 3.5 V8	Emanuele Pirro	39	4th
1990	Ford HBA4 3.5 V8	Alessandro Nannini		
		Roberto Moreno		
		Nelson Piquet	71	3rd
1991	Ford HBA4 3.5 V8	Roberto Moreno		
	Ford HBA5 3.5 V8	Michael Schumacher		
		Nelson Piquet	38.5	4th
1992	Ford HBA5 3.5 V8	Michael Schumacher		
	Ford HBA7 3.5 V8	Martin Brundle	91	3rd
1993	Ford HBA7 3.5 V8	Michael Schumacher		
	Ford HBA8 3.5 V8	Riccardo Patrese	72	3rd
1994	Ford ECA Zetec-R 3.5 V8	Michael Schumacher		
		JJ Lehto		
		Jos Verstappen		
		Johnny Herbert	103	2nd
1995	Renault RS7 3.0 V10	Michael Schumacher		
		Johnny Herbert	137	1st
1996	Renault RS8 3.0 V10	Jean Alesi		
		Gerhard Berger	68	3rd
1997	Renault RS9 3.0 V10	Jean Alesi		
		Gerhard Berger		
		Alexander Wurz	67	3rd
1998	Playlife GC37-01 3.0 V10	Giancarlo Fisichella		
		Alexander Wurz	33	5th
1999	Playlife FB01 3.0 V10	Giancarlo Fisichella		
		Alexander Wurz	16	6th
2000	Playlife FB02 3.0 V10	Giancarlo Fisichella		
		Alexander Wurz	20	4th
2001	Renault RS21 3.0 V10	Giancarlo Fisichella		
		Jenson Button	10	7th

Index

Palmer, Jonathan 72
Pandey, Manish 41
Panis, Olivier 96
Patrase, Riccardo 33, 134
Pembrey testing 148-151
Piquet, Nelson 29, 71, 137
Piquet Jr, Nelson 141-142
Pirro, Emanuele 35
Plank 84, 96-97, 103, 108, 115, 153
Portuguese Grand Prix 31, 117
Postlethwaite, Harvey 60
Prost, Alain 23, 51, 71

R

Ratzenberger, Roland 41, 44, 157
Reedie, Andrew 114
Refuelling 21, 29, 86-89, 92-94
Renault 142, 152
Roebuck, Nigel 72
Rover 139
Rubython, Tom 35

S

San Marino Grand Prix 41-47, 80-81
Schumacher, Michael – throughout
Semi-automatic gearbox 36
Senna, Ayrton 23, 25, 30-31, 34-35, 38, 41, 45-46, 50-52, 67, 71, 122, 135, 157
Senna movie 41
Seymour, Rob 153
Sheene, Barry 134
Silk, Christian 38, 84-85, 136
Silverstone testing 22, 29, 57, 112, 116
Simtek 36, 41, 64
Singapore Grand Prix 141
Spanish Grand Prix 38, 43, 58-65, 76, 94
Spires, Di 86
Stanford, Dickie 146, 152-153
Stop-go penalty 72
Symonds, Pat 32, 50, 64, 99, 129, 133, 142, 147

T

Titchmarsh, Ian 104
Todt, Jean 16, 33-34, 66
Toet, Willem 19, 25, 38-39, 52-53, 59, 85, 92, 100, 111, 117, 124, 145-146, 152-154
Toleman 35
Toyota 102
Traction control 11, 20, 34, 36, 80, 149-155
Tracy, Paul 116, 119
TWR 140
Tyrrel 37

V

Varsha, Bob 54
Verstappen, Jos 27, 29-30, 38, 67, 83-84, 85-87, 111, 116-119, 122, 124, 137
Villadelprat, Joan 66, 74, 91, 100, 107-108, 152
Vodac 83
Volvo 140

W

Walker, Murray 71
Walkinshaw, Tom 31, 60, 102-103, 139-142
Walters, Martin 24
Ward, Adrian 94,
Warwick, Derek 29, 51
Watkins, Sid 43, 56-57
Watson, John 59, 73, 86, 96, 116-117, 137
Wendlinger, Karl 47, 54-55
West, Paul 31, 118, 123, 131, 134, 136, 147
Whiting, Charlie 11, 19, 21, 32-34, 79, 103, 105, 156
Williams – throughout
 FW14B 11
 FW15D
 FW16 – throughout
Williams, Frank 11, 17, 44
Williams, Jonathan 44, 149
Williams, Richard 86
Wise, Richard 152
World Motor Sports Council 12, 74

Z

Zanardi, Alex 29, 50, 123

BIBLIOGRAPHY
Further reading

BOOKS

NO ANGEL The Secret Life of Bernie Ecclestone, Tom Bower (Faber & Faber)
MONACO: Inside F1's Greatest Race, Malcolm Folley (Arrow)
WATCHING THE WHEELS: My Autobiography, Damon Hill (Pan Macmillan Publishers)
HOW TO BUILD A CAR: The Autobiography of the World's Greatest Formula 1 Designer, Adrian Newey (HarperCollins)
LIFE AT THE LIMIT: Triumph and Tragedy in F1, Sid Watkins (Pan Books)
DAMON HILL'S GRAND PRIX YEAR: The Inside Story of an F1 Season, Damon Hill (MacMillan)
F1 AND BEYOND: The Autobiography, Max Mosley (Simon & Schuster)
LIFE IN THE FAST LANE: The Story of the Benetton Grand Prix Year, Steve Matchett (Weidenfeld & Nicolson)
MICHAEL SCHUMACHER: The Edge of Greatness, James Allen (Headline)
AUTOCOURSE: 1989/1990, Alan Henry (Osprey)
I JUST MADE THE TEA: Tales of 30 years inside Formula 1, Bernard Ferguson and Di Spires (J H Haynes & Co Ltd)

NO ORDINARY MAN: A Life of George Carman, Dominic Carman (Hodder & Stoughton Ltd)
MICHAEL SCHUMACHER: The Whole Story, Christopher Hilton (J H Haynes & Co Ltd)
WHAT DOES DOESN'T KILL YOU: My Life in Motor Racing, Johnny Herbert (Bantam Press)

PERIODICALS

Autosport
Motor Sport
F1 News
The Independent
Quattroruote
Motoring News
F1 Racing
L'Automobile Magazine
Autosprint

WEBSITES

www.racefans.net
www.linkedin.com
www.belfasttelegraph.co.uk
www.autosport.com
www.motorsportmagazine.com
www.ayrtonsennavive.blogspot.co.uk
www.mtv.fi

www.f1fanatic.co.uk
www.motorsport.com
www.grandprix.com
www.auto-motor-und-sport.de
www.gpupdate.net
www.bbc.co.uk
www.jomenvisst.de
news.sportauto.fr
www.telegraph.co.uk
www.youtube.com
www.formula1.com
www.thetimes.co.uk

TV PROGRAMMES

A Season with McLaren (John Gau Productions)
BBC and Eurosport's coverage of the 1994 Formula One World Championship (Formula One Management)
Speed Channel's retrospective of the 1993 Monaco Grand Prix (Formula One Management)
Legends of F1 (Sky F1)
Architects of F1 (Sky F1)

FILMS

Senna, Asif Kapadia/Manish Pandey (ESPN/Working Title)

ABOUT THE AUTHOR

Ibrar Malik

The book's author. In case you're wondering about the haircut, I've taken inspiration from F1 aerodynamicists like Willem Toet and Adrian Newey (who both had similar haircuts), and opted for a low downforce/drag set-up.
Photo: Elizabeth Mizon

Who am I and what makes me qualified to write this book? I am a massive F1 fan and 1994 holds special memories. It was the first full year I followed the sport and I spent my childhood playing *Grand Prix 2*, a computer game based on that season. This book arose because there are constant rumours Schumacher, Benetton and others may have cheated that year, so since 2015 I needed to find out the truth. Therefore I've painstakingly researched all the books, internet sources and magazines covering this subject and interviewed key figures at Benetton, Ford Electronics, and Williams. Furthermore, I've studied all the on-track action – because common sense evidence is often forgotten when discussing the 1994 allegations. This book is the fruits of all that hard work and research.

I've never written a book before, nor had any childhood aspirations to become a writer. The reason for this endeavour is to record and discuss the mind blowing and exclusive content unearthed, while placing it within the public domain. Hopefully helping to uncover the truth: was Senna fighting an illegal car when he crashed to his death? Or did the sport become paranoid that cheating was rife that year? The 25th anniversary of 1994 is as good a time as any to seek the answers to this and much more. Moreover, the amount of time passed is why key contributors have used this book to open up about the allegations, much more than previously.

Looking back, 1994 was a landmark year for F1 in so many respects. It was a season of tragedy, chaos, politics and technical disputes which involved some very colourful characters at the heart of the action. Whatever your thoughts on the controversies beforehand, do not be afraid to change them upon learning new facts. Since writing this book I have changed my mind on certain things, and learnt to appreciate opposing opinions. Perhaps after reading it you might do so to?

Ibrar Malik
July 2018